The End of the Ottoman Empire
1908–1923

TURNING POINTS
General Editor: Keith Robbins
Vice Chancellor, University of Wales Lampeter

THE END OF
THE OTTOMAN EMPIRE

This is the first title in an ambitious new programme of books under the direction of Professor Keith Robbins (already General Editor of Longman's very successful series of Profiles in Power*). It will examine moments and processes in history which have conventionally been seen as 'turning points' in the emergence of the modern world. By looking at the causes and long-term consequences of these key events, the books will illuminate the nature of both change and continuity in historical development. There are numerous titles in active preparation.*

The End of the Ottoman Empire 1908–1923

A.L. MACFIE

LONGMAN
London and New York

Addison Wesley Longman Limited
Edinburgh Gate,
Harlow, Essex CM20 2JE,
United Kingdom
and Associated Companies throughout the world.

*Published in the United States of America
by Addison Wesley Longman, New York.*

First published 1998

ISBN 0–582–28762–6 CSD
ISBN 0–582–28763–4 PPR

Visit Addison Wesley Longman on the world wide web at http://awl-he.com

British Library Cataloguing in Publication Data

A catalogue entry for this title is available from the British Library

Library of Congress Cataloging-in-Publication Data
Macfie, A.L.
The end of the Ottoman Empire, 1908–1923 / A.L. Macfie.
p.   cm.
Includes bibliographical references and index.
ISBN 0–582–28762–6. — ISBN 0–582–28763–4 (pbk.)
1. Turkey—History—Mehmed V, 1909–1918. 2. Turkey—History—
Revolution, 1918–1923. I. Title.
DR583.M38   1998
956.1′02—dc21   97–50575
                                                     CIP

Set by 35 in 10/12pt Baskerville
Produced by Addison Wesley Longman Singapore (Pte) Ltd.,
Printed in Singapore

Contents

List of Maps

Note on Population

The population of the Ottoman Empire on the eve of the Young Turk Revolution of 1908 has been estimated, very roughly, at about 30 million. Of these some 3–4 million lived in the Balkans, 14–16 million in Anatolia, including 10–12 million Turks, 4 million in Greater Syria, which then included Palestine and the Lebanon, 3 million in Iraq and 7 million in Arabia. The Greek population of the Ottoman Empire has been estimated at about 3 million, more than half of whom lived in Anatolia, mainly in the Izmir and Pontus regions. The Armenian population, mainly inhabiting the eastern provinces, has been estimated at 1–1.5 millions. In Macedonia, Bulgars made up about a half of the total population, Turks just over a fifth, Greeks a tenth, and Albanians, Jews and Vlachs another tenth. The population of Istanbul (Constantinople) was about 1 million, that of Salonica 120 000, including a large Jewish element. Despite the spread of education in the nineteenth century, the bulk of the population, some 90–95 per cent, mainly inhabiting the rural areas, remained illiterate.

Introduction

Turning points

Historians have identified many decisive turning points in history, moments when the historical landscape changes, or appears to change, opening up new vistas and foreclosing on the old. In the context of the Near and Middle East, the area of concern of this study, one might mention the defeat suffered by the Byzantines in a battle (1071) fought against a Seljuk army at Manzikert (Malazgird) in eastern Anatolia, a defeat which opened eastern Anatolia (Asia Minor) to an influx of Turcoman (Turkish) tribes from Central Asia; the foundation of a Seljuk state in Anatolia shortly thereafter; the collapse of that state as a result of a defeat inflicted on the Seljuks by a Mongol army at Kösedağ, also in eastern Anatolia (1243); the Mongol conquest of Mesopotamia and Syria, and the destruction of Muslim civilisation which that entailed; the foundation by the eponymous Osman Ghazi of a *ghazi* (Islamic warrior) state or principality in northwestern Anatolia, on the borderlands of the world of Islam, in the last quarter of the thirteenth century; the battle of Kosova (1389), which secured Ottoman control of the Balkans; the Ottoman conquest of Constantinople, the capital of the Byzantine Empire (1453); the Ottoman conquest of Syria and Egypt which followed; and finally the two Ottoman sieges of Vienna (1529 and 1683), which marked the limit of Ottoman expansion in Europe.[1]

Each of these turning points was, to a greater or lesser extent, significant in determining the course of history in the area now generally known as the Near and Middle East. But few, if any, can compare in the range and profundity of its consequences with the collapse of the Ottoman Empire, which occurred in the period of the Balkan and First World Wars (1908–23). In a few short years, one of the world's greatest empires (which as Alan Palmer, a historian

---

1. P.M. Holt, A.K.S. Lambton and B. Lewis (eds), *The Cambridge History of Islam* Cambridge: Cambridge University Press, 1970.

of Ottoman decline, has remarked, succeeded, despite all its evident inadequacies, in outliving imperial Spain, republican Genoa and Venice, the elective monarchy of Poland, British colonial America, the vestigial Holy Roman Empire, Bourbon and Napoleonic France, and even the Habsburg and Romanov Empires) collapsed, leaving in its stead merely a series of disparate and troubled kingdoms, republics, sheikhdoms and mandated territories, including, among others, Turkey, Iraq, Syria, Transjordan, Palestine and the Hedjaz (later absorbed by Saudi Arabia).[2]

The principal stages on the road leading to Ottoman collapse, in the period of the Balkan and First World Wars, are not difficult to identify. In 1908, following the so-called Young Turk Revolution, which brought about a restoration of the First Ottoman Constitution of 1876, Austria–Hungary annexed Bosnia and Herzegovina, the administration of which it had acquired in 1878; while Bulgaria, still nominally a tributary of the Ottoman Sultanate, proclaimed its independence; and Crete announced its *enosis* (union) with Greece. In 1910–11 the Albanians rose in revolt, and in 1911 Italy occupied Tripolitania (Libya). In 1912–13 a league of Balkan states, made up of Serbia, Bulgaria, Greece and Montenegro, launched an assault on the Ottoman Empire, with the object of expelling the Ottoman Turks from their remaining territories in Europe. This task the Balkan League very nearly accomplished. Following a series of brilliant victories, its armies succeeded in driving the Ottomans back to the Chatalja lines, some 40 miles from Istanbul; but following the outbreak of a second Balkan war, between Bulgaria and its erstwhile allies, aided now by Romania, the Ottomans succeeded in recovering possession of Edirne (Adrianople) and eastern Thrace. Finally, in the First World War, in which the Ottoman government made the fatal mistake of siding, not with the Triple Entente Powers (Britain, France and Russia), but with the Central Powers (Germany and Austria–Hungary), the Ottomans, after a long and bloody struggle, were expelled from Mesopotamia, Syria, Palestine and Arabia, and even parts of eastern Anatolia; though in 1917–18, following the outbreak of the Bolshevik revolution in Russia, and the collapse of the Russian armed forces which followed, they did succeed not only in recovering control of eastern Anatolia but also in securing control of parts of Azerbaijan and Transcaucasia. Such successes, however, proved short-lived. In the Armistice of Mudros (1918), which ended Ottoman participation in the First World War,

2. A. Palmer, *The Decline and Fall of the Ottoman Empire* London: John Murray, 1992, p. 32.

the Ottomans were obliged to agree to the demobilisation of the greater part of their armed forces, the surrender or withdrawal of all Ottoman units stationed in the Arab provinces, Azerbaijan and Transcaucasia, and an Allied occupation of a number of strategic points in Anatolia and eastern Thrace, including, in particular, the forts defending the Turkish Straits (the Bosphorus and Dardanelles), the narrow seaway linking the Mediterranean and the Black Sea.

The conclusion of the Mudros armistice marked the effective end of the Ottoman Empire as a substantial imperial power, ruling over extensive territories and numerous communities, nations and peoples. Nevertheless, a rump Ottoman state, however truncated, might yet have survived in Anatolia and eastern Thrace, had not the western Entente Powers, Great Britain and France, supported by their associate, the United States of America, intent on preventing an Italian occupation of Izmir (Smyrna), dispatched in May 1919 a Greek expeditionary force to occupy the area. As a result of this and other ill-advised decisions (these included an Allied occupation of Istanbul (Constantinople), the Ottoman capital, accomplished in March 1920, and an attempt to impose a draconian peace treaty, concluded at Sèvres on 10 August 1920) in the course of the following months the Ottoman political and military elite, led by Mustafa Kemal (Atatürk), the so-called founder of modern Turkey, was able to set up in the interior a Turkish national movement of remarkable strength and cohesion. In the course of the following years, this movement succeeded in establishing in Ankara a Grand National Assembly, based on the principle of the sovereignty of the nation; confronting, and even on occasion fighting, the occupation forces of the Allied Powers; expelling the Greek expeditionary forces from Anatolia; and eventually in July 1923 concluding at Lausanne a treaty of peace, freely negotiated with the Allies, recognising the existence of an independent Turkish state, incorporating the whole of Anatolia and eastern Thrace. In November 1922, following the defeat of the Greek expeditionary force and its expulsion from Anatolia, Mustafa Kemal, now generally recognised by the Turkish people as their supreme leader, had a bill introduced into the national assembly providing for the abolition of the sultanate, and shortly thereafter another, providing for the creation of a republic.[3]

3. For an account of the rise of the national movement and the creation of a Turkish republic see P. Kinross, *Atatürk: The Rebirth of a Nation* London: Weidenfeld and Nicolson, 1964; A.L. Macfie, *Atatürk* Harlow: Longman, 1994; and S.R. Sonyal, *Atatürk, The Founder of Modern Turkey* Ankara: Turkish Historical Society, 1989.

The process of Ottoman disintegration in the final phase of the empire's decline is clear enough. What is less clear is just why this process occurred at the time that it did. What factors gave rise to the Young Turk Revolution of 1908? Was the revolution itself a factor contributing to the collapse, or was it, as intended, a factor making for survival? How did it come about that the Ottoman army, traditionally so formidable in war, was routed by the powers of the Balkan League in the Balkan Wars? What part did the policies pursued by the Great Powers (Great Britain, France, Russia, Italy and Germany) play in bringing about the collapse of the Ottoman Empire; and what part did the Committee of Union and Progress (CUP, the secret society which organised the Young Turk Revolution of 1908, and later as a political party governed the empire until the end of the First World War) play? Finally, what factors persuaded the Ottomans to side not with the Central but with the Entente Powers in the First World War, a decision which, as things turned out, was to secure the empire's final demise? These are some of the questions which this study will attempt to answer, paying attention where possible to the views of contemporaries, mainly British, on the issues involved.

The leaders of the CUP, which ruled the Ottoman Empire throughout the greater part of its final phase, have not on the whole had a good press. To foreign commentators, mainly British, they constituted merely a spurious combination of self-seeking 'Jews, Socialists and Freemasons', representatives of the 'Jew Committee of Union and Progress', responsible for the collapse of the Ottoman army in the Balkan Wars; while to many traditional Muslims, they appeared as infidels and atheists, the victims of an overexposure to the decadent values of a degenerate Europe. To Mustafa Kemal, and a number of his colleagues, who led the national struggle in the period immediately following the defeat of the Ottoman Empire in the First World War, they were for the most part merely self-seeking opportunists, 'blagueurs' and 'beaux parleurs', who whilst engaging in corruption, war-profiteering and abuse on a massive scale, had by taking the Ottoman Empire into the First World War on the side of the Central Powers gambled irresponsibly with its future.[4]

The most extreme denunciation of the CUP leadership was perhaps that penned by Sir Mark Sykes, a British diplomat, traveller and politician, who was later to play an important wartime role in

---

4. E. Kedourie, 'Young Turks, Freemasons and Jews', *Middle Eastern Studies*, Vol. 7, No. 2 (1971), pp. 90–1; J. Deny, 'Les Souvenirs du Gazi Moustafa Kemal Pacha', *Revue des Etudes Islamique*, Vol. 1 (1927).

the history of the Middle East. In *The Caliph's Last Heritage* (1913) he referred to them variously as 'dissipated, half-educated, emasculated babus', exponents of 'atheism, Jacobinism, materialism and license', promoters of 'secret societies, lodges, oaths of brotherhood, assassinations, courts-martial, and strange, obscure policies', advocates of the 'licentious anarchism of the *apache* of Montmartre, the dark terrorism of the Portuguese Carbonari, the destructive idealism of the French Revolution, the half digested theories of Spencer, Nietzsche, and Hartman, and the paralysing influence of a perverted freemasonry'.[5]

Nor were the CUP leaders particularly fortunate in the role which fate reserved for them. Mahmud Shevket Pasha, never an actual member of the CUP but nonetheless the army commander responsible for the suppression of the 1909 counter-revolution, was assassinated in Istanbul in 1913. Mehmet Talaat, a dominant figure in the organisation from its foundation in 1906 to its liquidation in 1918, was assassinated by an Armenian in Berlin in 1921. Enver, a 'Hero of Freedom' of the 1908 revolution, and minister of war throughout the First World War, was killed in a skirmish with a Red Army unit in Turkestan in 1922. Ahmed Djemal, minister of marine and military governor of Syria in the First World War, was assassinated, again by an Armenian, in Tiflis in 1922. Mehmet Djemal Asmi, a director of the Salonica Law School, Unionist deputy and vali (governor of a *vilayet*) of Konya, was assassinated by Armenians in Berlin in 1922; and Said Halim, grand vizier from 1913 to 1916, by Armenian nationalists in Rome about the same time. Djavid Bey, a financial expert and minister of finance, was condemned to death by an independence court, set up by Mustafa Kemal, and executed in 1926, as were Dr Nazim, an influential figure, Filibeli Ahmet Hilmi, an early member of the CUP, and Ismail Canbolat, a founder member. Kara Kemal, the CUP party boss in Istanbul, committed suicide in 1926, in order to escape arrest.[6]

Rise of the Ottoman Empire

The Ottoman Empire, which collapsed so rapidly in 1908–18, started out as a *ghazi* principality established by Osman Ghazi in the marches

5. M. Sykes, *The Caliph's Last Heritage* London: Macmillan, 1913, p. 508.
6. *Encyclopaedia of Islam*, new edn, Enver Pasha; E.J. Zürcher, *The Unionist Factor* Leiden: E.J. Brill, 1984, pp. 37–9; C.J. Walker, *Armenia* London: Routledge, 1990, p. 344. Many of the assassinations of CUP leaders were carried out by Nemisis, a special task force set up by Dashnaksutiun.

of northwestern Anatolia in the thirteenth century. Following the conquest of Bursa (an early capital), Nicaea (Isnik) and Ismid, the Ottomans, as the followers of Osman Ghazi and his successors became known, having crossed the Dardanelles and secured control of the Gallipoli Peninsula, proceeded to occupy first Thrace and then southern Bulgaria, acquiring in the process possession of Edirne (Adrianople, also an early capital), Sofia and Salonica (Thessaloniki). In 1389 Sultan Murad defeated a coalition of Serb, Bulgar and Croat forces at Kosova, a victory which effectively established Ottoman control in the Balkans; and in 1453, Sultan Mehmed, known in Europe as the Conqueror, conquered Constantinople, a city quickly established as the new capital of the Ottoman state. Further expansion in the Balkans and eastern Europe followed. In the following years, Serbia, Hungary, Moldavia, Wallachia, Transylvania and the Morea were added to the empire. Meanwhile, in Anatolia, the Ottomans continued their advance; and in 1516–17, following a series of great campaigns fought against Shah Ismail, the ruler of Azerbaijan, western Persia and Iraq, and the Mamluk Beys of Egypt, Sultan Selim, known to his subjects as the Grim, conquered Syria and Egypt, acquiring in the process the titles of caliph (Muslim religious leader, successor of Muhammed) and Servitor of the Two Holy Sanctuaries (Mecca and Medina). As a result of these and other conquests, which included Mesopotamia and the greater part of North Africa (Algiers 1516, Tunis 1534 and Tripoli 1551) the Ottoman Empire emerged as one of the world's greatest empires, ruled over by a sultan (padishah), who, in language which betrays the complex character of the empire, claimed in the *khutba* (the Friday prayer) recited in his name, the titles of 'Master of the Two Lands and the Two Seas, the Breaker of the Two Armies, the Sultan of the Two Iraqs and the Servitor of the Two Holy Sanctuaries'.[7]

In order to rule over the extraordinary empire they had conquered, the Ottoman sultans developed a complex system of government, based on the principles of theocracy, hierarchy, centralisation and tradition. In this system the ruler, the sultan, assisted by the grand vizier (sadrazam), and the two principal ruling institutions, the army and the bureaucracy, ruled over the common people, who were divided up into groups according to their economic function: primary producers (for the most part peasant farmers), artisans,

7. P.M. Holt, *Egypt and the Fertile Crescent* Harlow: Longman, 1966, p. 40; H. Inalcik, *The Ottoman Empire, 1300–1600* London: Weidenfeld and Nicolson, 1973; Fuad Köprülü, *The Origins of the Ottoman Empire* New York: State University of New York Press, 1992.

traders and herders. Alongside the ruling institutions, enjoying equivalent status, stood the *ulema*, the corps of learned men trained in the law and theology of Islam who, led by the Sheikh al-Islam, were made responsible for the teaching of religion, the execution of the *Sheriat* (the holy law of Islam) and the preservation of tradition. Not that the Ottomans ever attempted to impose a universal system of government and administration on the empire. On the contrary, eminently aware of the need to adjust to circumstances, they frequently made a point of preserving the laws and customs of a particular community and accommodating its traditions. Thus local princes, potentates and tribal leaders were on occasion appointed as governors, fief holders or tax collectors, while, in conformity with Muslim law and tradition, Christians and Jews, the 'People of the Book', were allotted a place in the social system, deemed appropriate, as *dhimmis* (tolerated infidels). At the same time the minority religious communities were recognised as more or less autonomous *millets* (religious communities or nations), enjoying special privileges.[8]

Just how extensive was the autonomy enjoyed by the minority Christian and Jewish communities in the early days of the empire remains a matter of dispute, but there is no doubt that as time passed they came to enjoy the strong sense of corporate identity traditionally associated with the *millet* system. In Istanbul an Orthodox Patriarchate emerged, ruling over the *Millet-i Rum* or 'Greek' *millet*, which in fact incorporated all the Orthodox Christian subjects of the sultan, including Serbs, Romanians, Bulgarians, Vlachs, Orthodox Albanians and Arabs. Not that in the following years the Orthodox Patriarchate retained its authority over all the sultan's Orthodox subjects. On the contrary, in the nineteenth century, as nationality became a more significant factor than religion in determining identity, the Orthodox community split, largely along ethnic lines. In the 1830s the Patriarchate was forced to accept the *de facto* autonomy of the Serbian church; and shortly thereafter the effective independence of a Romanian church, formally recognised in 1885. In 1870 a Bulgarian Exarchate was created; and shortly thereafter the first tentative steps were taken to create an autocephalus church in Albania. As for the Armenian Patriarchate and the Chief Rabbinate, created about the same time as the Greek Orthodox Patriarchate, they never enjoyed the power enjoyed by their Greek

8. N. Berkes, *The Development of Secularism in Turkey* Montreal: McGill University Press, 1964, pp. 10–17.

counterpart, but they remained nonetheless significant as symbols of the autonomy enjoyed by their communities, an autonomy extended in 1830 to the Armenian Catholics.[9]

Decline

The Ottoman Empire, established by the successors of Osman Ghazi, proved remarkably successful in combining the disparate peoples, communities, clans and tribes of the Near and Middle East into a single more or less harmonious imperial system. But in succeeding generations the empire proved unable to sustain the system thus created. As a result, from at least the beginning of the seventeenth century onwards a process of internal fragmentation began, which enabled a series of local potentates and dynasties to secure a high degree of autonomy, and in some cases even independence. These included, in Anatolia, the Chapanoğlu of the Amasya–Ankara–Kayseri region, the Karaosmanoglu of the Aydin region, and the Janikli family of the Trabzon (Trebizond) region; in the Balkans the Tirsiniklioğlu and the Dagdevirenoğlu; and in Moldavia and Wallachia the Romanian Boyars. Elsewhere, in Egypt, the Mamluk Beys, who had recovered from their defeats of 1516–17, established powerful households; in Aleppo and Baghdad leading families, such as the Naqibal-Ashraf, descendants of the prophet, established control; while in North Africa a series of regencies acquired virtual independence. At the same time, in the desert areas of Mesopotamia and Arabia, where central control had from the beginning proved lax, pastoral groups, such as the Anaza, the Muntafiq and the Shammar, formed great tribes or confederations, led by sheikhs, some of whom were elected; while in central Arabia the Wahhabis, a fundamentalist Islamic sect, established a state which not only conquered Mecca and Medina but also rejected Ottoman sovereignty outright (the Ottomans were accused of atheism and idolatry); though Ottoman authority was later reestablished for a time in central Arabia by an army dispatched by the viceroy of Egypt, Mehmet Ali. Yet such cases of outright rejection of Ottoman sovereignty proved rare. For the most part local rulers, however independent, preferred to retain some sense of allegiance to the sultan-caliph,

9. B. Braude and B. Lewis (eds), *Christians and Jews in the Ottoman Empire* Vol. 1 London: Holmes and Meier, 1982.

maintaining connections, frequently lucrative, with the Ottoman capital, representing the interests of their followers there and serving in the sultan's army. In effect, therefore, the empire increasingly came to resemble a loose association of more or less autonomous states, regencies, tribes, clans and fiefdoms, held together not so much by an integrated system of government as by a common culture, though the prospect of a sudden and unexpected visitation by the sultan or one of his agents, accompanied by an Ottoman army, placed an effective limit on the pretensions of the more ambitious of the sultan's over-mighty subjects.[10]

The internal fragmentation of the Ottoman Empire, and the relative economic and military decline which this entailed, led in the eighteenth and nineteenth centuries to military defeat and loss of territory. At the same time it raised questions in Europe regarding the future viability of the empire and its possible partition, questions frequently encapsulated by European diplomats and others under the general title of the 'Eastern Question'.

The main stages on the long road of Ottoman defeat and decline, each of which might in itself rank as a turning point in the history of the Ottoman Empire warranting a chapter in the history of the Eastern Question, require rehearsing. By the Treaty of Carlowitz (1699), concluded following a long and debilitating war fought against a combination of European powers in the Balkans, the Ottomans were compelled to admit a substantial loss of territory in Hungary and Transylvania. By the Treaty of Kutchuk-Kainardji (1774), concluded following a war with Russia, they were compelled to concede a substantial loss of territory on the northern shores of the Black Sea and recognition of the independence of the Khanate of the Crimea, later annexed by Russia. In 1798 possession of Egypt, already tenuous, was temporarily lost to the French, when the Paris Directory dispatched an army, commanded by General Bonaparte, to occupy the delta and drive the British out of the Red Sea. By the Treaty of Adrianople (1829), concluded following a Greek rebellion in the Morea and a disastrous war fought against the Russians, in the course of which a Russian army marched to within striking distance of the Ottoman capital, the Ottomans were compelled to admit not only the loss of the Morea (where a Greek state was created) but also recognition of a Russian annexation of Georgia

---

10. 'Ottoman Reform and the Politics of the Notables', in A. Hourani (ed.), *The Modern Middle East* New York: I.B. Tauris, 1993; K. Karpat, 'The Transformation of the Ottoman State, 1789–1908', *International Journal of Middle Eastern Studies*, Vol. 3 (1972).

and eastern Armenia, and a number of other changes favourable to Russia.

Further humiliation followed. By the terms of the Treaty of Unkiar-Skelessi (1833), concluded with Russia following an invasion of Syria and the Lebanon by the forces of Mehmet Ali, the viceroy of Egypt, the Ottomans were obliged, in return for assurances of Russian protection, to accept effective Russian control of the Straits; though following a second crisis, provoked by an Ottoman attempt in 1839 to recover control of Syria and the Lebanon, the Ottomans, with British, French and Austrian assistance, did succeed in recovering both a degree of independence and control of the lost territories. Moreover, in 1841, the Russians were obliged to agree to the conclusion of a Straits Convention, formally recognising the determination of the sultan to conform to the 'ancient rule' of the Ottoman Empire, whereby in time of peace and in time of war, Turkey being neutral, the Straits would remain closed to foreign warships. Nor did victory in war necessarily halt the process of contraction. In the Treaty of Paris (1856), concluded following the defeat of Russia by an alliance of western powers in the so-called Crimean War (1853–6), the Ottomans were obliged to admit not only the right of the contracting powers to establish a protectorate over Serbia and the principalities, but also the right of the principalities, still nominally subject to Ottoman suzerainty, to create an 'independent and national' organisation – a concession which not surprisingly quickly led to complete independence.

In the Treaty of Paris (1856) the contracting parties agreed to respect and guarantee the independence and integrity of the Ottoman Empire; but it rapidly transpired that such guarantees were worthless. In 1878, following yet another Russo-Turkish war, provoked by Christian uprisings and massacres in Bosnia, Herzegovina and Bulgaria, in the course of which a Russian army once again marched to within a few miles of the outskirts of the Ottoman capital, the Ottomans were obliged, as part of a settlement drawn up by the Great Powers at the Congress of Berlin (1878), to accept substantial losses of territory, both in the Balkans and eastern Anatolia, including Bosnia and Herzegovina (the administration of which passed to Austria), Kars, Ardahan and Batum, though thanks to the efforts of Britain and France the creation of a greater Bulgaria, enjoying an outlet to the Aegean, a principal Russian objective, was prevented. At the same time the Ottomans were obliged to admit the complete independence of Serbia, Romania and Montenegro, already effectively conceded; and in a separate convention, agreed with Britain, they were obliged to agree to a British occupation of Cyprus, granted in return for promises of British support for the Ottoman position in eastern Anatolia.[11]

The decline of Ottoman power and independence did not find expression merely in military defeat and loss of territory. From the middle years of the nineteenth century, the Ottomans found themselves increasingly dependent on the European capitalist system. In 1875, following a period of hectic borrowing on the London and Paris exchanges, generated in part by the extravagance of Sultan Abdulaziz and in part by a series of bad harvests, accompanied by famine, in Anatolia, the Ottoman government was obliged to default on the interest payments due on a part of the Ottoman public debt; and in 1881 to agree to the creation of an Ottoman public debt administration, controlled by a council of the public debt, elected mainly by European bond holders. As a result of the strict supervision thus imposed, in the decade or so preceding the Young Turk Revolution of 1908, more than one-third of Ottoman revenue was made available to make payment on the Ottoman public debt. Meanwhile European capitalists, exploiting concessions and monopolies granted by the Ottoman government, gained control of the greater part of the Ottoman transport system, and a number of other industries, including tobacco, gas, electricity and water. Not that foreign influence and control was exercised merely by military and economic means. In the nineteenth century a number of the Great Powers, building in some cases on claims put forward in the eighteenth century, even asserted a right to protect whole communities, in the case of Russia the Greek Orthodox, France the Maronite and Armenian Catholic and Britain the Druze. At the same time the system of extra-territorial rights, known as the capitulations, enjoyed mainly by foreigners and members of the minority communities, granted by earlier sultans, was further extended, to the great disadvantage of the Ottoman state. In these circumstances it is not surprising that, in the period of the Young Turk Revolution of 1908 and even earlier, Ottoman reformers and others should have become increasingly obsessed with the need to reestablish Ottoman independence.[12]

11. For a wide-ranging account of the Eastern Question see M.S. Anderson, *The Eastern Question* London: Macmillan, 1960. For a shorter version see A.L. Macfie, *The Eastern Question* Harlow: Longman, 1989.

12. B. Lewis, *The Emergence of Modern Turkey* Oxford: Oxford University Press, 1961, p. 156; M.E. Yapp, *The Making of the Modern Near East* Harlow: Longman, 1987, pp. 31–3.

Ottoman commentators were in no doubt regarding the causes of Ottoman decline, already evident in the sixteenth century. As befits the exponents of a system of government based on the religious principle, they concluded that the essential cause lay in moral failure: in the failure of the sultan and his chief officers to preserve the political and administrative system. Thus Kochu Bey, an Ottoman official of Macedonian or Albanian descent, writing in 1630, identified four principal causes of decline: the withdrawal of the sultan from direct supervision of the affairs of state; the debasement of the office of grand vizier by the appointment of favourites and other unsuitable candidates; the corruption of the imperial household by the appointment of 'Turks (Anatolian peasants, yokels) Gypsies, Jews, people without religion or faith, cut-purses and city riff-raff'; and the corruption of the military, economic and social systems which these appointments entailed. As a result the judges were hated, the treasury empty and the peasantry ruined.[13] Hadji Khalifah, a finance official, writing in the 1650s, likewise identified four causes of decline: the failure of the sultan to protect the peasantry from extortion and oppression, his failure to enforce justice, his failure to control the size of the army (growing at an alarming rate) and his failure to preserve fiscal probity; though following Ibn Khaldun, the Arab philosopher, he did make a point of emphasising that decline was inevitable in all human institutions. Being created by God, they were, like other created beings, subject to the laws of growth and decay.[14]

Later, mainly western historians of Ottoman decline, on the other hand, the products for the most part of an essentially materialistic culture, have been inclined to reverse the process of causation and see Ottoman moral decline not as a cause but as a consequence of economic, political and military decay. Thus Bernard Lewis, in *The Emergence of Modern Turkey* (1961), has argued that many of the problems identified at the time by Kochu Bey and others, far from being a consequence of the moral failure of the leadership, were in fact a principal cause of that failure. Ottoman society, in other words, failed to respond adequately to the changed circumstances brought about by the closure of the Balkan frontier, a growing population, changes in the pattern of trade brought about by the discovery of a sea route to India, and the sudden influx of American silver, which occurred in the first half of the sixteenth century – failures further exacerbated by an ingrained Ottoman contempt

13. B. Lewis, 'Ottoman Observers of Ottoman Decline', *Islamic Studies*, Vol. 1 (1962) pp. 74–8.
14. Ibid., pp. 78–82.

for trade and manufacture (the business of Christians and Jews) and by a lack of interest in all things technological. Halil Inalcik, in a chapter in the *Cambridge History of Islam*, Volume I (1970) (one of the best accounts of Ottoman decline) and Stanford and Ezel Shaw, in *A History of the Ottoman Empire and Modern Turkey* (1977) adopt an essentially similar approach; while Alan Palmer, in *The Decline and Fall of the Ottoman Empire* (1992), an essentially narrative account, identifies many factors making for decline, including the loss of military supremacy, economic failure, the rise of nationalism, the spread of secular values and the rise of Russia.[15]

Such easy assumptions of Ottoman decline, frequently encapsulated in the nineteenth century by the expression 'Sick Man of Europe', have by no means received universal assent. In a recent study, entitled *An Economic and Social History of the Ottoman Empire* (1994) Halil Inalcik and Donald Quataert have pointed out that throughout the seventeenth century the Ottoman Empire remained a formidable military power, more than capable of defeating its enemies; and that following the crisis years of the early 1600s, when the so-called *Jelali* troubles broke out in Anatolia, a noticeable recovery occurred, as did a longer and more pronounced upswing in the period following the defeats (in Hungary and Transylvania) and disasters (further troubles in Anatolia) of the period 1683–99.[16] Malcom Yapp, in *The Making of the Modern Middle East* (1987), goes even further, arguing that the concept of decline, embodied in the thesis of the 'Sick Man of Europe', represented merely a historical fiction, a sort of orientalist fantasy elaborated by western European historians, writers and diplomats heavily biased against Islam. Far from being an empire in decline, Yapp argues, the Ottoman Empire in the nineteenth and early twentieth centuries might more appropriately be described as an active reforming state, capable of reforming its army, reorganising its institutions and imposing its authority throughout the greater part of its territory. The question that should be asked, Yapp concludes, is not why the Ottoman Empire eventually collapsed, but why it survived for so long.[17]

The task of reforming the Ottoman army and reestablishing control in the provinces was undertaken primarily by the sultans Selim III (1789–1807) and Mahmud II (1808–39). In 1792–3, Sultan Selim,

---

15. Lewis, *The Emergence of Modern Turkey*, Ch. 2; E. Shaw and S. Shaw, *A History of the Ottoman Empire and Modern Turkey* Vol. I, Cambridge: Cambridge University Press, 1977, Chs 4–7; Palmer, *Decline and Fall of the Ottoman Empire*.

16. H. Inalcik and D. Quataert (eds), *An Economic and Social History of the Ottoman Empire, 1300–1914* Cambridge: Cambridge University Press, 1994, pp. 552–6.

17. Yapp, *Making of the Modern Middle East*, pp. 92–6.

as part of a series of reforms known collectively as the New Order, created a new corps of regular infantry, trained and equipped along modern European lines; and in the following years he established military and naval schools, staffed in part by foreign, mainly French, instructors. Initially reform proved difficult; but in 1826 Mahmud II, building on the foundations laid by Selim III, first had the members of the Janissary Corps, stationed in Istanbul, exterminated (the Janissaries had in the early years of the empire been an elite force recruited from Christian prisoners of war, but subsequently they had become a lawless and unruly rabble) and then created a new army, similar to that created by Selim III. In the meantime he took vigorous steps to reimpose Ottoman authority throughout the empire. In 1812–13 he had the notables of the Black Sea coastal region, including the Janikli, suppressed; and in 1814–16 the Chapanoglu and the Karaosmanoglu. In 1820 Ali Pasha of Janinna, a rebellious governor, was suppressed; and in 1831 Da'ud Pasha, the Mamluk ruler of Baghdad. Finally, in 1834 Ottoman authority was restored in the Kurdish provinces and Mosul; and in 1835 in Tripoli.

The task of reforming (westernising) the Ottoman system of government was undertaken mainly by Sultan Abdul Medjid (1839–61) and a series of great reforming grand viziers, Reshid, Ali, Fuad and Midhat. In a series of reforms known collectively as the *Tanzimat* (reform or reorganisation) a new system of central government was introduced, based on the western model; and a reformed system of provincial administration. New schools were set up, again based on the western model; and new systems of law, commercial, penal and civil, introduced. Moreover, in 1839 and 1856 imperial rescripts were issued, promising respect for the life, honour and property of the subject, reform of the tax system, regular and orderly recruitment for the armed forces, fair and public trial of persons accused, and equality before the law, irrespective of race or religion. And in 1876, in the midst of the Eastern Crisis, Midhat Pasha, determined to shift power from the Palace to the Sublime Porte (the central office of the Ottoman government, including the offices of the grand vizier, the ministry of foreign affairs and the council of state), and prevent further Great Power intervention in the internal affairs of the empire, had a constitution, based on the Belgian, French and Prussian constitutions, proclaimed. Henceforth, according to the articles of this constitution, effective power would be placed in the hands of a council of ministers, appointed by the sultan, and legislative power in the hands of a chamber of deputies, elected indirectly by the people, and a senate, appointed by the sultan; though sovereignty would in principle remain with the sultan. In order to secure popular support for the new order, a new ideology of Ottomanism was promoted, the principal tenet of which was that henceforth the subjects of the sultan would be expected to identify, not as heretofore with the *millet*, Greek, Armenian or Muslim, but with a new entity, the Ottoman nation.[18]

Many of the reforms introduced in the period of the *Tanzimat*, particulary those concerning the apparatus of the state and the reform of the armed forces, proved, as the stubborn resistance mounted by the Ottomans in the Russo-Turkish war of 1877–8 showed, reasonably effective. But those concerned with the creation of a constitutional system of government, based on the western model, proved ineffective, for Ottoman Muslims for the most part refused to acknowledge the principle of equality on which the reforms were based, preferring instead to stick to the old order, based on the principle of Muslim supremacy enshrined in the *Sheriat*. As a result, in 1878, Abdul Hamid, proclaimed sultan in the midst of the Eastern Crisis, taking advantage of the mood of national humiliation and despair that defeat in the war against Russia had evoked, was enabled not only to suspend the constitution and send the chamber of deputies packing, but also to reassert the traditional authority of the sultan, recently undermined by the *Tanzimat* reforms. The regime thereby created, which was to become a byword in Europe for despotism and reaction, was to last for more than 30 years.[19]

The policies adopted by Abdul Hamid in the remaining years of his reign were the natural outcome of his decision to reject constitutional reform and opt instead for the preservation of the traditional system of government, based on the absolute sovereignty of the sultan and the supremacy of the Muslim *millet*. In the first place, assisted by the elaborate paraphernalia of a police state, he endeavoured to prevent the spread of western, liberal, secular and nationalist values, particularly those associated with constitutional and political reform. In the second, he endeavoured to reassert the essentially Islamic character of the empire. To this end attention was given to a revitalisation of the caliphate, the principal institutional embodiment of the faith, and court paid to the Muslim

18. For a history of the Ottoman Reform movement see Lewis, *Emergence of Modern Turkey*, Ch. 4; and Shaw and Shaw, *A History of the Ottoman Empire and Modern Turkey*, Vol. 2, Chs 1 and 2.
19. J. Haslip, *The Sultan* London: Cassel, 1958.

peoples of the empire, particularly the Arabs; while throughout the Islamic world pan-Islamic policies were promoted, designed to stimulate opposition to the advance of the great imperial powers, Britain, France and Russia, in Central Asia, the Middle East and North Africa, and where possible secure the liberation of the enslaved Muslim peoples of the world. Throughout the empire the more conservative members of the *ulema* were promoted, and members of the Muslim mystic brotherhoods, with whom Abdul Hamid liked to associate, appointed. Yet paradoxically, throughout the long years of reaction, the process of westernisation and modernisation, and the parallel process of centralisation, promoted in the period of the *Tanzimat*, continued unabated, driven not so much by western ideology as by technology, its material embodiment.

The speed with which western technology was introduced into the Ottoman Empire in the decades immediately preceding the First World War was remarkable. In the closing years of the nineteenth century, an elaborate telegraph system, linking all parts of the empire, was completed; and a railway network, linking Istanbul, Ankara and Konya. In 1901 construction of the Hedjaz railway, financed by voluntary subscription, was commenced; and in 1903 construction of the notorious Baghdad line. Elsewhere, in Damascus, Beirut and Jerusalem, new roads and buildings were constructed, which as Elie Kedourie has remarked, turned Syria into one of the most civilised parts of the empire.[20] Meanwhile, in the seas surrounding the empire, new shipping companies, for the most part foreign owned, were set up; and on the Tigris and Euphrates rivers navigation companies. In this way many parts of the empire, previously remote and isolated, were opened, not only to international trade but also to effective government control, hitherto for the most part unknown.[21]

Thanks largely to his vigorous promotion of traditional Islamic values, Abdul Hamid enjoyed substantial support among the Muslim peoples of the Ottoman Empire; and in the years following the conclusion of the Treaty of Berlin (1878) he was generally successful in holding the front against the great imperial powers, though he did lose Tunis, still nominally a part of the Ottoman Empire, to France in 1881; and Egypt and the Suez Canal (opened in 1869) to Britain in 1882. But he could not for ever stem the tide of western, liberal, secular and nationalist ideas, already in full flood in the

20. E. Kedourie, *Arabic Political Memoirs and Other Studies* London: Frank Cass, 1974, p. 125.
21. Karpat, 'Transformation of the Ottoman State'.

Balkans. In 1893 a group of Bulgarian nationalists, resident in Salonica, intent on securing first autonomy for Macedonia and then union of the unredeemed territories with Bulgaria, formed an organisation known as the Bulgarian Macedonian-Edirne Revolutionary Committees and later as the Internal Macedonian Revolutionary Organisation (IMRO); while in 1895 a group of Macedonian refugees, resident in Bulgaria, intent on securing immediate union, formed the Macedonian Supreme Committee. At the same time Greek and Serbian elements, equally determined to protect the interests of their communities in Macedonia, set up similar societies, such as *Ethniké Hetairia* and the Society of St Sava. As a result there broke out in Macedonia a fierce struggle for power, fought out for the most part by Bulgarian, Serbian and Greek *chetniks* (guerrillas), seeking to secure control of the local churches, the focal point of national identity, and the allegiance of their congregations. Not that the conflict was entirely confined to local action. In 1895 IMRO attempted to provoke a general rising in Macedonia; and in 1903, it organised a similar rising in Salonica, known as the St Ilias Day (Ilinden) rising, designed to provoke Great Power intervention.[22]

The difficulties created by the spread of western, liberal, secular and nationalist ideas and ideologies in the Ottoman Empire were by no means confined to the European provinces. In eastern Anatolia, Armenian nationalists organised by Henchak (Bell), a nationalist organisation set up by Armenian students in Geneva in 1887, and by Dashnaksutiun (the Armenian Revolutionary Federation), founded in Tiflis in 1890, mounted a series of campaigns calling for either independence or autonomy, with the result that in 1894–6 there occurred a terrible massacre of Armenians, not only in the eastern provinces but also in Istanbul, carried out for the most part either by the *Hamiddiyye* (Kurdish cavalry regiments set up by Abdul Hamid) or by local riff-raff.[23]

The disorder created in Macedonia and the eastern provinces by the failures of the Hamidian regime and the spread of nationalist ideology led in the closing years of the nineteenth century to the

22. Anderson, *Eastern Question*, Chs 8 and 9; D. Dakin, *The Greek Struggle in Macedonia* Salonica: Institute for Balkan Studies, 1966; Ilber Ortayli, 'Formation of National Identity among the Balkan Peoples', *Turkish Review of Balkan Studies*, Vol. 1 (1993); E. Barker, *Macedonia* Westport, Connecticut: Greenwood Press, 1980; C.J. Walker, *Armenia* London: Routledge, 1980, Ch. 1.
23. See A.O. Sarkissian, *History of the Armenian Question to 1885* Urbana, Illinois: Illinois University Press, 1938 and L. Nalbandian, *The Armenian Revolutionary Movement* Berkeley, California: University of California Press, 1963, for histories of the Armenian question.

foundation of a series of opposition movements in the Ottoman Empire, aimed at a restoration of the constitution. In 1889 a group of students at the Military Medical College in Istanbul (a centre of secular and anti-religious opinion) formed an Ottoman Unity Society, calling for a restoration of the Ottoman constitution. During the following years, this society, the membership of which included many high-ranking officers, officials and members of the *ulema*, spread rapidly; and in 1896, now renamed the Society of Ottoman Union and Progress, it attempted a coup. But the plot was quickly discovered and the conspirators arrested. Meanwhile, attempts made by leading members of the Ottoman elite, including Kiamil Pasha, a leading advocate of reform, and Ismail Kemal Bey, an Albanian notable, to secure British backing for a radical change in the system of government, involving a transference of power from the Palace to the Porte, and the possible deposition of Abdul Hamid, proved equally unsuccessful, for the British refused to intervene. As a result Abdul Hamid's regime, seemingly threatened on every side in the period of the Armenian massacres of 1894–6, survived intact. Indeed, victory in the Greco-Turkish War of 1897, which broke out shortly thereafter, actually improved its standing with the Muslim peoples of the empire.

Following the defeat of the 1896 coup d'état and the victory of the Ottomans in the Greco-Turkish War of 1897, Ottoman opposition activity, effectively suppressed at home, shifted to Europe, where for more than a decade Young Turk emigrés had been busy promoting ideas of reform and even revolution. In 1902 the Young Turk emigrés, and other discontented elements, organised a Congress of Ottoman Liberals in Paris; but the conference quickly split into two groups, the one (inspired it may be supposed by the French model) calling for the promotion of an Ottoman national identity and increased centralisation, and the other (inspired by the Anglo-Saxon model) calling for decentralisation. But events within the empire soon conspired to shift attention back to the centre. As a result of the St Ilias's Day Rising and other events in Macedonia, the Great Powers decided to intervene and oblige the Ottomans to agree to the creation of a local gendarmerie, led by European officers; and in 1905 they obliged the Ottomans to agree to the appointment of an international finance commission, again controlled by European directors, whose task it would be to reform the finances of the Macedonian provinces. As a result of these and other developments, in the early 1900s there occurred an explosion of conspiratorial activity in the Ottoman Empire, particularly among the officer corps of the army. In 1904 a group of cadets at the War College formed a *Jeunes Gens* (Jön Jan) society. In 1905–6 a group of Turkish officers, stationed in Syria, including Mustafa Kemal (Atatürk), the later president of Turkey, set up a Fatherland Society (Vatan) later known as the Fatherland and Freedom Society; and about the same time Redjeb Pasha, the vali of Tripoli (a province that was a centre of disaffection: scores of dissidents had been exiled there) attempted, unsuccessfully as it turned out, to organise a coup d'état, involving the dispatch of an army from Tripoli to the Gallipoli Peninsula and the delivery of an ultimatum to Abdul Hamid, demanding the restoration of the constitution. Finally, in 1906, a group of civil servants and army officers, led by Talaat Bey, the chief clerk of the correspondence division of the Salonica Directorate of Posts, founded a society in Salonica, known initially as the Ottoman Freedom Society and later as the CUP, committed to the restoration of the Ottoman constitution and the reform of government. During the following years membership of this society spread rapidly, particularly among the officer corps of the Second and Third Army Corps, stationed in Edirne and Salonica. As a result, when in 1908 events conspired to promote a mutiny among units of the Third Army Corps in Macedonia, the leadership of the society found itself well placed to take advantage of the situation and engineer the so-called Young Turk Revolution, an event which, in the eyes of some scholars at least, marked a major turning point in the history of the Ottoman Empire, heralding not only the demise of the Hamidian regime but also the eventual collapse of the empire as a whole.[24]

24. Lewis, *Emergence of Modern Turkey*, Ch. 6; M. Şükrü Hanioğlu, *The Young Turks in Opposition* Oxford: Oxford University Press, 1995, Ch. 3; S. Akşin, *Jön Türkler ve Ittihat ve Terrakki* Istanbul: Gerçek Yayinevi, 1986, pp. 57–8; S. Story (ed.), *The Memoirs of Ismail Kemal Bey* London: Constable, 1920, p. 309; Zürcher, *Unionist Factor* Ch. 1. The attempted coup d'état of 1896 was by no means a marginal affair. In the wave of arrests that followed more than 350 people were held, including Kiazim Pasha, the Military Commander of Istanbul, Hüsni Bey, the police commissioner, and Salih Bey, the commander of the gendarmerie; though they were not necessarily all implicated in the plot.

CHAPTER ONE

The Young Turk Revolution of 1908

Events

The course of events leading up to the so-called Young Turk Revolution of 1908 appears in retrospect clear enough; though several aspects remain obscure. On 28 June 1908 Ahmed Niyazi, an adjutant major serving with his unit in Resna, in Macedonia, fearing arrest as a result of the infiltration of his conspiratorial group by one of the sultan's spies, and concerned regarding the possibility of Great Power intervention in Macedonia (at that very moment the British monarch, Edward VII, and the Russian tsar, Nicholas II, were meeting at Reval in the Baltic, supposedly to discuss the issue) called a meeting of his co-conspirators in Resna at which it was decided that action of some kind could no longer be postponed. As a result on 3 July, with the support and approval of the Monastir branch of the CUP, as the Ottoman Freedom Society had become known, Niyazi, accompanied by some 240 or so regular soldiers and a similar number of civilians, many of Albanian descent, liberally supplied with money, arms and ammunition seized from the local treasury and armoury, took to the hills above the town, calling in the meantime, in appeals addressed to the Palace Secretariat, the inspector general of Rumelia and the vali of Monastir, for immediate action to combat injustice and inequality and secure a restoration of the constitution. Niyazi's example was soon followed by a number of other officers, for the most part members of the CUP, including Major Enver, an officer attached to the staff of the inspector general of Macedonia, and later leader of the CUP, while local troops, commanded by officers for the most part loyal to the Unionist cause, refused to fire on the mutineers, as did others later dispatched from Anatolia. Moreover, on 6 July, Hakki Pasha, a member of a commission appointed by the sultan to enquire into unrest in the Third Army Corps, stationed in Macedonia, was assassinated, as were other senior officers loyal to the sultan in the following weeks. On 7 July Şemsi Pasha, the general dispatched by the sultan to put down the rebellion, was shot by an agent of the CUP in the main street of Monastir, as he was getting into his carriage outside the post office, where he had just telegraphed the Palace to inform them of his plans. On 12 July Sadik Pasha, the sultan's aide-de-camp, was shot on board a ship, returning to Istanbul, and about the same time Osman Hidâyet Pasha, commandant of the Monastir garrison, was struck down. Further outbreaks and demonstrations followed, for the most part organised by agents of the CUP, including one in Firzovik in Albania, where Unionist agents succeeded in subverting a local demonstration against the presence of members of an Austro-Hungarian Railway school at a festival in the area. Then on 20 July the Muslim population of Monastir rose; and on 22 July Osman Pasha, who had replaced Şemsi Pasha as the sultan's special envoy, was kidnapped by the rebels. As a result of these and other developments, on 24 July Abdul Hamid, now convinced of the hopelessness of his position (he was informed that should he refuse to comply at once to demands for the restoration of the constitution, 100 000 men would march on the capital to secure his deposition) decided that discretion was the better part of valour and announced his intention of acceding to the wishes of the people. On the same day an *irade* was published, calling for preparations to be made for the holding of elections, so that a chamber of deputies might be convened, in accordance with the articles of the constitution, which as Abdul Hamid was quick to point out remained effective.[1]

Origins and causation of the Young Turk Revolution

Contemporary observers generally assumed that the Young Turk Revolution of 1908 was organised, or at least inspired, by the Young

1. F. Ahmad, *The Young Turks* Oxford: Clarendon Press, 1969, Ch. 1; W. Miller, *The Ottoman Empire, 1801–1913* Cambridge: Cambridge University Press, 1913, Ch. 14; H. Bayur, *Türk Inkilâbi Tarihi* Istanbul: Maarif Matbaasi, 1940, Pt. 1, pp. 217–20; A. Mango, 'The Young Turks', *Middle Eastern Studies*, Vol. 8, No. 1 (1972). For a more detailed, and slightly different, account of the events leading up to the Young Turk Revolution of 1908, see A. Kansu, *The Revolution of 1908 in Turkey* Leiden: E.J. Brill (1997), Ch. 3.

Turk emigrés abroad, though they remained uncertain how so extraordinary an achievement was accomplished. As an anonymous writer in the *Fortnightly Review* of September 1908 put it:

> At the moment of the interest excited throughout the world by the political struggle in Russia, the Young Turks transferred their operations from Paris to Salonica, which has remained the real headquarters. What happened for a long period afterwards is what no man has yet attempted to tell. When our partial knowledge of methods and results begins we find ramifying throughout Macedonia a vast conspiracy already almost complete.

Such an easy assumption of expatriate organisation can no longer be sustained. According to Nicolae Batzaria, an Ottoman Vlach, who joined the Ottoman Freedom Society, possibly at Enver's invitation, in 1907, and who was acquainted with virtually all of the CUP leaders, including Enver, Talaat, Djavid, Hafiz Hakki and Djemal (he was later made minister of public works in the CUP cabinet appointed following the coup d'état of January 1913) the Young Turk Revolution of 1908 was exclusively the work of branches of the CUP, locally established in Salonica and Monastir.[2] It should not, however, be assumed that no connection existed between the emigré organisation established in Europe and the Ottoman Freedom Society. On the contrary, in 1907 Talaat, wishing to establish an outlet for his society's propaganda abroad, had made contact with the Young Turk organisations in Europe, in particular with Ahmed Riza's group in Geneva; and to this end he had dispatched two agents, Ömer Naci and Hüsrev Sami, to establish a publication there. Shortly thereafter Ahmed Riza dispatched one of his followers, *Selanikli* Dr Nazim, to Salonica (disguised it is said as a Dervish Hodja), to negotiate a merger between the two organisations, an arrangement completed in September 1907. It was as a result of this agreement that the Ottoman Freedom Society became known as the CUP. Nevertheless, according to Batzaria, contact between the two organisations remained minimal, as the emigré groups were generally distrusted by the Salonica and Monastir branches, who were inclined to believe that they had for the most part either been infiltrated by the sultan's spies or simply bought off.[3]

2. K. Karpat, 'The Memoirs of N. Batzaria: The Young Turks and Nationalism', *International Journal of Middle Eastern Affairs*, Vol. 6 (1975). Recent researches, carried out by Aykut Kansu, would suggest that contact between the CUP organisation in Europe and the branches of the organisation in Macedonia and Anatolia was somewhat more extensive than Nicolae Batzaria supposed. See A. Kansu, *The Revolution of 1908 in Turkey*, Chs 2 and 3.

3. E.J. Zürcher, *The Unionist Factor* Leiden: E.J. Brill, 1984, pp. 41–2.

Contemporary observers were generally agreed that the immediate causes of the Young Turk Revolution lay in the fear of the conspirators of the CUP that they were about to be discovered and their concern regarding the possibility of Great Power intervention in Macedonia, daily expected. But with regard to the underlying causes, it was agreed that they lay elsewhere, in the rottenness of the Hamidian regime, generally despised, the disaffection of the army, frequently observed, the discontent of the Ottoman bourgeoisie and intelligentsia, noted by among others Leon Trotsky, the Russian revolutionary, a close observer of Balkan affairs,[4] and the atmosphere of revolutionary change prevalent at the time, not only in Europe but also in Asia.[5] The following extract from an article by E.J. Dillon, entitled 'The Reforming Turk', published in the *Quarterly Review* of 1909, may be taken as typical:

But worse than all that was the intolerable system of military espionage which tended to foster jealousy, to crush out initiative, and to kill all *esprit de corps*. Officers might not have dealings or cultivate acquaintance with foreigners, commanders could not win battles or attain popularity in any way, without running the risk of being entered on the spies' black list and persecuted or made away with. Promotion for military merit and active service was falling into desuetude; and no one, however deserving, was raised to higher rank if the report of a spy declared him unworthy. . . . It was this crime against the nation in the person of its heroic defenders that contributed most to turn the scale in favour of reform. Officers and men were profoundly disaffected towards the Government, and began to show their feelings openly. During the past three years several cases of 'spontaneous combustion' had been recorded, explained, and forgotten. In 1907 there was a mutiny of the reserves at Adrianople, and a strike of reserves in Monastir. Last June, in Adrianople, forty artillery officers seized the telegraph office and communicated with the Sultan, complaining of not having received their well-earned pay and of not being promoted according to merit. The Padishah kept them four days waiting for a reply, and then promised to redress their grievances if they would return to duty.

At last the army would brook these things no longer. The officers, many of them young men educated abroad, sent special messengers to their comrades in other parts of the country to concert means of redress. A widespread organisation was thus created without the use of paper and ink. But in time the spies got wind of the Young Turkish conspiracy. The court party rigged out a punitive expedition and

4. For Leon Trotsky's views on the Young Turk Revolution see *The War Correspondence of Leon Trotsky: The Balkan Wars, 1912–13* London: Pathfinder, 1991, pp. 9–15.
5. Viator, 'Turkey: the Problems of the Near East', Pt. 1, *Fortnightly Review*, (1908), pp. 364–5.

despatched it to Monastir under the command of Shemzy Pasha. There was no time to lose. The plot, although not yet quite mature, had to be executed at all risks. Niazy Bey, one of the most accomplished officers of the army, deserted at Monastir, leading 200 men with him, and took to the woods. Thereupon the movement began. A few murders, mutinies, proclamations of constitutional government, and the first act of the drama was over. The Sultan could devise no expedient; his stalwarts, at their wits' ends, did nothing; activity was confined to the revolutionists, who scored a decisive victory. The Hamidian régime might be likened to a vast tree of which the inside is eaten away and the bark alone lives. Suddenly it receives a slight impact and falls for ever.

Recent research, carried out mainly in the French archives, has confirmed the validity of Dillon's observations, particularly those concerning the part played in the outbreak by discontent in the army, which in the decade or so preceding the revolution had reached unprecedented levels. Two factors, in particular, it would seem, loomed large in the catalogue of grievances which gave rise to this discontent: the non-payment of the troops and unwarranted delays in their demobilisation. In August 1896 eight officers protested at the ministry of war in Istanbul that they and their families were dying of starvation, for want of pay. In January 1904 soldiers returning from the Yemen mutinied in Beirut, again demanding pay. In March 1905 400 soldiers, stationed in Tripoli, gathered in the Jaama-el Bacha mosque, demanding that they be sent home, as their period of active service (normally three years, followed by six years in the active army reserve, and nine years in the reserve) was completed. In August 1906 conscripts serving in the Yemen, conscripted in 1898, mutinied, pillaging towns and villages. In February 1907, 280 soldiers serving in Benghazi, who had completed seven years' service, retired to a mosque, demanding that they be sent home. In May some 100 serving in Üsküb mutinied when informed that they were to serve longer without pay; and in June–August troops serving in the Yemen, joined by new recruits and by their officers, mutinied, complaining that the money allocated for their pay was being used to buy off the Arab chiefs involved in the Seyed Yahya revolt. Some of the conscripts, it is said, had served in the Yemen for 25 years.

In the period immediately preceding the Young Turk Revolution discontent if anything increased. In March 1908 two regiments of cavalry stationed in the Edirne area (the class of 1903), complained of not being paid and of delays in their demobilisation.

Shortly thereafter 70 artillery officers organised a demonstration, protesting against the lack of promotion and the elevation of unqualified colleagues; while similar outbreaks occurred in Denizli, Salihli and Kula. In April 1908 1,500 reservists from the province of Ankara assembled at Üsküb, demanding to be sent home. In May 1908, in Scutari, 300 soldiers handed in their arms and occupied the telegraph office, complaining to the *serasker* of their problems; while in June two regiments of infantry, joined by members of an artillery regiment, and their officers, occupied the telegraph office, complaining to the sultan that they had not been paid. Meanwhile similar outbreaks occurred in Monastir, Manisa, Izmir (including soldiers returning from Yemen), Nazilli, Akhisar and Alashehir. On the eve of the Young Turk Revolution, therefore, not only were acts of indiscipline and mutiny commonplace, but the essential bond of loyalty, on which the sultan depended for the exercise of his authority, had to a large extent been destroyed.[6]

Not that unrest in the period preceding the outbreak of the Young Turk Revolution of 1908 was confined to the army. In the period 1906–7, as Aykut Kansu, the Turkish historian, has recently shown, there occurred in Anatolia a series of tax revolts and demonstrations in which peasants, shopkeepers, merchants and other groups, aggravated beyond endurance by the imposition of extra taxes and the rapacity of the local tax collectors, boycotted elections, petitioned the Sultan requesting a remission of taxation, organised demonstrations, and on occasion occupied government buildings and assassinated officials. In January 1906, in Kastamonu, a group of leading merchants and artisans dispatched a petition to the Sultan in Istanbul demanding the abolition of poll taxes recently imposed on people and domestic animals. And when their petition remained unanswered they organised a demonstration attended by more than 4,000 people, Moslem, Greek and Armenian, in front of the government buildings in the town. At the demonstration calls were made for the dismissal of the Governor and the Tax Commissioner. In February 1906, in Sinop (Sinope), several thousand people marched on the government offices, occupied the telegraph office and forcibly placed the Sub-Governor on a ship bound for Istanbul. And in March 1906, in Erzerum, a group of local shopkeepers, merchants and artisans, encouraged by agents of the CUP and the local Mufti (Muslim priest or expounder of the law) petitioned the Sultan, requesting a remission in taxation, organised a demonstration,

6. M.-Ş. Güzel, 'Prélude à la Revolution', *Varia Turcica*, Vol. 13 (1991).

attended by thousands, occupied the telegraph offices and attacked the Governor's residence.

Government attempts to suppress the tax revolts in Kastamonu, Sinob and Erzerum proved largely ineffective. In Kastamonu the local Military Commander and Police Chief, both it would seem supporters of the CUP, refused to take action against the demonstrators when called upon by the Government to do so. In Sinob likewise no action was taken against the demonstrators; and in the east Zeki Pasha, the Commander of the Fourth Army Corps, stationed in Erzincan, refused to dispatch troops to suppress the revolt in Erzerum when requested to do so by the Council of Ministers. As a result, during the following months tax revolts and demonstrations broke out in many other towns in Anatolia, including Trabzon, Giresun, Samsun, Ankara, Kayseri, Sivas, Bitlis and Zeytun; the authority of the Sultan, already undermined by the failure of the military authorities to maintain discipline in the army, was further eroded.

Historians have likewise accepted that fear of discovery and concern regarding the outcome of the Reval meeting were decisive factors inspiring the uprising at Resne. As Feroz Ahmed has explained in *The Young Turks* (1969), in the spring of 1908 the CUP, concerned regarding the success of Abdul Hamid's espionage system, had already decided to take action against the agents of the Palace in Macedonia; and on 11 June, in an attempt to prevent further investigation, they had had Colonel Nâzim, an officer responsible for the interrogation of law students at the Salonica Law School who were accused of conspiracy, shot (he was badly wounded but survived). In these circumstances it is scarcely surprising that Major Niyazi, convinced that his organisation had been penetrated by a Palace spy, should have decided to act, and that others, equally fearful of discovery, should have decided to follow suit.[7] As for the significance of the Reval meeting, Niyazi is said to have had three sleepless nights following the conclusion of the meeting; and both Enver and his fellow Unionist Fethi later identified it as a factor influencing their decision to take to the hills.[8] As Sir Gerard Lowther, the British ambassador in Istanbul, remarked, the Reval meeting was the 'match' which set off the explosion.[9]

Not that the uprising was entirely spontaneous. In the early days of the association Unionist leaders had decided to seek an understanding with the minority organisations in Macedonia and

---

7. Ahmad, *Young Turks*, pp. 2–4.
8. Ibid.
9. *British Documents on Foreign Affairs*, Pt. I, Series B, Vol. 20, Annual Report for 1908.

elsewhere, in order that they might present the sultan with a united front and compel him to reinstate the constitution. In 1907, according to Kiazim Karabekir, an early member of the society and later leader of the Turkish national movement, plans had been made (or at least considered) to assassinate Abdul Hamid; while Kiazim Karabekir himself had put forward a plan to organise an Army of Freedom, which would march on the capital, depose the sultan and clean out the Palace.[10] Finally, in the spring of 1908 plans were made for a revolution, to be carried out in September.[11] Surprisingly, in view of the apparent need for secrecy, in May a memorandum drawing attention to the existence of the society and to its intention to take action against the despotism of Abdul Hamid, was dispatched to the representatives of the Great Powers in the Ottoman Empire.[12]

Organisation of the Ottoman Freedom Society (CUP)

The Ottoman Freedom Society, later known as the CUP, influenced by other revolutionary organisations, in particular it would seem IMRO, and also by the rituals and practices of the various masonic lodges then active throughout the Near East, was from the beginning a hierarchical association with a cellular structure. Members were generally proposed by existing members. Thoroughly vetted, they were then initiated in elaborate ceremonies involving secret houses, blindfolds and oaths sworn on copies of the Koran, revolvers and knives. Traitors, it was made clear, would be ruthlessly hunted down and killed. All Ottoman subjects were entitled to join, irrespective of race or creed (though some accounts suggest that only Muslims were entitled to do so). Members frequently met in masonic lodges, some of which enjoyed extra-territorial status, and in the houses of Greeks sympathetic to their cause. (Not all Greeks at that time wanted union with Greece. Some aimed rather at the reform and possible Hellenisation of the Ottoman state. Only a reformed Ottoman state, it was believed, would be capable of opposing the advance of the Slavs.)

10. S. Akşin, 'Notes on Kiazim Karabekir's Committee of Union and Progress', *Varia Turcica*, Vol. 13 (1991).
11. Ahmad, *Young Turks*, p. 2.
12. O. Koloğlu, 'Les Jeunes Turcs Face à l'Affaire Macedonienne en Mai–Juillet 1908', *Turkish Review of Balkan Studies*, Vol. 1, Annex 2 (1993).

Designed ultimately to create an organisation capable of penetrating every level of the state administration, from village to province, membership of the CUP spread rapidly, particularly among
the officer corps of the Second and Third Armies, based in Salonica
and Edirne, and of the navy. Founder members included Talaat,
Midhat Shükrü and Ismail Canbolat, while early members included
Kiasim Karabekir, Süleyman Askeri and Enver. At the time of the
proclamation of the constitution in 1908 membership of the Salonica
branch numbered some 505, of which 319 were officers and 186
civilians. Membership of the Monastir and Istanbul branches, formed
by Karabekir, Enver and others, was of a similar order. Members
willing to sacrifice their lives for the cause (*fedais*) formed a special
branch of the association, controlled by a designated official. *Fedais*
might initiate projects, but they had on no account to carry them
out without permission. Those who initiated activities detrimental
to the interests of the organisation would be tried by its central
committee, and if found guilty reprimanded, fined or executed.
Families of *fedais*, left in need, would be supported.[13]

Following the Young Turk Revolution, the CUP attempted to
change its status to that of a political party, and to this end sub-
committees or branches (including it would seem a number of
masonic lodges) were set up in every quarter of the capital, and in
the provinces. Each sub-committee or branch was entitled to elect a
delegate to attend an annual congress, or general assembly, which
together with a central committee would be made responsible for
determining policy; though in practice power remained for the
most part firmly in the hands of the central committee. Members
of the CUP elected as members of the chamber of deputies might
operate in the name of the CUP.[14]

Aims and objectives

According to the memorandum dispatched to the representatives
of the Great Powers in May 1908 the immediate aims of the CUP
were both clear and simple: the removal of the corrupt regime

13. Akşin, 'Notes on Kiasim Karabekir's Committee'; Karpat, 'Memoirs of
N. Batzaria'.
14. Zürcher, *Unionist Factor*, pp. 38–40; A.B. Kuran, *Inkilâp Tarihimiz ve Jön Türkler*
Istanbul: Tan Matbaasi, 1945 and *Inkilâp Tarihimiz ve Ittihad ve Terakki* Istanbul: Tan
Matbaasi, 1948; H. Ertürk, *Iki Devrin Perde Arkasi* Istanbul: Pinar Yayinevi, 1969.

installed by Sultan Abdul Hamid and the restoration of the constitution. Thereafter, as the title of the CUP suggests, the society would seek 'union' and 'progress'; that is, a 'union of the peoples' which would in due course facilitate political, social and economic progress. In this way liberty, equality and justice would be secured, not only for the Muslims but also for the Christian minorities. As Enver is said to have remarked at a meeting of his supporters held in Salonica on the eve of the restoration of the constitution: 'Henceforth we are all brothers. There are no Bulgars, Greeks, Romanians, Jews, Mussulmans; under the blue sky we are all equal, we glory in being Ottomans.'[15]

Agreement regarding the aims and objectives of the CUP, however, was not matched by agreement regarding the means by which those aims and objectives might be achieved. While a majority of the supporters of the CUP, particularly those of Turkish Muslim descent, believed that union and progress might be secured most effectively by a greater degree of centralisation in the system of government, a significant number, made up mainly of minority elements, looked for a greater degree of decentralisation, involving perhaps the creation of some kind of federal system. Moreover, according to Nicolae Batzaria, a number of Young Turks belonging to the minority communities looked on constitutional reform not as a means of promoting Ottomanism and securing union and progress, but as a stepping stone to independence; while others looked on the whole process merely as a means of securing personal advancement.

The question of centralisation was not the only significant issue dividing the members of the CUP. While the so-called westerners believed that, in order for the Ottoman Empire to survive it would be necessary for the Ottoman people to adopt the culture and values of western civilisation wholesale, others, notably the so-called Islamicists, argued that, as the Islamic faith was itself essentially rational, western science and technology could be adopted freely, without the need to adopt other western values, secular, liberal and national, considered unacceptable. Ottoman decline, in other words, was not a consequence, as some of the westerners believed, of the dominance of Islam and the obstacle to progress that this supposedly created, but of its very opposite, a failure fully to adopt the faith. The solution lay, the Islamicists concluded, not in a diminution of the influence of Islam, but in its promotion. A third group,

15. W.T. Castle, *Grand Turk* London: Hutchinson, 1942, p. 79.

small but growing, the so-called Turkists, generally agreed with the westerners that in order for the Ottoman Empire to prosper it would be necessary for it to adopt the new civilisation of the west more or less wholesale, but they argued that for this task to be accomplished effectively it would be necessary first to create a distinct national culture, in which the religion of Islam, the foundation of Ottoman (Turkish) culture, might play a part. The solution to the problem of Ottoman decline lay, therefore, not in a superficial adoption of western culture and civilisation, but in the promotion of a strong national culture, on which foundation the scientific and technological structures of western civilisation might be erected.[16]

It is evident that the aims and objectives of the Young Turks of the CUP – at least those who genuinely looked to promote union and progress – differed little from those of the statesmen of the *Tanzimat* period, who had first promoted Ottomanism and promulgated the First Ottoman Constitution. Where the Young Turks differed from their predecessors was in their determination to tackle the problems of the empire head on, to abandon the policies of compromise and procrastination pursued, sometimes with considerable skill, by the statesmen of previous eras, and opt instead for a 'rule of thorough'. Young, enthusiastic and full of energy, they intended, as Enver later put it, to root out corruption, rally the Muslims (and presumably the Christians and Jews) and 'come to grips with the European monsters who are crushing Islam'.[17]

'Jews, Socialists and Freemasons'

Contemporary observers were virtually united in their conclusion that the Young Turk Revolution of 1908 was the product of a conspiracy mounted by Young Turks, Jews, Socialists and Freemasons. An anonymous author writing in the *Fortnighty Review* in 1908 referred to the 'political freemasons' of Macedonia. Aubrey Herbert, an honorary consul at the British embassy in Istanbul, who published *Ben Kendim* in 1924, remarked that the Jews of Salonica, generally known as 'Jünme' (*dönme*, converts, members of a Judaeo-Islamic syncretist sect founded in the seventeenth century), were the real parents of the constitution. Colonel Sadik, a leader of the

---

16. N. Berkes, *The Development of Secularism in Turkey* Montreal: McGill University Press, 1964, Ch. 11.
17. Castle, *Grand Turk*, Ch. 8.

opposition to the CUP, accused the CUP leadership in 1911 of being irreligious, self-seeking, pro-Zionist and in league with the freemasons. Halil Halid, according to W.S. Blunt, a shrewd observer of Middle Eastern affairs, blamed the 'freemasons of the CUP' for the loss of Tripolitania to Italy in 1911. More significantly, Sir Gerard Lowther, the British ambassador, much influenced it would seem by G.H. Fitzmaurice, the indefatigable dragoman (translator) at the British embassy, referred, in a letter written to Sir Charles Hardinge, the permanent under-secretary at the British foreign office, in July 1909, to the 'Jew Committee of Union and Progress'; and in a letter written in April 1910 to the 'Jews, Socialists and Freemasons' who now dominated the government of the Ottoman Empire. In another letter, written shortly thereafter, he refers scathingly to that 'combination of self-seeking spurious freemasons and Jews that represent the Committee of Union and Progress'.[18]

The assumption that freemasons, Jews and Socialists played a significant part in the setting up of the CUP and in organising the Young Turk Revolution of 1908 found its clearest expression in a letter written by Lowther to Hardinge on 29 May 1910. In this letter Lowther remarks:

> As you are aware, the Young Turkey movement in Paris was quite separate from and in great part in ignorance of the inner workings of that in Salonica. The latter town has a population of about 140,000, of whom 80,000 are Spanish Jews, and 20,000 of the sect of Sabetai Levi [*sic*] or Crypto-Jews, who externally profess Islamism. Many of the former have in the past acquired Italian nationality and are Freemasons affiliated to Italian lodges. Nathan, the Jewish Lord Mayor of Rome, is high up in Masonry, and the Jewish Premiers Luzzati and Sonnino, and other Jewish senators and deputies, are also, it appears, Masons. They claim to have been founded from and to follow the ritual of the 'Ancient Scottish'.
>
> Some years ago Emannuele Carasso, a Jewish Mason of Salonica, and now deputy for that town in the Ottoman Chamber, founded there a lodge called 'Macedonia Risorta' in connection with Italian Freemasonry. He appears to have induced the Young Turks, officers and civilians, to adopt Freemasonry with a view to exerting an impalpable Jewish influence over the new dispensation in Turkey, though ostensibly only with a view to outwitting the Hamidian spies, and

---

18. A. Herbert, *Ben Kendim* London: Hutchinson, 1924, p. 15; F. Ahmad, 'Unionist Relations with the Greek, Armenian, and Jewish Communities of the Ottoman Empire, 1908–1914', in B. Braude and B. Lewis, *Christians and Jews in the Ottoman Empire* London: Holmes and Meier, 1982.

gave them the shelter of his lodge, which, meeting in a foreign house, enjoyed extra-territorial immunities from inquisitorial methods. Adbul Hamid's spies got cognisance of the movement, and a certain Ismail Mahir Pasha, who was mysteriously murdered shortly after the revolution in July 1908 – an accident after dark – appears to have learnt some of their secrets and reported on them to Yildiz Palace. Spies were posted outside the lodge to take down the names of officers and others who frequented it, a move which the Freemasons countermined by enrolling of the secret police as 'brethren'. The inspiration of the movement in Salonica would seem to have been mainly Jewish, while the words 'Liberté', 'Egalité' and 'Fraternité', the motto of the Young Turks, are also the device of Italian Freemasons. The colours of both, red and white, are again the same. Shortly after the revolution in July 1908, when the Committee established itself in Constantinople, it soon became known that many of its leading members were Freemasons. Carasso began to play a big rôle, including his successful capture of the Balkan Committee, and it was noticed that Jews of all colours, native and foreign, were enthusiastic supporters of the new dispensation, till, as a Turk expressed it, every Hebrew seemed to become a potential spy of the occult Committee, and people began to remark that the movement was rather a Jewish than a Turkish revolution.[19]

Historians of the Young Turk movement have generally remained unconvinced by such accounts. Elie Kedourie, who first published extracts from Lowther's correspondence on the subject in 1971, saw them merely as 'fuddled fantasies', examples of the kind of simple-minded credulity the British and other foreign observers were from time to time wont to display: 'Rule by doctrinaire officers such as the Young Turks was, of course, an ominous development in the Ottoman Empire; but to represent it as the outcome of a Judaeo-masonic conspiracy was entirely to miss its significance. It was to be gulled by fuddled fabulosities.'[20] Bernard Lewis, in *The Emergence of Modern Turkey* (1961), was equally scathing. In his view such asseverations were the product of a prejudice originating in a 'line of clerical and nationalist thought' familiar on the continent at the time. The Young Turk Revolution could no more be explained in terms of Jewish influence and freemasonry than it could in terms of the activities of the agents of 'the Roman Catholic Church, the positivists, the house of Orleans, the German general staff and the British foreign office', also charged on occasion with

---

19. E. Kedourie, 'Young Turks, Freemasons and Jews', *Middle Eastern Studies*, Vol. 7, No. 2 (1971), Appendix.
20. Ibid., p. 92.

responsibility for the uprising.[21] It was none of these things: 'The Young Turk revolution . . . was a patriotic movement of Muslim Turks, mostly soldiers, whose prime objective was to remove a fumbling and incompetent ruler and replace him by a government better able to maintain and defend the empire against the dangers that threatened it.'[22] Certainly, a number of Jews, such as Emmanuel Carasso (Karasu), a Salonica lawyer, and Djavid Bey, a leading CUP figure and later minister of finance, did play a significant part in the Unionist movement; but Carasso's part was at best marginal, while Djavid Bey was merely a *dönme*. Not that, in Lewis's view, it made much difference. Turks of the Young Turk period were 'far from thinking in such terms as "pure-blooded Turks"'.[23]

Freemasons

Recent research would suggest that historians such as Lewis and Kedourie may have been premature in discounting so completely the part played by freemasons in the organisation of the various opposition movements in the Ottoman Empire, in particular the Ottoman Freedom Society, later known as the CUP. As Şükrü Hanioğlu, the Turkish historian, has shown, masonic organisations, mainly Greek, proliferated in the Ottoman Empire in the quarter century or so preceding the Young Turk Revolution. Under Abdul Hamid they were for a time suppressed, but in the mid-1890s they resumed their activities, seeking the promotion of liberal reform and a restoration of the constitution; and even in some cases the creation of a new multi-national state, in effect a resurrection of the Byzantine Empire. In 1901, the Comité Libéral Ottoman (Osmanli Hürriyetperverân Cemiyeti), supposedly the political arm of the freemasons in Istanbul, petitioned King Edward VII, himself a freemason of long standing, on behalf of the former sultan, Murad V, then imprisoned in the Yildiz Palace; and masonic elements are said to have played a part in the formation of a coalition, fashioned by Prince Sabahaddin, the Young Turk leader, and Ismail Kemal, the Albanian notable, at the Paris conference in 1902. Nor was the circle of Ahmed Riza, the Young Turk emigré, immune from their influence: Prince Muhammad Ali Halim, the leader of the

21. B. Lewis, *The Emergence of Modern Turkey* Oxford: Oxford University Press, 1961, p. 207 n. 4.
22. Ibid., p. 208.
23. Ibid., p. 207 n. 4.

movement in Egypt, for one, was a prominent freemason. Talaat, who corresponded with Ahmed Riza, joined the Macedonia-Risorta lodge in 1903; and in 1907 or thereabouts it is said that the Ottoman Freedom Society, later the CUP, was organised into two masonic lodges.[24] It is therefore possible to argue that, as Kemal Karpat, the eminent Turkish historian, has remarked, 'the Freemason lodges . . . played important roles in shaping the ideology and politics of the Union and Progress Society, at least during its formative years in the Balkans'.[25]

The significance of the part played by the freemasonry movement in the rise of the CUP, however, should not be exaggerated, for the principal objective of the masons was the creation of a new, decentralised, multi-national state, in effect a restoration of the Byzantine Empire, whereas the principal objective of the CUP, whatever their public statements, was the creation of a strong, centralised Ottoman state, based on the supremacy of the Muslim-Turkish element. As Şükrü Hanioğlu has remarked: 'In spite of the co-operation between them, the depiction of the Young Turk revolution as a Freemason conspiracy – a notion popular between the two world wars – is erroneous. The inescapable reality was that these movements were following divergent paths.'[26]

Jews

A reasonable case can also be made out in support of the contention that a number of Ottoman Jews, in particular those belonging to the Salonica community, played a small but by no means insignificant part in shaping the ideas and organisation of the CUP; though it would be misleading to suppose that they played anything like the part assumed for them by Lowther and others, who might reasonably be accused of propagating the anti-semitic attitudes

24. M. Şükrü Hanioğlu, *The Young Turks in Opposition* Oxford: Oxford University Press, 1995, Ch. 3; and 'Notes on the Young Turks and the Freemasons', *Middle Eastern Studies*, Vol. 25, No. 2 (1989); P. Dumont, 'La Turquie dans les archives du Grand Orient de France: les loges maçonniques d'obedience Francaise à Istanbul du milieu du XIXe siècle à la veille de la Première Guerre Mondiale', in *Colloques internationaux du CNRS*, No. 601; J.M. Landau, 'Muslim Opposition to Freemasonry', *Die Welt des Islams*, Vol. 32, No. 2 (1996). Freemasonry lodges continued to operate in Turkey in the period of the War of Independence. See P. Dumont, 'French Free Masonry and the Turkish Struggle for Independence, 1919–1923', *International Journal of Turkish Studies*, Vol. 3, No. 2 (1985–6).
25. Karpat, 'Memoirs of N. Batzaria', p. 280.
26. Şükrü Hanioğlu, *Young Turks in Opposition*, p. 41.

common in Britain at the time. Haim Nahoum, an influential rabbi, later appointed chief rabbi, is said to have maintained close contacts with the committee. Emmanuel Carassu, the Salonica lawyer, was not only grand master of the Macedonia-Risorta lodge but also a leading member of the organisation, representing the CUP in the chamber of deputies on a number of occasions. During the First World War he became one of the food controllers, amassing it is said a considerable personal fortune. Moses Cohen, an Istanbul intellectual and student of Ottoman politics, writing under the name Tekin Alp, was later to become a leading exponent of the ideology of pan-Turkism, adopted by the CUP, or at least by some of its leaders, in the First World War. That the designation 'Jew Committee of Union and Progress' conveys an entirely erroneous picture of the organisation is not in doubt; but it would seem unnecessary to deny Ottoman Jews, many of whom were among the best educated members of Ottoman society, any effective influence on the course of Ottoman politics in the period of the Young Turk Revolution.[27]

Circumstantial evidence might suggest that members of the various Jewish communities in the Ottoman Empire supported the CUP in order to secure the objectives of the Zionist movement, then active in Europe and America. At the turn of the century Theodor Herzl, a leading Zionist activist, had approached Abdul Hamid on several occasions, offering to 'regulate the whole finances of Turkey' (i.e., pay off the Ottoman national debt) in return for a grant of land in Palestine.[28] Following the Young Turk Revolution, Zionists opened an office in Istanbul; and according to Lowther newspapers advocating the creation of a Jewish colony appeared there about the same time. But there is in reality little or no evidence to support this contention. On the contrary, Ottoman Jews for the most part remained throughout loyal to the ideology of Ottomanism, convinced that the continued existence of the empire, in which they had on the whole prospered, offered the best guarantee of security. Salvation, it was argued, lay not in the creation of a Jewish colony in an obscure corner of the empire, but in a restoration of Ottoman power and prosperity. Nor were the Jews in any way inclined to support the creation of a federal system,

---

27. J.M. Landau, 'Les Jeunes-Turcs et le Sionisme', *Varia Turcica*, Vol. 13 (1991); Ahmad, 'Unionist Relations with the Greek, Armenian and Jewish Communities of the Ottoman Empire'; A. Mango, 'Remembering the Minorities', *Middle Eastern Studies*, Vol. 21, No. 4 (1985).
28. M. Lowenthal (ed.), *The Diaries of Theodor Herzl* Gloucester, Mass.: Peter Smith, 1978, pp. 121–38.

based on the principle of minority self-government, for this would merely encourage the territorial ambitions of the principal minorities, Greek, Bulgarian and Armenian – ambitions which posed as great a threat to the survival of the Jews as to that of the Muslim Turks. Finally, support for the Zionist programme would encourage anti-semitism, an ever-present danger.[29]

Had Ottoman Jews been tempted to offer their support to the Zionist project, advocated so persuasively by Theodor Herzl, the Zionist leader, then the extraordinary response elicited from Abdul Hamid on one occasion would certainly have given them pause for thought:

> The Sultan told me [Nevlinski, a contact of Herzl, informed him]: if Mr. Herzl is your friend in the same measure as you are mine, then advise him not to go a single step further in the matter. I cannot sell even a foot of land, for it does not belong to me but to my people. They have won this Empire and fertilized it with their blood. We will cover it once more with our blood, before we allow it to be torn from us. Two of my regiments from Syria and Palestine allowed themselves to be killed to a man at Plevna. Not one of them yielded; one and all remained, dead, upon the field. The Turkish people own the Turkish Empire, not I. I can dispose of no part of it. The Jews may spare their millions. When my Empire is divided, perhaps they will get Palestine for nothing. But only our corpse can be divided. I will never consent to vivisection.[30]

Socialists

Quite what contemporary commentators intended by the use of the word Socialist in their descriptions of the Young Turks of the CUP is not clear. For the most part they no doubt intended to convey merely a sense of disapprobation; but they may also have wished to indicate that it was the intention of the CUP to employ the powers of the state to secure political, economic and social reform. Not

---

29. Ahmad, 'Unionist Relations with the Greek, Armenian and Jewish Communities of the Ottoman Empire'; Landau, 'Les Jeunes-Turcs et le Sionisme'; *British Documents on Foreign Affairs*, Pt. I, Series B, Vol. 20, pp. 270–1. Lowther and his colleagues admitted that the ideology of Ottomanism, advocated by the CUP, could not be reconciled with the ideology of Zionism. Nevertheless, they argued that Salonica Jews, who played a significant part in the organisation of the CUP, used the movement to further Zionist ideals. See *British Documents on Foreign Affairs*, Pt. I, Series B, Vol. 20, Memorandum respecting the New Regime in Turkey.

30. Lowenthal (ed.), *Diaries of Theodor Herzl*, p. 152.

that Socialist ideas were unknown in the Ottoman Empire at that time. On the contrary, in the closing years of the nineteenth century they had spread rapidly, particularly among the minority communities inhabiting the western parts of the empire. Henchak and Dashnaksutiun, for instance, were inclined to refer to themselves as Marxist or Socialist organisations; and Socialists played a significant part in the organisation of IMRO. In 1905 Socialists opposed to the policies pursued by IMRO formed a Social Democratic Organisation of Macedonia and Edirne. Meanwhile Bulgarian Socialists, members of the Bulgarian Workers' Social Democratic Party, formed groups and organisations, published newspapers and journals, and organised strikes. Following the Young Turk Revolution, in which Socialists played a small but by no means insignificant part, a veritable explosion of such activities occurred. In Salonica a Workers' Federation was set up, whose membership, mainly Jewish, was numbered in hundreds; and in Istanbul an Ottoman Socialist Party and a Socialist Centre.

Membership of most of the socialist parties and organisations set up in Macedonia in this period was open to all nationalities, but in practice the parties and organisations tended to divide on national and ethnic lines. Nevertheless it was generally agreed that the social question should have priority over the national question. The problems of the Ottoman Empire, it was argued, might be most effectively resolved by the creation of a reformed empire, organised along federal lines, or by the creation of a federation of Slavonic states. All workers should unite against the despotic policies pursued by the Ottoman government and the exploitative practices of the Ottoman bourgeoisie.[31]

The extent of Socialist influence in Macedonia was quickly made evident in the period immediately following the Young Turk Revolution of 1908, when a wave of strikes and demonstrations occurred. In August 1908 a strike of longshoremen paralysed the port of Salonica for several days, and in September strikes – in effect a general strike – occurred in the transport, printing, tobacco, baking and tailoring industries. In May 1909 members of the Workers' Federation of Salonica organised a mass demonstration in the city; and in June 6,000 people marched in protest against a bill, introduced into the Ottoman parliament, limiting the right of workers to organise trade unions and go on strike. Other strikes and

31. M. Tunçay and E.J. Zürcher, *Socialism and Nationalism in the Ottoman Empire* London: British Academy Press, 1994, Chs 2–6.

demonstrations followed, in both Istanbul and Salonica; but increasingly, as the Unionists secured their hold on government, all such freedoms were curtailed.[32]

In the period preceding the Young Turk Revolution Ottoman Socialists belonging to the minority communities were by no means disinclined to associate with the CUP in its opposition to the hated Hamidian regime. In Macedonia and the Armenian provinces IMRO, Henchak and Dashnaksutiun maintained contact with the organisation and even on occasion offered it active support. They welcomed the outbreak of the revolution when it occurred. In the period of euphoria that followed the revolution Bulgarian, Greek and Armenian *chetniks* and *fedais*, committed to the Socialist ideology, were among the first to come down from the hills and lay aside their weapons; and they welcomed the suppression of the counter-revolution of April 1909. But it quickly transpired that the aims and objectives of the Socialists, with the possible exception of Jewish Socialists (the creation of a radically transformed Ottoman state, based on the federal principle) could not be so easily accommodated to those of the CUP (the creation of a strong centralised Ottoman state, based on the ideology of Ottomanism). Nor was any accommodation possible on the question of trade-union activity, for what the CUP, increasingly identified with the bourgeois and semi-feudal classes that dominated Ottoman life, wanted was social discipline, the necessary prerequisite, in their view, of 'union' and 'progress'. So concerned, indeed, were the leaders of the CUP with the outbreak of strikes and demonstrations that occurred following the Young Turk Revolution, that in the second half of 1909 they had a series of draconian laws introduced into the Ottoman parliament, designed to control public meetings, forbid strikes and prevent the formation of political parties and other organisations based on the ethnic or national principle. In 1910 the Ottoman Socialist Party was closed down, and a syndicate of tobacco workers banned. Finally, in the period of the Balkan and First World Wars all forms of Socialist and trade-union activity were suppressed. Not until the period of political and economic collapse that followed the defeat of the Ottoman Empire in the First World War were Ottoman workers and Socialists again to enjoy the extraordinary freedoms they had enjoyed for a brief spell in the aftermath of the Young Turk Revolution.[33]

32. Ibid., Chs 3 and 5; Zürcher, *Unionist Factor*, p. 99; Miller, *Ottoman Empire*, p. 476.
33. Tunçay and Zürcher, *Socialism and Nationalism in the Ottoman Empire*, Chs 3–6.

CHAPTER TWO

Counter-revolution

Immediate impact of the Young Turk Revolution

Most contemporary observers, particularly those resident in the European provinces of the empire, agreed that the success of the Young Turk Revolution and the restoration of the constitution which it brought about, was welcomed with an immense, and even at times surreal, enthusiasm. According to Aubrey Herbert, in Istanbul, a city tense with excitement, Muslims walked the streets arm in arm with Christians; the old order and the new mingled; and high hopes were held for the future. Baksheesh was refused, thieving stopped, murders no longer took place: the millennium, in short, had arrived. In Albania a Muslim band played outside a Greek cathedral, while enthusiastic supporters fired ball cartridges into the air. In Monastir and Salonica festivities organised to celebrate the coming of the constitution lasted for three days; in Tripoli Turks and Arabs joined in a thanksgiving service; and in Antakia and Iskenderun, where local committees were quickly formed, without distinction of race or creed, the event was celebrated with illuminations. In Beirut a Maronite priest four times kissed a Muslim sheikh; and the Muslim sheikh responded by four times kissing the priest.

Elsewhere in Macedonia Greek, Bulgarian and Serbian armed bands, including, by the end of the first week in August, some 26 Greek bands (217 men) and 55 Bulgarian bands (707 men) laid down their arms, as did some 340 Albanian rebels. As Hikmet Bayur, the Turkish historian, has remarked, seldom in the history of the world can a revolutionary movement have given rise to such high expectations.[1]

The accuracy of such accounts is not in doubt; but in recent years historians have come to question the validity of the picture of universal enthusiasm and rejoicing they convey, particularly in the case of the Arab provinces. Recent researches in consular archives and other sources suggest that, far from being received with universal rejoicing, the revolution was frequently greeted with scepticism. In Baghdad, it was reported, the announcement that the parliament was to reassemble, after a lapse of more than 30 years, and that elections were to be held immediately, was received without the smallest sign of enthusiasm. Local people (a well-known chronicler declared) rejected the aims of the CUP, which they interpreted as an attempt to end Muslim supremacy, out of hand. What need was there to introduce constitutional rights as long as the *Sheriat* was in existence, and what need to protest against the rule of the sultan, whose government was administered with a light hand? In Aleppo the report was received with astonishment bordering on incredulity: such a sudden break with the past was 'wholly unexpected'.[2] In Beirut the news was received with 'a certain amount of incredulity and scepticism'.[3] In Mosul, where opposition to the constitution was pronounced, a riot, inspired by the *ulema*, occurred, in which scores of peoples were killed or injured.[4] In Bussorah the news was 'as usual' received with astonishment. In Van, Diarbekir and Mosul, where Kurdish notables feared that the new dispensation might interfere with their right to despoil and oppress the Armenians at will, opposition was widespread. In Haifa, the Naqib al-Ashraf, an old man of 80, roundly cursed the constitution. Later, when he was tried for the offence, he was acquitted; and a crowd of 1,000 Muslim supporters gathered, chanting 'Long live the nation of Mohammed and the Sultan'. In Jerusalem the announcement had 'little effect'; though the *fellahin* welcomed the proposed changes in the system of government, which they believed implied an end

1. A. Herbert, *Ben Kendim* London: Hutchinson, 1924, p. 257; F. Ahmad, 'Unionist Relations with the Greek, Armenian, and Jewish Communities of the Ottoman Empire', in B. Braude and B. Lewis (eds.), *Christians and Jews in the Ottoman Empire* London: Holmes and Meier, 1982; D. Dakin, *The Greek Struggle in Macedonia* Salonica: Institute for Balkan Studies, 1966, pp. 378–84; *British Documents on Foreign Affairs*, Pt. I, Series B, Vol. 20, Docs 1–12.

2. E. Kedourie, 'The Impact of the Young Turk Revolution on the Arabic-speaking Provinces of the Ottoman Empire', in *Arabic Political Memoirs and Other Studies*. London: Frank Cass, 1974, p. 129.

3. Ibid.

4. Ibid., pp. 142–3.

to all taxation. In Ta'if, in Arabia, where the promulgation of the constitution was not even announced until some months later, a number of men 'found talking of the constitution' were flogged by order of the grand sharif.[5] In Benghazi the news was said to have made 'little or no impression': people seemed indifferent as to the form of government and sceptical as to reform, 'tolerating Turkish rule as a Muslim rule, and harbouring some veneration for the Sultan as religious head of the Ottoman Empire'.[6] In Tripoli, where a governor (Redjeb Pasha) sympathetic to the CUP had organised a demonstration to celebrate the promulgation of the constitution, the event was received with 'surprising indifference'. As for the Senussis (members of a Sufi order that controlled large parts of Tripolitania), they remained totally ignorant regarding the aims and objectives of the supporters of the CUP, whom they identified merely as idolators, committed to the destruction of the Ottoman state. Finally, in Macedonia many Greek *commitadjis* and others looked on the revolution merely as a nine-day wonder, unlikely to influence the course of events.[7]

The struggle for control

In the weeks immediately following the revolution the leaders of the CUP acted with both speed and determination to extend their influence and control to every corner of the empire. In Istanbul, vigorous steps were taken to destroy the palace clique surrounding Abdul Hamid, dismiss the horde of acolytes and parasites dependent upon him, abolish the secret police and secure amnesties for the hundreds of political prisoners and exiles created by his regime. At the same time CUP representatives were dispatched to the provinces to explain the aims and objectives of the movement (Mustafa Kemal Atatürk was one such); and telegraph messages dispatched, calling on the people to demonstrate their support, dismiss corrupt and unreliable officials and otherwise exert control. The response was nothing if not enthusiastic. In Jerusalem a local branch of the movement was set up to supervise the actions of officials and remove those suspected of disloyalty to the new regime. In Beirut the local CUP faction, already well established, took over control of the administration; though the governor general,

5. Ibid., p. 130.
6. Ibid.
7. Dakin, *Greek Struggle in Macedonia*, pp. 378–84.

mayor and chief of police were allowed to hold on to their offices (later the mayor was obliged to resign and the police chief and commander of the gendarmerie arrested and sent under guard to Salonica). In Aleppo a committee, made up of 21 designated officers, was formed. In Hodeida, in the Yemen, a branch of the society, previously formed, seized the *mutasarrif* (governor of a *sandjak*) and had him expelled from the area. In Mecca, when news of the revolution eventually arrived, the junior officers obliged the sharif to parade in the barracks, swear an oath of loyalty to the constitution, and promise to abandon evil practices, detrimental to the interests of the people. In Baghdad CUP supporters organised a demonstration against the Naqib, Sayyid Abd al-Rahman, and threatened violence if he did not join the society. In Damascus, where crowds of young men armed with swords and rifles roamed the streets terrorising the inhabitants, supporters of the organisation quickly established a branch. In Trabzon, on the Black Sea coast, a demonstration was organised, calling for the dismissal of the vali. Finally, in Bursa and Konya supporters of the movement secured the dismissal of corrupt officials and the arrest of Abdul Hamid's spies and other agents. As a result, in the months following the revolution, a substantial network of CUP organisations was set up which, together with those already established in Macedonia and Anatolia, quickly gained effective control of a substantial part of the administration of the empire.[8]

With regard to policy too, swift action was taken. In the first week in August 1908 a series of imperial decrees was issued and reform programmes published, promising a full implementation of the constitution, including the articles concerning the right of the grand vizier to appoint ministers (but not the ministers of war and marine whose appointment was reserved to the sultan, subject to the advice of the grand vizier and the council of ministers), a relaxation of the strict censorship laws, freedom of travel, freedom of association, annual budgets, which should henceforth be balanced, measures to encourage education and science and a substantial reorganisation of the administration, both central and provincial. As a result of these and other measures in the period following the revolution an explosion of political activity, previously suppressed, occurred, in the course of which numerous newspapers were set up

8. Kedourie, 'Impact of the Young Turk Revolution on the Arabic-speaking Provinces of the Ottoman Empire'; *British Documents on Foreign Affairs*, Pt. 1, Series B, Vol. 20, Doc. 26: F. McCullagh, 'The Constantinople Mutiny of 13 April', *Fortnightly Review*, Vol. 86 (1909); V.R. Swanson, 'The Military Rising in Istanbul, 1909', *Journal of Contemporary History*, Vol. 5 (1970).

and political parties formed. Prominent among the political parties formed was the Ottoman Liberal Union Party (Osmanli Ahrar Firkasi), set up by Sabahaddin Bey and his supporters, which was henceforth to form the principal vehicle of opposition.[9]

It is evident that in the period immediately following the Young Turk Revolution the leaders of the CUP proved adept at extending the influence and control of their organisation. Yet paradoxically in this period they appear to have made no attempt to secure direct control of the government. Convinced that they were as yet too young and inexperienced to take direct control themselves, and fearful of the breakdown in order which they believed such a public seizure of power might entail, they decided rather to leave the government, for the moment at least, in the hands of members of the Ottoman elite (the officers and civil servants of high rank, frequently rewarded with the title of pasha, who traditionally ruled in the Ottoman Empire), themselves taking only indirect control; though the grand vizier, Ferid Pasha, was replaced, first by Said Pasha (22 July–4 August 1908) and then by Kiamil Pasha (5 August 1908–14 February 1909), both Ottoman statesmen of wide-ranging knowledge and experience. As a result, in the following months there occurred a fierce struggle for power between the established elite, centred on the Porte, the CUP, the Palace and the numerous political parties opposed to the CUP, in particular the Ottoman Liberal Union Party – a struggle not finally resolved until January 1913, when, following a period of intense conflict, involving mutiny, counter-revolution, massacre and war, the CUP launched a coup d'état and emerged victorious, in control of all the effective instruments of power in the state.[10]

The initial events in the long period of political conflict which occurred in the years following the Young Turk Revolution, display all too clearly the struggle for power then taking place, mainly in the Ottoman capital, between the principal institutions, parties, groups and factions concerned. In August 1908, following a dispute regarding the right of the sultan to appoint not only the grand vizier and the Sheikh al-Islam (granted in the 1876 constitution), but also the ministers of war and marine (claimed by Abdul Hamid

9. B. Lewis, *The Emergence of Modern Turkey* Oxford: Oxford University Press, 1961, Ch. 7. For a detailed account of the reform programme announced by the new government and other changes introduced, see A Kansu, *The Revolution of 1908 in Turkey* Leiden: E.J. Brill, 1997, Ch. 4.

10. Ibid., pp. 15–19. *Kibrisli* Mehmed Kiamil, who had been born in Cyprus and started his career as a translator in the service of the khedive of Egypt, had been four times grand vizier. Mehmed Said Pasha, sometimes known as *Küçük* (little) Said, born in Erzerum, had been seven times grand vizier.

in a decree of 1 August 1908) – appointments which would have placed control of the armed forces firmly in the hands of the Palace – the CUP, which had just dispatched a committee of seven, including Talaat, Djemal, Djavid and Rahmi, to Istanbul to represent the interests of the organisation there, secured not only the dismissal of *Küçük* Said Pasha, now distrusted, and the appointment of Kiamil Pasha, considered more amenable, as grand vizier, but also the appointment of Redjeb Pasha, the *vali* of Tripoli, a loyal CUP man, as minister of war. In October 1908 when, following a demonstration in Istanbul provoked by the Austrian annexation of Bosnia and Herzegovina, in the course of which calls were made for the abolition of the constitution, the restoration of the *Sheriat*, the closing down of drinking houses and theatres and a declaration of holy war, *Mizandji* Murad Bey, the editor of an anti-CUP journal entitled *Mizan* (Balance), and others attempted to form an anti-constitution group, the Porte, with the support of the CUP, had Murad and his supporters arrested, tried and either imprisoned or exiled. And in November, Kiamil Pasha, who believed, mistakenly as it turned out, that he could use the CUP as an instrument to exert his control over the Palace without risking a substantial increase in the power exercised by the organisation, had Manyasizade Refik, a leading Unionist, appointed minister of justice and Hüseyin Hilmi Pasha, a Unionist sympathiser, minister of the interior.[11]

It is not clear why Kiamil Pasha should have been so contemptuous of the CUP, for in the elections for the chamber of deputies, held in November–December 1908, CUP-backed candidates won a substantial majority of the seats (though as events were soon to show many of the CUP-backed candidates were less than fully committed to the Unionist cause) being won by the Ottoman Liberal Union Party. Not that CUP power and influence was used in this period to exclude the minorities. On the contrary, a substantial effort was made to provide them with representation, so that in the assembly, out of 281 deputies elected, approximately 53 were Arabs, 27 Albanians, 22 Greeks, 14 Armenians, 10 Slavs and 4 Jews.[12]

Following its overwhelming victory in the election, the CUP took immediate steps to weaken the sultan's control over the senate,

11. Lewis, *Emergence of Modern Turkey*, pp. 19–26; S. Akşin, *Jön Türkler ve Ittihat ve Terrakhi* Istanbul: Gerçek Yayinevi, 1980, pp. 91–2.

12. F. Ahmad, *The Young Turks* Oxford: Clarendon Press, 1967, pp. 27–8; H. Kayali, 'Elections and the Electoral Process in the Ottoman Empire, 1876–1919', *International Journal of Middle Eastern Studies*, Vol. 27 (1955); A. Kansu, *The Revolution of 1908 in Turkey*, Brill, Leiden, 1997, Ch. 6.

forcing him to exclude supporters of the old regime. Moreover, when in February 1909 Kiamil Pasha, in a move which the CUP interpreted as a bid for personal power, attempted to have his own men appointed ministers of war and marine, they took immediate steps (including the resignation of Manyasizâde Refik and Hüseyin Hilmi Pasha) to provoke a political crisis and bring about his downfall. In this they were successful. In a vote of no confidence, held in the chamber of deputies, the deputies (intimidated it is said by CUP officers, roaming the lobbies, wielding revolvers) voted against the grand vizier by 198 to 8 votes. As a result Kiamil Pasha was forced to resign and Hüseyin Hilmi Pasha was appointed in his place.[13]

If Kiamil's removal from office was intended to produce a resolution of the conflict in favour of the CUP, it failed to do so. On the contrary, during the following weeks political tension was if anything even further intensified, as the various parties concerned mounted press campaigns accusing their political enemies of treachery, organised demonstrations and even on occasion engaged in assassination. On 6 March Hasan Fehmi, the editor of *Serbesti*, an anti-CUP paper owned by the sultan's brother, Reshad Effendi, published material supposedly implicating the CUP in the blackmail of corrupt officials belonging to the old regime. On 12 March Riza Nur, the deputy for Sinop, a supporter of the Ottoman Liberal Union Party, wrote an inflammatory article accusing the CUP of the use of dictatorial methods; and on 6 April Hasan Fehmi, the editor of *Serbesti*, was murdered, possibly by agents of the CUP. At Hasan Fehmi's funeral, held on 7 April, opponents of the CUP seized the opportunity offered to mount a huge demonstration of support for their cause, attended, according to one report, by as many as 5–10 000 people. Finally on 13 April there broke out in Istanbul a mutiny or counter-revolution of major proportions, which for a time threatened to bring about not only the defeat of the CUP but even its complete extinction.[14]

Counter-revolution

The events of the mutiny or counter-revolution of 13 April 1909 (31 March old calendar) appear in retrospect clear enough; though

13. Sommerville Story (ed.), *The Memoirs of Ismail Kemal Bey* London: Constable, pp. 324–5.

14. Akşin, *Jön Türkler ve Ittihat ve Terrakhi*, pp. 121–3.

their precise origins and character remain obscure. On 13 April troops belonging to the fourth *avci* (sharpshooter) battalion stationed at the Tashkishla barracks, Istanbul, generally discontented with their lot and roused by fundamentalist ideas preached by the recently formed Muhammedan Union and its fiery leader Dervish Vahdeti, a Nakshibandi *hafiz* (one who has committed the Koran to memory) from Cyprus, locked up their officers, mostly college trained, and marched into the city in order to protest their grievances. While some marched to Beshiktash and others to Yildiz, the majority gathered in front of the Sultan Ahmet mosque, calling all the while for a restoration of the *Sheriat.* Later joined by other troops stationed in the capital, *softas* (theological students), ranker officers and other discontented elements opposed to the CUP, they began to call not only for a restoration of the *Sheriat,* but also for the dismissal of all college-trained officers, the reappointment of dismissed ranker officers and the proclamation of an amnesty for the mutineers. Later still they called for the dismissal of the grand vizier, the ministers of war and marine and the president of the chamber of deputies, and even for the dissolution of the CUP. Faced with this substantial breakdown in order and discipline, the grand vizier, Hüseyin Hilmi Pasha, and the ministers of war and marine responded, not by ordering the suppression of the mutiny – the course advised by Muhtar Pasha, the commander of the First Army Corps, who had quickly assembled reliable units, including artillery and machine-gun detachments, at the war ministry – but by ordering that no action should be taken against the mutineers (Muhtar Pasha accordingly resigned). Moreover, when Ziaeddin, the Sheikh al-Islam, sent out to request the mutinous troops to return to barracks, reported that they would not do so unless the entire cabinet resigned, Hüseyin Hilmi Pasha caved in completely, tendering his resignation and that of his cabinet.[15]

The conciliatory approach adopted by Hüseyin Hilmi Pasha and his colleagues proved remarkably effective. Following the appointment of a new cabinet, led by Ahmed Tevfik Pasha, a former minister of foreign affairs (the new cabinet included several ministers from the previous cabinet and a number of Liberal Unionists) and the appointment of a new commander of the First Army Corps, Nazim Pasha, known as a strict disciplinarian, order was quickly restored; though in the meantime a number of college-trained

15. Lewis, *Emergence of Modern Turkey*, pp. 211–12; Ahmad, *Young Turks*, pp. 40–1; *British Documents on Foreign Affairs*, Pt. I, Series B, Vol. 20, Annual Report on Turkey for the Year 1909.

officers, CUP deputies and others (including the minister of justice, Nazim Pasha, supposedly mistaken for the minister of war) were killed, and the offices of the CUP and two of its newspapers in Istanbul ransacked and destroyed.[16]

The events of 13 April 1909 were by no means confined to the capital. In Erzincan and Erzerum in eastern Anatolia, mutinies broke out, similar to that which had occurred in the capital; but they were quickly brought under control by the officers concerned, who for the most part remained loyal to the CUP. Meanwhile, on the night of 14 April an incident occurred in Adana, in Cilicia, which sparked off a massacre of Armenians of major proportions, which in the end, spreading to the surrounding areas, was to cost some 15–20 000 lives; while in Damascus, Aleppo, Mosul, Beirut and a number of other towns and villages in the Arab provinces mobs of Bedouin Arabs, Kurds and Circassians paraded, threatening Christians. In Damascus in particular a crowd of some 2,000 assembled in the town centre, armed to the teeth and intent, it is said, on killing members of the CUP, who happened at the time to be attending a meeting in the Grand Mosque.[17]

Origins and character of the counter-revolution

Contemporary observers offered several explanations for the events of 13 April 1909. The counter-revolution was, it was suggested, the product of a conspiracy organised by Abdul Hamid and the Palace *camarilla* which surrounded him; the work of the Muhammedan Union and other reactionary Islamic elements determined to overturn the new order established by the 1908 revolution; the work of the Ottoman Liberal Union Party and other opposition groups, supported by redundant army officers and civil servants, and disappointed placemen; and even the product of a plot organised by the CUP itself, designed to justify a seizure of power and the imposition of a dictatorship. The following account of the events leading up to the outbreak, written by J.L. Garvin and published in the *Fortnightly Review* in May 1909, may be taken as typical:

> Discontent might have continued muttering without daring to strike, when a savage crime brought intrigue and conspiracy to a head. Some personal and dramatic touch is most apt in these cases to

16. Swanson, 'Military Rising in Istanbul'.
17. *British Documents on Foreign Affairs*, Pt. I, Series B, Vol. 20, Annual Report on Turkey for the Year 1909.

kindle a slowly smouldering prejudice into sudden flame. Hassan
Fehmi Effendi, editor of the *Serbesti*, was among the boldest and most
violent critics of the Committee. At midnight on April 6th, he was
passing with a companion across the Galata Bridge when a murderer
fired shots into his back. The assassin escaped in a boat. The victim
died on the bridge. His companion had been dangerously wounded.
Hassan Fehmi, it is important to note, was an Albanian, a country-
man therefore of Ismail Kemal, most prominent of the Opposition
deputies, and of the fiercest and formerly most pampered Prætorians
in the Sultan's bodyguard. It was this barbarous crime which raised
the temperature of the situation to flash-point. Without a particle of
proof the guilt was laid to the charge of the Committee. The Young
Turks were accused of attempting to suppress free speech and to set
up in their turn a bloodstained tyranny. The occasion was unscrupu-
lously exploited by Opposition journalism. A mob of students and
others gathered before the Porte to demand the discovery and punishment of the murderer. Hilmi Pasha met with a mixed reception on
appearing to harangue the crowd. The funeral passing through the
city, and attended by five thousand persons, was well calculated to
work upon the emotions of the masses in Stamboul. And every day
was now adding to the heap of inflammable stuff. The Government
had at last gained the Sultan's consent to the removal from Yildiz of
its famous Prætorian Guard. The Albanians, Arabs, Kurds, and Lazes
were to be transferred as nearly as possible to their native regions.
Abdul Hamid and his guards were at one in regarding with bitter
hostility the project of disbandment. Thus, on the eve of the mutiny,
there was no mystery in the situation. The Liberal Union was working on the non-Turkish nationalities, and they on it. The Opposition
Press was accusing the Young Turks of murderous tyranny. They
were charged with measureless irreligion by the members of the
Mohammedan League whispering among the troops. The Sultan was
full of fresh resentment and was oppressed by a new dread as he
thought of the utter helplessness and isolation to which he was soon
to be reduced. The garrisons of Stamboul and Yildiz for various
reasons, professional and fanatical, were saturated through and
through with insubordination. The clergy were now inimical, and the
very mob was hostile. The murder of Hassan Fehmi lighted, as it
were, the match that sent up in flame and thunder the whole mass of
combustible material. The crime on the Galata Bridge was committed on April 6th. Within a week the counter-revolution had exploded,
and amid shouts of 'Long live the Sultan,' the Hilmi Cabinet was
overthrown and the Young Turks were swept out of Constantinople.
A more sudden and complete *débâcle* so far as the capital was concerned has not been known in the record of revolutions.[18]

18. J.L. Garvin, 'Review of Events', *Fortnightly Review*, Vol. 85 (1909).

Historians of the events of 13 April 1909 have for the most part concluded that such wide-ranging accounts have been written with too broad a brush. Far from being a counter-revolution, inspired by opposition to the CUP and the changes brought about by the 1908 revolution, the events, it has been argued, represented merely a mutiny of a type common enough in the Ottoman Empire in that period, inspired on this occasion mainly by the failure of college-trained officers, remote and inexperienced, to provide the leadership and commitment that their men expected. According to this view, what turned the mutiny into something approaching a counter-revolution was the abject failure of Hüseyin Hilmi Pasha and his colleagues to deal effectively with the situation. As Abdul Hamid is said to have remarked: 'If Hüseyin Hilmi Pasha and his friends had not been so weak and hesitant, the 13 April incident would not have lasted on hour.'[19]

Much evidence has been adduced in support of the contention that the mutiny was the product of a discontented soldiery. It began, for a start, not among units loyal to the old regime, but among crack Macedonian troops, specifically brought to Istanbul to defend the constitution. Largely deserted by their college-trained officers, who preferred to participate in the heady political life of the capital rather than attend to their duties, and aggrieved at the imposition of new training schedules which deprived them of the opportunity to perform their ablutions and pray at the appropriate times, it is generally agreed that in the weeks preceding the uprising these troops suffered a breakdown in morale and a collapse of discipline that made them highly receptive to the ingenious propaganda propagated by Dervish Vahdeti and the Muhammedan Union.[20] As Mahmud Muhtar Pasha remarked after the uprising: 'The educated officers whom I had gradually introduced into the cadres in place of the ranker officers did not, unfortunately, make any efforts to study the psychology of the soldiers and to make themselves appreciated and loved by them.'[21] And as Abdul Hamid remarked: 'The soldiers whom they themselves brought in from Salonica have rebelled against them. They oppressed them and caused them to rebel.'[22]

The uprising of 13 April 1909 was then essentially a mutiny, which as a result of the weakness of the authorities was permitted to

19. Swanson, 'Military Rising in Istanbul', p. 183.
20. Ibid.; Akşin, *Jön Türkler ve Ittihat ve Terrakhi*, pp. 128–30.
21. Swanson, 'Military Rising in Istanbul', p. 175.
22. Ibid., p. 181.

get out of hand. Yet the interpretation of events presented by J.L. Garvin and other contemporary observers should not be entirely discounted, for the troops of the Istanbul garrison were by no means unaffected by the tide of political argument then sweeping through the Ottoman capital. In February 1909 the troops of the garrison had been made aware of the political crisis caused by Kiamil Pasha's attempt to undermine the influence of the CUP; and they had been kept well informed by the agents of the Muhammedan Union and the press of the danger which the organisation was believed to pose to Islam and the traditional system of government. On 3 April Dervish Vahdeti, who had only recently published the official programme of his party in *Volkan*, a newspaper he had established, held a meeting in Hagia Sophia Square, at which he called on his followers to demand a restoration of the *Sheriat* and the rejection of the secularist policies of the CUP.[23] And in an article in *Volkan*, published immediately following the assassination of Hasan Fehmi, he declared: 'Here is cruelty! Here is constitution! The remedy is a general consensus of opinion. The nation expects the immediate assistance of her soldiers.'[24] In these circumstances it is scarcely surprising that the Istanbul garrison, convinced that the new regime represented a threat to the established order, should have risen, creating a situation threatening the very survival of the CUP.[25]

Responsibility for the troubles in Adana was likewise laid at the door variously of the sultan, the Ottoman Liberal Union Party and the Muhammedan Union. Halil Halid, for example, writing in *The Nineteenth Century and After* in May 1909 blamed the Ottoman Liberal Union Party and the 'pestilential press' which supported it:

> Had the authority of the Turkish Government under Hilmi Pasha not been undermined by the Liberal Union agitators, I am firmly convinced that the unfortunate attacks on the Armenians, the most useful and, after the true Turks, the most patriotic community of the

23. Akşin, *Jön Türkler ve Ittihat ve Terrakhi*, pp. 121–3. Dervish Vahdeti had spent 15 years or so as a minor civil servant before entering the heady world of politics in Istanbul. In December 1908, frustrated by the failures of the existing political order (and it would seem by his own failure to secure promotion) he founded *Volkan*, a newspaper committed to political and social reform and the promotion of the faith. Shortly thereafter he set up the Muhammedan Union, membership of which increased rapidly. Although generally opposed to the despotic policies pursued by Abdul Hamid, it is believed that, as an opponent of the CUP and freemasonry, he received several subsidies from the Palace.

24. Swanson, 'Military Rising in Istanbul', p. 177.

25. See A. Mango, 'The Young Turks', *Middle Eastern Studies*, Vol. 8, No. 1 (1972), for an account of earlier mutinies in Istanbul, successfully dealt with by the authorities.

Ottoman Empire, could not have been carried out in the distant provinces of Asiatic Turkey.[26]

The British ambassador, in his annual report for 1909, however, laid most, but by no means all, of the responsibility at the door of Armenian and Muslim agitators, carried away by the emotions of the moment, and of the government, which in his own view displayed 'lamentable weakness':

> To lay the responsibility for the Adana massacres at the door of the ex-Sultan, as was at first done, is now impossible; no evidence of any sort has been produced to incriminate His Majesty or Izzet Pasha, though there can be no doubt that a number of hodjas and reactionaries did all they could to fan the flame of Moslem fanaticism. Nor is there any ground to assume that the Armenians were planning an insurrection, or that the Moslems had been preparing a carefully premeditated massacre. The causes of the massacre are rather to be found in the vain-glorious talk of equality on the part of the young Armenians who were all in theory revolutionaries and advocates of home rule, in the fear which their attitude inspired among the Moslems of some definite act of aggression, a fear which was somewhat justified by the constant stream of arms which flowed into the country for the use of the non-Moslem population, in the extravagance of the orators on both sides, and in the lamentable weakness of the Government authority. Through these causes came the events of the 13th April in the capital, and the murder of two Turks by an Armenian as a pretext for the outbreak at that particular time, and once the massacres had begun the cowardice of the vali and the ferik's action in arming the reserves, made the Moslems believe that the Government were encouraging the slaughter and urging them on to plunder and kill.
>
> The outbreak of the second massacre in Adana gave rise at the time to ugly stories of the complicity of the Roumelian troops, there is no truth in these reports; it was in reality started by some desperate Hundchakist revolutionaries, who, in the wild hope of provoking foreign interference, attacked and killed fifteen Roumelian soldiers newly arrived and picketed in the Armenian quarter; and it was chiefly owing to the soldiers' ignorance of the topography of the town that the bashi-bazouks and other riotous elements were able to descend under cover of night and continue the interrupted work of plunder, murder, and arson.[27]

26. H. Halid, 'The Origin of the Revolt in Turkey', *The Nineteenth Century* Vol. 65 (1909), p. 759.

27. *British Documents on Foreign Affairs*, 1909, Pt. I, Series B, Vol. 20, p. 145. For a more detailed account of the events in Adana see C.J. Walker, *Armenia* London: Routledge, 1990, pp. 182–8.

Factors contributing to the outbreak of the mutiny or counter-revolution of 13 April 1909, and the massacres in Adana, were not confined merely to the internal affairs of the Ottoman Empire. In October 1908 the empire suffered a series of humiliating reverses, as a number of European powers seized the opportunity offered by the outbreak of the Young Turk Revolution to resolve what they saw as political anomalies. On 5 October Prince Ferdinand of Bulgaria, supposedly slighted by an Ottoman failure to invite the Bulgarian agent in Istanbul to a dinner party given on the occasion of the sultan's birthday, had Bulgaria declared an independent kingdom. On 6 October Austria–Hungary proclaimed the annexation of Bosnia and Herzegovina, the administration of which it had secured in 1878. And on 7 October Crete announced her intention of uniting with Greece. As a result of these developments the Ottomans, deeply concerned, took immediate steps to strengthen their forces, and even contemplated war; while the Austro-Hungarians and the Bulgarians mobilised, the Serbians called out their reserves and the British, as was their wont in such situations, dispatched a fleet to the eastern Mediterranean. But there was in fact little the Ottomans, bankrupt and disorganised, could do to defend their interests in the relevant territories, supposedly protected by the Treaty of Berlin (1878) and other agreements. The Great Powers refused to call a congress and the Ottoman army, so Kiamil Pasha was informed, was unprepared for war. In the course of the following months, therefore, Kiamil Pasha and his successors were obliged to remain content with the dispatch of diplomatic notes and protests; and in the end to conclude agreements with Austria–Hungary and Bulgaria, effectively conceding defeat; though a successful boycott of Austrian, Greek and Bulgarian goods was mounted, which considerably strengthened the hand of the Ottomans at the negotiating table. In February 1909 an agreement was arrived at with Austria–Hungary, providing for an Austrian evacuation of the *sandjak* of Novibazar, the payment of a substantial sum in compensation for the annexation of the two provinces, and a promise of Austrian support for the abolition of foreign post offices in the Ottoman Empire; and in April an agreement, engineered by the Russians, was arrived at with Bulgaria, providing for a payment of compensation by Bulgaria not to the Ottoman Empire but to Russia, in return for a Russian cancellation of 40 of the last 74 payments due on an Ottoman war indemnity, owing from the time of the Russo-Turkish War of 1877–8. As for the future of Crete, this difficult issue was left for discussion at a future conference.[28]

28. *British Documents on Foreign Affairs*, Pt. I, Series B, Vol. 20, Docs 12–25.

Little or no evidence can be adduced in support of the contention that Abdul Hamid was responsible for instigating the mutiny or counter-revolution on 13 April 1909, an allegation widely credited at the time; though he remained generally sympathetic to the cause of the Muhammedan Union and its supporters. As Kiamil Pasha is said to have remarked:

> He [Abdul Hamid] was a broken man, broken in health and in spirits. I had continued intimate relations with him for many months, and I knew that he could not have engineered this Mutiny, as he was in extreme fear for his life and would have been very well satisfied if allowed to remain on the throne, no matter how much his power was circumscribed.
>
> The Mutiny was the result of a ferment in the army, provoked partly by the mistakes of the Committee and partly by the reactionary propaganda of the Mohammedan Association; the dislike which the soldiers entertained for the Young Turk officers; the intrigues of the discharged 'ranker' officers; the comparatively overworked condition of the rank and file; perhaps the memory of the old Janissary revolts which men yet living have seen; and a hundred other causes.
>
> If money was found on the soldiers, it was given them by the Mohammedan Association, not by the Padishah; but little money was found, if any.
>
> The Sultan was more frightened than anybody else when the revolt broke out; and, when Hilmi Pasha handed in his resignation, what could the Sovereign do but appoint a new Cabinet, and take that Cabinet's advice on the question of amnesty?
>
> The present Government sought in Yildiz for proofs of the late Sultan's guilt, but, so far, it has failed to find any proofs.[29]

Suppression

The success of the various opposition parties, groups and factions opposed to the CUP in exploiting the events of 13 April 1909 in order to secure the appointment of a government more sympathetic to their aims and objectives, proved short-lived. Well aware that, if unchecked, the new government might succeed not only in restoring the authority of the sultan and the Porte, but also in securing the extinction of the CUP (a probable aim of the uprising), the

29. F. McCullagh, *The Fall of Abdul Hamid* London: Methuen, 1910, pp. 48–9. In memoirs written following his deposition, Abdul Hamid wrote: 'I had absolutely no connection with the incident of 13 April. I did not condescend to profit from this opportunity which they themselves (the CUP) provided. If I had been involved in it, or if I had tried to profit from the mutiny, then today I would still be living in Yildiz Palace and not at Beylerbey.'

central committee of the CUP, based in Salonica, acting in conjunction with the officer corps of the Second and Third Army Corps, mainly CUP, responded immediately by organising a *Hareket Ordusu* (Mobile or Action Army), which it was hoped would prove capable of marching on the capital, restoring order and discipline in the garrison there, and securing the reappointment of Hüseyon Hilmi Pasha as grand vizier. At the same time, in order to justify the resolute action it intended to take, the CUP bombarded the capital and provinces with telegrams accusing Abdul Hamid of destroying the constitution and calling for the dismissal of the 'unconstitutional' cabinet and the arrest of a number of supposed leaders of the uprising, including *Mizandji* Murad, Ismail Kemal, elected president of the chamber of deputies in place of Ahmed Riza, and Said Pasha, Kiamil's son. The constitution was destroyed, they declared, the new ministry illegal, and only forceful action by the army would succeed in saving the day.[30]

The campaign launched by the central committee and its supporters in the army – a number of Young Turk officers, including Enver, Fethi and Mustafa Kemal, who had been posted abroad or elsewhere, rushed back to participate in the campaign – proved remarkably effective. On 17 April 1909 the Action Army departed from Salonica. On or about 22 April it surrounded the capital, and on 23–24 April, following a series of skirmishes with rebel units, it occupied the city. Deputations sent by the new cabinet to negotiate an end to the conflict and avoid violence were either ignored or arrested. As Mahmud Shevket Pasha, the commander of the army, remarked in a proclamation issued on 23 April, the issue was merely a military one, concerned with the restoration of discipline. Political questions could be left till later. Meanwhile, as the Action Army advanced, members of the two chambers of the Istanbul parliament who, following a period of intense confusion, had assembled in Yeshilköy (San Stefano) just outside Istanbul, where they had assumed the guise of a national assembly, passed a resolution approving the army's entry into the city, the restoration of order and the punishment of rebels. And on 27 April, in an attempt to ingratiate themselves with the Action Army and the CUP, they declared their intention to secure the deposition of Abdul Hamid, held responsible for the uprising, and his replacement by his more amenable brother, Mehmed Reshad.[31]

30. Ahmad, *Young Turks*, pp. 43–5.
31. Ibid., pp. 43–6.

Following its victory in the conflict, which was by no means uncontested, the Action Army and the CUP set about imposing 'discipline' on the Istanbul garrison. Martial law was declared and three courts martial were set up to try those accused of involvement in the mutiny. Many rebels were sentenced to death; and for a time, it is said, the lamp-posts of the Galata Bridge were festooned with dangling bodies. At the same time steps were taken to bring the opposition parties to heel. The offices of the Ottoman Liberal Union Party, which was assumed (probably rightly) to have played a significant part in the organisation of the uprising, were raided in search of evidence of complicity; and later the party was closed down, as were the Muhammedan Union (Dervish Vahdeti was executed) and several newspapers and cultural associations sympathetic to the opposition cause. In the mopping-up operation which followed, which involved, as the British ambassador put it, the 'usual arrest and pursuit of suspected persons', hundreds of reactionary officers, officials, *softas, hodjas* and members of the Ottoman Liberal Union Party and the Muhammedan Union were picked up.[32] Finally, on 27 April a CUP delegation led by Talaat, having secured the appropriate *fetwa* from the Sheik al-Islam, attended Abdul Hamid in Yildiz Palace to inform him of his deposition; and on 5 May, in an act designed to give a public demonstration of the restoration of its authority, the CUP had Hüseyin Hilmi Pasha reappointed grand vizier.

32. *British Documents on Foreign Affairs*, Pt. I, Series B, Vol. 20, p. 135.

CHAPTER THREE

Politics, Constitution, Rebellion and War

Politics and constitution

Paradoxically, the suppression of the counter-revolution of 13 April 1909 did not lead to an immediate CUP seizure of power, but to a prolonged period of military rule, in the course of which Mahmud Shevket Pasha, the victorious commander of the Action Army, having had himself appointed first inspector general of the three principal army corps (based in Instanbul, Salonica and Edirne) and then minister of war, attempted, in conjunction with the CUP, to reestablish order not only in the army but also in government and society. The steps taken proved initially reasonably successful. But in due course, as the opposition parties, profiting from the support of thousands of discharged army officers, officials and other discontented elements, including the minorities – the minorities for a variety of reasons became disenchanted with the regime – reorganised their forces, the regime suffered a series of reverses, leading first to the defeat of the CUP in the chamber of deputies (the CUP bloc in the chamber split into a series of parties, groups and factions) and then, in the summer of 1912, to the complete exclusion of the organisation from power.

The measures taken by Mahmud Shevket Pasha and the CUP to reestablish order in the army, government and society were both vigorous and far reaching. Steps were immediately implemented to secure a reorganisation of the army, the dismissal or demotion of army officers promoted above their qualifications or experience, the exclusion of army officers, where possible, from politics, the creation of special 'pursuit battalions' for employment in Macedonia (a measure earlier advocated by Enver), the punishment and possible execution of persons convicted of carrying arms or participating in armed bands, the prevention of brigandage and the conscription of non-Muslims. At the same time a series of laws was passed providing for the control of the press and printing establishments, the banning of groups and organisations based on, or bearing the title of, ethnic or national groups (the so-called Law of Associations), the control of vagabondage and suspected persons and a reform of the constitution. Henceforth, according to the newly amended constitution, the grand vizier, appointed as heretofore by the sultan, would, subject to the approval of the sultan, appoint ministers, including the ministers of war and marine. Ministers would now be made responsible not only for their departments but also for the overall policy of the government. Should a disagreement arise between the cabinet and the chamber of deputies then the cabinet should either submit or resign. Should the new cabinet appointed in place of the previous one again fail to secure the support of the chamber of deputies then the cabinet should again resign and the sultan order a dissolution of parliament and the holding of new elections. Henceforth the president and vice-president of the chamber of deputies, previously appointed by the sultan, would be elected. The sovereignty of the sultan would be made dependent on the new sultan swearing an oath, on the occasion of his succession to the throne, to respect the constitution and the *Sheriat*.[1]

The reverses and setbacks suffered by the CUP in the period following the suppression of the counter-revolution reveal all too clearly both the initial weakness and lack of experience of the organisation and the nature and extent of the opposition raised against it. In the summer of 1909, when the CUP sought to have the constitution changed in order to allow deputies loyal to the movement to hold government office as undersecretaries – the central committee had decided that the CUP should after all seek direct representation in the administration, if only in order to enable its members to acquire experience in the art of government – it failed to have the measure carried. As a result it was obliged to seek instead the appointment of CUP deputies as ministers, permitted by the constitution: in June 1909 Djavid was appointed minister of finance, and in August Talaat was made minister of the interior. In February 1910, the supporters of the CUP in the chamber of deputies, who the previous summer had published an official charter setting out their aims and objectives, split, a substantial group of some 40 or

1. F. Ahmad, *The Young Turks* Oxford: Clarendon Press, 1969, pp. 57–62; B. Lewis, *The Emergence of Modern Turkey* Oxford: Oxford University Press, 1961, pp. 213–14; *Encyclopaedia of Islam*, new edn, Düstur London: Luzac & Co, 1965.

so, many of Albanian descent, forming a new party, the People's Party (Ahali Firkasi). In January 1911, following the outbreak of a large-scale insurrection in Albania, the remaining supporters of the CUP again split, a group this time forming the New Party (Hizb-i Cedid). This party was formed under the leadership of Colonel Sadik, a traditionalist of the old school, who believed that the CUP, which he identified with freemasons, atheists, pro-Zionists and self-seekers, should adopt a more moderate policy, based on a respect for traditional values and a recognition of the 'sacred rights of the Caliphate and the Sultan'. So great, indeed, was the degree of dissension within the chamber of deputies and so great the opposition without, that in February 1911 Talaat, held responsible for the hard-line policies pursued in Albania, Macedonia and the Yemen, felt obliged to resign; and in May Djavid, embroiled in a conflict with Mahmud Shevket Pasha over financial control of the ministry of war, followed suit. In November 1911, following the Italian occupation of Tripolitania, seen as a severe setback both for the military regime and the CUP, the principal opposition parties formed the Liberal Party of Freedom and Understanding, generally known as the Liberal Union or Entente Libéral, in effect an alliance of all the elements opposed to the CUP. Finally in December in a by-election held in Istanbul, a candidate standing in the name of the Liberal Union won a resounding victory, defeating the CUP candidate.

The response of the CUP to the challenge it faced, as a result of the collapse of its support in both the chamber of deputies and the community in general, was both ruthless and unprincipled. In January 1912, confident of its organisational superiority in the provinces, it engineered a dissolution of the chamber of deputies, and in the election, known as the 'big stick' election, which followed, using every means of bribery and intimidation at its disposal, it swept the board, winning all but six of the 275 seats available. But success in the 'big stick' election did not enable the CUP to quell the opposition. Following the election a number of young officers serving in Macedonia, concerned regarding the situation in Albania and Tripolitania, and opposed to the authoritarian policies pursued by the CUP, took to the hills. Then in May–June 1912, in a bizarre replay of the events of July 1908, a group of conservative and traditionalist officers in Istanbul formed a secret society, known as the Saviour Officers (Halâskar Zabitân Grubu), committed to a restoration of constitutional government and an end to radical politics. Henceforth, they declared, the army should stay out of politics. Quickly gaining control of a number of army units in Macedonia, in July the Saviour Officers issued a manifesto calling for the expulsion of the CUP from government, dispatched a declaration to the sultan and the army council threatening action if their demands were not met, and initiated a series of military manoeuvres designed to intimidate the government. Their demands, as simple as they were significant, included the selection of the grand vizier by the sultan, the appointment of Nazim Pasha, a man of great personal courage and independence, who despite several discrete approaches the CUP had failed to win over to their side, as minister of war, and the inclusion of Kiamil Pasha, the old enemy of the CUP, in the government. The results of the action taken by the Saviour Officers were as spectacular as they were unexpected. On 9 July Mahmud Shevket Pasha, having failed to impose his authority on the rebellious soldiery, resigned. On 17 July the grand vizier, equally dispirited, followed suit; and on 21 July the sultan, having dutifully sought the advice of the presidents of the chamber of deputies and the senate, as the constitution required, and considered several possible candidates for the post, appointed Ghazi Ahmed Muhtar Pasha, an elder statesman and hero of the Russo-Turkish war of 1877–8, grand vizier. In the new cabinet appointed by Ghazi Ahmed Muhtar Pasha, known as the Great Cabinet because it included a number of previous grand viziers, Nazim Pasha was appointed minister of war and Kiamil Pasha president of the council of state.[2]

That it was the intention of the new government, which enjoyed the support not only of the conservative officer class but also of the Liberal Union, to secure the suppression of the CUP is not in doubt. On 5 August 1912 the sultan, in response to a request issued by the Saviour Officers, dissolved the chamber of deputies and called for new elections. On 8 August, the cabinet had martial law proclaimed (martial law had only recently been suspended), and on 3 September it had *Tanin*, the principal organ of the CUP, suspended. But all such efforts proved unavailing, for on 30 September, before it was possible for a new election to be held, the Balkan states mobilised; and on 8 October the Ottoman Empire found itself once again engaged in war.

CUP and the minorities

Among the minority communities, the extraordinary enthusiasm generated by the Young Turk Revolution was soon dissipated;

2. Ahmad, *Young Turks*, Chs 4 and 5; Lewis, *Emergence of Modern Turkey*, pp. 209–19; S. Akşin, *Jön Türkler ve Ittihat ve Terrakhi* Istanbul: Gerçek Yayinevi, 1980, pp. 184–206.

though the speed with which attitudes changed varied according to circumstances. Among the Greeks and the Armenians, who had initially expected to benefit from the restoration of constitutional government and the implementation of the ideology of Ottomanism promised by the CUP, old attitudes soon reappeared, as the patriarchs and their supporters, mainly the wealthy merchant classes, sought to preserve existing privileges, and as the common people, all too often the victims of Ottoman army 'security' measures, began once again to dream of autonomy and even independence. In August 1909, Yuvakim Efendi, the Greek patriarch, supposedly committed to the Ottoman ideal, issued a proclamation urging the Ottoman government to guarantee freedom of person and conscience, confirm the ecclesiastical and educational rights and privileges traditionally enjoyed by the *millets* and ensure that, in implementing the proposed law for the conscription of non-Muslims, recruits from the minority communities would be permitted to serve in special battalions, stationed in their home provinces – hardly a resounding vote of confidence in the principle of equality on which the ideology of Ottomanism was supposedly based. In debates on education, the economy and constitutional reform, held in the chamber of deputies, many non-Muslim deputies argued strongly in favour of the preservation of existing privileges – again hardly a resounding endorsement of the principle of equality. In the elections of 1908 and 1912, the Greek Patriarchate worked tirelessly to obtain not so much fair as proportional representation for the Greek Orthodox *millet*; and in the period of the counter-revolution most Greeks sided not with the CUP but with the Istanbul garrison and its supporters. As an article in *Neologas*, a leading Greek journal, remarked: 'The army has gained the great prize for patriotism, and 13 April 1909 ought to be henceforth marked with no less splendour than 24 July 1908'.[3] Meanwhile, in Macedonia and the eastern provinces, many *commitadjis*, *chetniks* and other guerrilla fighters, disappointed at the pace of Ottoman reform, returned to the hills. Only among the Jews, particularly those located in Salonica and Izmir, whose very survival was threatened by the rising tide of Greek, Bulgarian and Serbian nationalism, did support for the ideology of Ottomanism remain firm, and even there it was increasingly undermined by the spread of socialism. As Djavid Bey is said on one occasion to have

3. F. Ahmad, 'Unionist Relations with the Greek, Armenian, and Jewish Communities of the Ottoman Empire, 1908–1914', in B. Braude and B. Lewis (eds), *Christians and Jews in the Ottoman Empire* London: Holmes and Meier, 1982, Vol. 1, p. 410.

remarked sadly, it was evident that a sense of Ottomanism had not yet replaced that of communal identity among the inhabitants of the empire.[4]

It has generally been assumed that the harsh policies pursued by the Ottoman government and the CUP with regard to the minorities, in particular the policy of Ottomanisation, which required the teaching of Ottoman Turkish and the promotion of Ottoman culture in schools and colleges, were mainly responsible for the decline of minority support for the CUP in the period following the Young Turk Revolution; and indeed there is some truth in this assertion, particularly with regard to the Albanians. But it may be doubted that the policies pursued by the government and the CUP were indeed quite as harsh as they have sometimes been made to appear. When in the autumn of 1908 Yuvakim Efendi expressed fears regarding the government's policy concerning the Greek *millet*, the CUP sent a representative to assure him that they had no intention of curtailing in any way the special privileges his community enjoyed. In the elections of 1908 and 1912 the authorities were at pains to satisfy Greek complaints regarding the working of the electoral system; and they took steps to ensure that the minorities would receive a fair representation. Policies of Ottomanisation, far from being extreme, were for the most part merely a logical extension of the ideology of Ottomanism which many in the minority communities had agreed to adopt; and in any case the minority elites were for the most part already well acquainted with Ottoman language and culture; though of course attempts to enforce the use of the Ottoman Turkish language and the Arabic script and codify syllabuses did frequently provoke opposition. As for the imposition of the new conscription law, when the minorities expressed concern, the CUP, which had in fact little if any desire to undertake the difficult task of integrating Christian recruits into the armed forces, took immediate steps to enable the non-Muslims (and also incidentally Muslims) to buy their way out by paying a special tax, similar to the tax that recruits wishing to avoid military service had previously been expected to pay.[5]

Following the Adana massacre, which did so much to damage relations between the Ottoman government and the Armenians, the government took immediate steps to restore order, appointing

---

4. Ibid., pp. 405–25. For further information on relations between the CUP and the minorities, see A. Kansu, *The Revolution of 1908 in Turkey* Leiden: E.J. Brill, 1997, Ch. 5.

5. Ibid., pp. 405–18.

a commission to investigate the event and providing T.L. 30 000 for the relief of victims. Thereafter, measures already instituted to ameliorate the situation in the eastern provinces were stepped up; and in February 1912 Said Pasha, the grand vizier, allotted T.L. 100 000 for the settlement of Armeno-Kurdish land disputes in the area, in the expectation that dispossessed Armenians might be reinstated in their lands and Kurdish squatters expelled. In the 'big stick' election of 1912, while the position of a number of the minorities was adversely affected, the Armenians, with the support of the CUP, succeeded in holding on to all 14 of their seats. Finally, in the period following the Balkan Wars, even the policy of central-isation pursued by the CUP, earlier considered vital, was to some extent relaxed: in March 1913 a new law concerning provincial administration was introduced, providing for greater local control by provincial councils and increased autonomy with regard to administrative and financial affairs.[6]

The surviving records of the CUP, such as they are, and other sources, reveal something of the way the policy of the CUP regard-ing the minorities and other issues evolved in this period. At the 1908 congress, which was held in secret in October–November, attention was given mainly to the organisational problems associ-ated with the rapid expansion of the CUP, and the need to clarify its character and aims, which it was made clear would now include a rapid expansion of the economy and education. According to the regulations of the society there adopted, the Ottoman Turkish lan-guage, the official language of the empire, should be taught to all Ottoman subjects and employed in all official correspondence: 'Turkish language must be taught in elementary education.'[7] In the 1909 congress, held again in secret following the suppression of the counter-revolution, attention was concentrated mainly on the ques-tion of whether army officers should be permitted to play a part in politics. Nevertheless, small but significant changes were made in the constitution of the CUP, designed to show that the society, still effectively a secret organisation, did not intend to operate outside the law now that the constitution was restored. According to the regulations of the society, once again adopted at the congress, Ottoman Turkish should be the language taught in both elemen-tary and higher education; but in secondary schools local languages

6. Ibid., pp. 418–24; J. Heller, 'Britain and the Armenian Question', *Middle East-ern Studies*, Vol. 16, No. 1, 1980.

7. M. Arai, *Turkish Nationalism and the Young Turk Era* Leiden: E.J. Brill, 1992, p. 46.

might also be taught. In the 1911 and 1912 congresses, more substantial changes in the organisation, programme and constitution of the CUP were introduced, designed to show that the society was truly a constitutional party committed to the ideology of Ottomanism. Reforms would be introduced to secure for every citizen, without distinction of race or religion, the right to religious freedom and equality before the law. Finally, at the 1913 congress held in Istanbul, following the defeat of the Ottoman Empire in the Balkan Wars, a clause was introduced into the party programme, declaring that, although in elementary public and secondary schools Turkish should be taught as the only language, 'the mother tongues of every province will be used as the medium of teaching'.[8]

Unfortunately the various resolutions and amendments adopted by the CUP at its annual congresses cannot be taken as a true and accurate reflection of CUP policy. In 1910, it is said, under the influence of extremist elements led by Talaat, a radical change of direction occurred. Henceforth, members were informed at a 'secret conclave' of the society held in August 1910, the CUP would no longer seek to secure racial liberty and equality, but seek instead to uphold Muslim supremacy. Ottoman Turkish would be the supreme language and Christians would as far as possible be excluded from office. All important posts would be occupied by Muslims, nominated by the CUP. As Talaat is reported to have remarked:

> We have made unsuccessful attempts to convert the *Ghiaur* into a loyal Osmanli and all such efforts must inevitably fail, as long as the small independent states in the Balkan Peninsula remain in a position to propagate ideas of separatism among the inhabitants of Macedonia. There can therefore be no question of equality, until we have succeeded in our task of Ottomanising the Empire – a long and laborious task, in which I venture to predict that we shall at length succeed after we have at last put an end to the agitation and propaganda of the Balkan States.[9]

It is not clear for how long the 'extremist' policies secretly advocated by Talaat and his supporters remained effective. It may be supposed that, following the outbreak of the Albanian revolt (to which they were undoubtedly a contributory factor), and the marginalisation of the CUP which followed, they were to some

---

8. Ibid.
9. Lewis, *Emergence of Modern Turkey*, p. 214; *British Documents on Foreign Affairs*, Pt. I, Series B, Vol. 20, Doc. 32, Memorandum respecting the New Regime in Turkey.

extent modified. Yet the suspicion must remain that through-out the period that followed they remained central to the CUP approach.

The Albanian revolt

The Albanian people, 70 per cent Muslim, did not initially seek independence, merely local self-government, relief from excessive taxation (which to some Albanians meant any taxation) and relief from conscription. This did not mean that the Albanian people were immune to the spread of nationalist ideology. On the con-trary, in the closing years of the nineteenth century elements within the leadership had called for the creation of an Albanian state, united by culture and language, incorporating the four *vilayets* of Janina, Kossova, Vitola and Shkodër; and in 1905 a group of young intellectuals had established a secret society in Bitola (Monastir), with branches throughout Albania. Nevertheless the majority of the people remained loyal to the Ottoman sultan. Only when, follow-ing the Young Turk Revolution of 1908, the Unionists, reneging on promises of greater autonomy, started to increase taxes, impose conscription, enforce the use of Ottoman Turkish and the Arabic script in schools and other institutions, withdraw the privileges tra-ditionally enjoyed by the Beys and enforce Ottoman authority even in the remotest corners of the country, did the Albanian people become disenchanted. A number of Albanian leaders then decided to raise a revolt, first in Priština and then throughout the *vilayet* of Kossova.

The response of the Ottoman government to the Albanian revolt was both vigorous and effective: the rising was quickly put down and the leaders arrested. But in the following months a number of tribes and clans, inhabiting remote, mountainous areas, supported by others offended by the brutal methods employed by the Ottomans in the supression of the revolt, decided to rise. As a result the Porte, unable to impose its will, was forced to offer the rebels a series of concessions, including a reduction in taxes, the posting of Albanian conscripts to their home regions, the appoint-ment of officials able to speak the local language, the free use of the Albanian language and script, and an amnesty for those guilty of political offences. For a time these concessions brought peace, but following the 'big stick' election of 1912 revolts again broke out, particularly in the south; and in August 1912 the rebels, encouraged by the Italians and Macedonians, took Skopje. As a result negotiations regarding a possible settlement were resumed; but, before an agreement was arrived at, the Balkan Wars broke out and the Ottomans were expelled from the area.[10]

The Albanian provinces were not the only parts of the Ottoman Empire disturbed by the centralising policies pursued by the CUP in this period. In Macedonia a harsh application of the Law on Vagabondage and Suspected Persons, the suppression of the constitutional clubs set up following the Young Turk Revolution, and the brutal measures taken to secure the disarmament of the Christian minorities (but not the Muslims), led first to an increase in tension and then to a renewal of the conflict that had plagued the area for a decade and more. Meanwhile in the Yemen, where tribal chiefs and imams had never ceased to resist Ottoman attempts to secure control, trouble once again broke out, as Imam Yahya, Seyyid Idris and others struggled for supremacy.[11]

For the Ottomans in general, and for the CUP in particular, the outbreak of the Albanian revolt came as a profound shock, for it showed that nationalist aspirations were not confined merely to the Christian *millets*, as hitherto believed. At the same time it suggested that the centralising reforms associated with the ideology of Ottomanism, far from uniting the empire, might actually be contributing to its further disintegration. Following the failure of the Ottoman government to suppress the revolt, therefore, the CUP took immediate steps to modify the programme of vigorous centralisation they had instituted; and to consider what alternative courses might be open to them to secure the survival of the Ottoman state. But before they could make much progress in that direction they found themselves once again embroiled in war, this time not against a rebellious vassal, but against a major European power, Italy. In September 1911, the Italians, taking advantage of the evident weakness of the Ottoman position, dispatched an expeditionary force to occupy the North African provinces of Tripoli and Benghazi, sometimes known as Tripoli in Barbary or Tripolitania.

10. B. Jelavich, *History of the Balkans* Cambridge: Cambridge University Press, 1983, Ch. 3; S. Pollo and A. Puto, *The History of Albania* London: Routledge and Kegan Paul, 1981, pp. 121–45; *British Documents on Foreign Affairs*, Pt. I, Series B, Vol. 20, Annual Reports, 1909–11.

11. Jelavich, *History of the Balkans*, Ch. 3; P. Dresch, *Tribes, Government and History in Yemen* Oxford: Clarendon Press, 1989, pp. 219–24. The Ottomans, having lost control of the Yemen, had reoccupied the country in 1872.

The Tripolitanian War

The Italian occupation of Tripolitania was not unexpected. For almost 30 years the Italians, convinced that they had lost out in the 'scramble for Africa', had been engaged in expanding their influence, both political and economic, in the area; and they had sought the agreement of the other Great Powers to an eventual annexation. In the renegotiation of the Triple Alliance, completed in 1887, they had made Austrian and German support for Italian expansion in the area a condition of their continued participation; and in the negotiation of the Mediterranean Agreements, concluded with Britain in the same year, they had sought British support. In 1890 they had raised the issue with the French, and in 1900 agreed with them that in return for Italian recognition of France's interests in Morocco, France would recognise Italy's interests in Tripolitania. In 1902, during a second renegotiation of the Triple Alliance, they had secured further Austrian assurances of support. Finally in 1909, at a meeting held at Racconigi, they had secured from Isvolsky, the Russian foreign minister, an agreement to the effect that Russia would support Italian aspirations in Tripolitania in return for Italian support for a Russian initiative, mounted by Isvolsky at the time, to secure the opening of the Turkish Straits to Russian ships of war.[12]

Nor was there any doubt regarding the nature of Italian motivation in seeking the annexation of the North African provinces. Only by acquiring an African colony or colonies, it was frequently argued at the time, would Italy preserve its status as a 'great' power. If Italy did not act at once to 'cash the Libyan cheque', then another power, Germany, France or Britain, might seize the opportunity to intervene, thereby disturbing the eqilibrium of the eastern Mediterranean and threatening Italian interests in the area, vigorously pursued in recent years by the Banco di Roma. Above all the acquisition of an African colony would enable Italy to solve her population problem, which in the recent past had led to substantial migration.

Yet surprisingly when in the autumn of 1911 the invasion of Tripolitania finally came about it appears to have been largely unexpected by the Ottoman leadership, who had just reduced the size of the Ottoman garrison there (though Ottoman diplomats in Rome,

---

12. T.W. Childs, *Italo-Turkish Diplomacy and the War over Libya, 1911–1912* Leiden: E.J. Brill, 1990; E.D. Akarli, 'The Defence of the Libyan Provinces', *Studies in Ottoman Diplomatic History*, Vol. 5, Istanbul: Isis Press, 1990.

Berlin and Vienna had warned of a possible Italian action). On 28 September an Italian fleet was sighted off the Tripoli coast, and on 29 September the Ottoman government was presented with an ultimatum, explaining that Italy intended to occupy Tripoli forthwith. Should the Ottomans fail to acquiesce in the occupation within 24 hours, then they would face war. On 5 October, following a short bombardment, Tripoli was occupied; and shortly thereafter Derna and Tobruk. On 18 October Italian troops landed at Juliana, where they were attacked by a large Turkish force, losing some 200 killed and many wounded; and on 21 October Benghazi was bombarbed and taken. Finally on 5 November, following a battle fought at the Bumelian Wells, in which a force of some 9,000 Turks and Arabs almost succeeded in breaking the Italian lines, Italy, having secured control of the coastal towns but not of the interior, proclaimed the annexation of the Tripolitanian provinces.

Ottoman interest in Tripolitania, as in the other North African territories, had never been considered a matter of vital importance to the Ottoman Empire. Indeed, it was only in 1835, following the French occupation of Algiers, that the Ottoman government had bothered to reassert its control over the area, previously lost; and it had never succeeded in securing effective control of the interior, where the Senussi Brotherhood reigned supreme. There was, therefore, little likelihood that the Ottoman government would place the security of the empire at risk by mounting a major attempt to recover possession. Nor was there any likelihood that they would have succeeded, had they so decided. The dispatch of a substantial force, sufficient to expel the Italians, was at the time simply not feasible. In recent months the rebellion in the Yemen had required the dispatch of a special force (some 30 000 men), including troops withdrawn from the Tripoli garrison; and in any case the dispatch of a substantial force would require command of the sea, not available. Initially, therefore, the reaction of the Porte to the Italian occupation was conciliatory. Italy, it was suggested, might be permitted to occupy and administer Tripolitania, provided the sultan's sovereignty were recognised and a substantial indemnity paid, a proposal later expanded to include Italian concessions regarding the abolition of the capitulations. But the CUP, which happened at the time to be holding its annual congress in Salonica, took a different line. Believing that any Ottoman failure to defend Muslim-Arab territory might lead to a substantial loss of support in the Arab provinces, and in any case determined to fight, the congress at once inaugurated a committee of national defence, designed to muster support for the war effort; and at the same time it instituted a boycott of Italian goods. Moreover, in the course of the following weeks hundreds of volunteers, including Enver, who returned at once from Berlin, where he had been serving as military attaché, Nuri, his brother, Mustafa Kemal (Atatürk), Suleyman Askeri (later the head of the Teşkilati Mahsusa, special organisation), Fethi, who had been serving as military attaché in Paris, and Yakup Djemil (who later assassinated Nazim Pasha during the coup d'état of 23 January 1913), made their way, for the most part by the land route, to the front which had quickly been established by the Ottoman garrison and the Arab tribes in the interior, mainly in the vicinity of Derna, Tripoli, Benghazi and Tobruk. The object of the operation, as Fethi Bey made clear at the time, was to fight a prolonged guerrilla war, designed to prevent the Italians securing control of the country, and eventually to drive them out, or at least force them to negotiate:

> It would be madness [Fethi wrote] – with the forces we dispose of – to wait for the Italians under the walls of Tripoli and immediately offer them a battle in open country. One of the prime qualities of the Turks is to be tenacious and patient, and we will try to be both. Despite what the Italians think, we can rely on the collaboration of the Arabs.
>
> The important thing for us is to organize these auxiliary troops sufficiently . . . our plan is simple. Without deeply committing ourselves, we shall fight in retreat after the occupation of Tripoli . . . the munitions and arms which we had at Tripoli have already been shipped to the interior . . . There will also be concentrated the troops which we had stationed on the Tunisian frontier or in the South. Within a few weeks we will thus have gathered 10 000 regular troops and twenty or thirty thousand well-armed Arabs. Only then will the real struggle begin.
>
> We will fight in retreat at first, but soon we will be able to go energetically over to the offensive . . . in small actions incessantly giving the enemy no rest.[13]

The tactics adopted by the Turks and their Arab supporters in the war proved remarkably effective. In the following months the Italians found themselves bogged down in the main towns, while the Italian fleet, as one observer put it, sailed up and down the coast, sprinkling shells, often without doing 'any more damage than

---

13. Childs, *Italo-Turkish Diplomacy and the War over Libya*, pp. 76–7; J. Wright, *Libya; A Modern History* London: Croom Helm, 1981.

Messrs. Brock's pyrotechnical displays at the Crystal Palace'.[14] Thus frustrated in their efforts to force the Ottomans to admit defeat, on 19 November 1911 Italian warships shelled Aqaba; and on 24 February 1912 Beirut, an action which resulted in the partial expulsion of Italians resident in the empire. On 18 April 1912 an Italian fleet attacked the fortresses guarding the Dardanelles, thereby bringing about a five-week closure of the Straits to neutral shipping; and when this initiative, which caused Britain and Russia much concern, failed to persuade the Ottomans to submit, the Italians occupied the Dodecanese islands. But such half-hearted attempts to broaden the scope of the war made little impression on the Ottomans, who for the most part remained fixed in their determination to preserve Ottoman sovereignty in Tripolitania, or at least to secure a negotiated withdrawal and the payment of substantial compensation. Only in October 1912, when the outbreak of the Balkan Wars threatened the very survival of the empire, were the Ottomans obliged to give way.

The treaty ending the Tripolitanian War, concluded, following lengthy negotiations, at Ouchy, a suburb of Lausanne, on 18 October 1912, was by no means humiliating. According to the agreement there arrived at, the Ottomans were committed to an immediate cessation of hostilities and a withdrawal of all Ottoman troops and other functionaries from the area. In return the Italians were obliged to agree to a withdrawal of their forces from the Dodecanese, amnesties for the inhabitants of all the territories concerned, an increase in Ottoman customs duties, support for the ending of the capitulations and the payment of a substantial indemnity.

Not that the Treaty of Ouchy concluded the struggle for control of the North African provinces. Whilst the Ottomans did order a recall of their troops and other functionaries, many stayed on to organise resistance. As a result resistance continued in Tripoli and elsewhere for more than 20 years, under the leadership of Sulayman al-Barani, the Ottoman parliamentary deputy for Jebel, who set up a Tripolitanian national government. Nor did the Italians fully implement the terms of the agreement. Using the supposed involvement of Ottoman officers and others in the resistance as an excuse, they refused to evacuate the Dodecanese; and thereafter on several occasions used their possession of the islands as a bargaining counter in negotiations with the Ottoman government regarding economic concessions they hoped to secure.

14. *The Athenaeum*, No. 4405, 30 March 1912, Review of E.N. Bennett, *With the Turks in Tripoli* London: Methuen, 1912.

The Italian occupation of Tripolitania and the war which followed exposed to all concerned the extreme weakness of the Ottoman Empire, particularly in the Aegean, where the Italian fleet reigned supreme. At the same time it exposed the unwillingness of the Great Powers, not involved in the war, to intervene to protect the empire, whose independence and integrity they were supposedly committed to preserving. Of all the Great Powers only Germany appeared sympathetic to the Ottoman cause; and German sympathy had, of necessity, to be sacrificed to the need to keep Italy in the Triple Alliance. Yet in a war fought in the most difficult circumstances, against a major European power, a disparate group of Ottoman volunteers, with the support of the Arab Senussi tribes and others, inspired by a sense of common cultural identity and the Islamic faith, had succeeded in confining an Italian expeditionary force of superior technical strength to the coastal towns. Contemporary observers of the Ottoman scene might, therefore, with some justification, have expected that, in the war launched by the Balkan League in October 1912, the Ottoman army, recently reformed and reorganised, would perform adequately, at least. If such were the case they were to be quickly disillusioned.

CHAPTER FOUR

The Balkan Wars

Events

The outbreak of the Tripolitanian War in the autumn of 1911 had an electrifying effect in the Balkans, where the Balkan states had for some time been seeking an opportunity to attack the Ottoman Turks and drive them from their remaining territories in Europe. In March 1912 Serbia and Bulgaria, following talks regarding a possible partition of Macedonia, concluded a treaty, a secret annex of which stipulated that if disorder were to break out in the Ottoman Empire, endangering the national interests of the contracting parties or otherwise disturbing the status quo, then the two participating countries would meet to discuss joint military action. In the event of Serbia and Bulgaria emerging victorious from any war which might ensue, territory would be partitioned between the contracting parties, while unresolved boundary disputes would be adjudicated by the Russian tsar. In May Serbia and Bulgaria concluded a military convention, defining the number of troops each power might deploy in the expected campaign; and in October the alliance, having in the mean time been joined by Greece and Montenegro, whose king, Nicholas, had in the last weeks of peace organised a series of carefully orchestrated frontier disputes on the Ottoman border, ordered its forces to advance.

In the campaigns which followed the powers of the Balkan League, as the alliance of Balkan powers became known, won a series of spectacular victories. In less than a month they overran almost all the remaining Ottoman territories in Europe, causing an exodus of sick, wounded and impoverished Turkish refugees, most of whom congregated in Istanbul. In the west the Greeks took parts of southern Macedonia, including Salonica, and southern Albania, while the Serbs, advancing as far as the Adriatic, occupied parts of Macedonia and northern Albania. In the east the Bulgarians, following a series of easy victories, advanced as far as the Chatalja lines, a mere 40 miles from the Ottoman capital. As a result, in December 1912 the Ottomans were compelled to seek an armistice; and thereafter to engage in peace talks promoted by the Great Powers; but to no avail. In January, following a coup d'état (the so-called Bab-i Ali coup d'état of 23 January 1913) in the Ottoman capital, talks were broken off. Shortly thereafter the Bulgarians occupied Edirne, the great fortress town defending the approaches to Istanbul; and in April a second armistice was signed; though the Montenegran army continued fighting for a time, until it captured Scutari. By the terms of the Treaty of London, concluded on 30 May 1913, the Ottoman Empire was compelled to cede to the victorious Balkan powers all of its remaining territories in Europe, lying to the west of a line running from Enos on the Aegean to Midia on the Black Sea, together with Crete.

Following the conclusion of the Treaty of London, fate, previously unsympathetic to the Ottoman cause, chose to afford the Ottomans an unexpected favour. Unable to agree among themselves regarding a division of the spoils – Serbia and Greece, excluded from Albania, which the Great Powers declared independent, sought to occupy territories in western Macedonia previously allotted to Bulgaria – the members of the Balkan League quickly came to blows. In the ensuing struggle, known as the Second (or according to some accounts the Third) Balkan War, Bulgaria fought not only against her old allies, Serbia, Greece and Montenegro, but also against Romania, a latecomer to the feast. Her defeat was both speedy and decisive. In the Treaty of Bucharest of 10 August 1913 she was compelled to admit the loss not only of the greater part of her recent gains in Macedonia, but also southern Dobrudja, which passed to Romania; and in the Treaty of Constantinople of 29 September 1913 she was compelled to admit the loss of Edirne, which units of the Ottoman army, led by Enver, taking advantage of the opportunity offered by the collapse of the Balkan League, had quickly reoccupied.[1]

1. M.T. Florinsky, *Russia* London: Macmillan, 1967, Vol. 2; B. Jelavich, *History of the Balkans* Cambridge: Cambridge University Press, 1983, Vol. 2, pp. 95–100; S. Shaw and E. Shaw, *History of the Ottoman Empire and Modern Turkey* Cambridge: Cambridge University Press, 1977, Vol. 2, pp. 292–8.

Causes of the Ottoman defeat

Numerous explanations have been offered for the disastrous defeats suffered by the Ottoman forces in the Balkan Wars. The defeats were due, it has been suggested, to the lack of experience of the leaders of the CUP, who had secured control of the Ottoman government in the period following the Young Turk Revolution; to the secularising policies they had adopted, and the weakening of the religious principle; to the introduction of Christians into the army; to the hostility of the Great Powers, who wished to secure the expulsion of the Turks from Europe; to the decadence of the Ottoman army; to defective rail communications; to the absence of good roads; to failures of supply; to the adoption of the 'German military system', supposedly inferior; and finally, to the shortsightedness of Nazim Pasha, who had been appointed minister of war in the Great Cabinet. In August 1912, it is said, Nazim Pasha, hoping to counteract discontent among the army rank and file who were provoked by the onerous and often unjust terms of service, had dismissed all reservists and men in excess of the normal peacetime establishment, with the result that many battalions had been reduced to less than half of their normal strength. Then in September the government, having ordered a partial mobilisation of the army, had, on the advice of the ministry of foreign affairs, immediately countermanded the order, in order to 'prove to Europe that Turkey desired peace'.[2]

All these explanations are no doubt apposite, but a more profound analysis of the causes of defeat may be found in a note written at the time by Field Marshal von der Goltz, the German general, who had been responsible for supervising military reform in the Ottoman Empire in 1883–95, and in an article written by Lieutenant General Imhoff, who under von der Goltz had been entrusted with the task of reorganising the Ottoman artillery. In his note, which was published in the *Fortnightly Review* in 1913, von der Goltz had explained that until 1908, the year of the revolution, the Ottoman army had consisted only of Muslims, for the most part untrained. In the reign of Abdul Hamid, indeed, Ottoman troops were deprived even of rifle practice and drill, except under the most restricted circumstances.

---

2. S. Akşin, *Jön Türkler ve Ittihat ve Terrakhi* Istanbul: Gerçek Yayinevi, 1980, pp. 216–18; T.W. Childs, *Italo-Turkish Diplomacy and the War over Libya, 1911–1912* Leiden: E.J. Brill, 1990, pp. 202–3.

Only after 1908 had steps been taken to create a modern army; and even then the 'unfortunate mutiny of 1909' had interrupted the process. As a result the time available for the reform had been quite inadequate, though some progress had been made. What was required was a long period of tranquillity, uninterrupted by war, insurrection or disorder. In the Balkan Wars defeat of the Ottoman army, untrained, badly supplied and ill equipped, fighting a highly trained and numerically superior force, was inevitable.

In his article, originally published in *Vossische Zeitung*, and later published in a revised version, also in the *Fortnightly Review* of 1913, Lieutenant General Imhoff went even further. In the Russo-Turkish War of 1877–8, he remarks, the Ottoman army, despite a lack of organisation and leadership, had performed creditably. But under the Hamidian regime, all attempts to create a modern army, properly trained, had been frustrated:

> It is notorious that until July, 1908, there was no such thing as a modern army in Turkey in the strict sense of the term, and that any efforts to improve military organisation under the old *régime* were looked upon as little short of a crime. The period of four years that elapsed before the outbreak of the war was obviously inadequate, even with the best of intentions, for the purpose of training an army of about a million men – a total which Turkey was in a position to provide. The very promising beginning that had been made was marred in consequence of internal and political differences, and seeds of discord were sown such as to render all further work hopeless. Moreover, the frequent risings in Albania, Syria, Arabia, and also the Tripoli war, were disturbing factors, and contributed to no small extent in rendering impossible the task of organising and training, in time of peace, an army efficient for war on a great scale. Efforts in this direction were further hampered by the dissensions that existed among the officers.
>
> The fanatical, wild, and brave Turkish Army, which in former times constituted a homogeneous whole as regards nationality and religion, had absorbed elements having absolutely no interest in the maintenance of the Ottoman Empire, and, indeed, whose sympathies were frankly on the side of the enemy. Observers who in 1908 shed tears of joy on witnessing the fraternisation of the various nationalities with the Turks, stand aghast to-day at the swift change which has come over the scene. It must be left to one more competent than myself to describe and explain this extraordinary phenomenon. But there remains the significant fact that the change did occur. The predicted brotherhood of all the races within the Ottoman Empire has not been realised; events, indeed, have proved it to be nothing more than a dream.

While the inner coherence of the Army had already been shaken in consequence of conditions described above, the causes of the demoralisation of the officers' corps were to be attributed to an altogether different influence, an influence which arose from the circumstance that its members were entirely engrossed in politics and political strife. Proof of this statement is to be found in the fact that the junior officers no longer accorded to their seniors the consideration due to their rank. Moreover, the younger officers received promotion out of all proportion to their merits, and consequently acquired not a little influence. The lavish praise that was for some reason bestowed upon the Turkish Army produced in them an exaggerated self-esteem, so much so that many officers seriously entertained the belief that they had reached a degree of efficiency which placed them above all further teaching. Having myself been an officer upon whom devolved the duty of instructing the Turkish forces, I am filled with sorrow when I reflect that this once famous and brilliant army has, in the short space of time that has elapsed since 1909, split into various parties and factions – the Old and Young Turks quarrelling together, the Committee with its good intentions and its great defects, the Sadik movement, the secret societies, the cabal of officers identified with the political murder of Zekki Bey, the clubs and all the evil consequences arising therefrom. As a result of these pernicious influences, authority and discipline became undermined, a great gulf divided officers and men, and it was little wonder that serious work in time of peace no longer appealed to a class of men who had become what might perhaps best be described as 'political officers.' We arrive, then, at the conclusion that the rein given to political passions had the effect of completely destroying that discipline so essential to the maintenance of an efficient army.

Within the last few years the authority of the Government has been greatly impaired. After the deposition of Abdul-Hamid Cabinet changes became still more frequent. The leaders of the Government, too, were continually changed, with the result that constant friction arose between Ministers and ex-Ministers. What could be more natural than that the people, responding to the clamour of irresponsible criticism levelled at the highest officials, should lose faith in the Government! As a result of the popular agitation which ensued, whole parts of the standing army were subsequently relegated to the Reserves. No wonder, therefore, that the principle upon which State and Army had been founded was irrevocably damaged.

For the writer, an old instructing officer, the question of the inadequate training of officers and men is a somewhat delicate one to deal with. As an interested party, I shall refrain from offering any detailed criticism, and will content myself with referring to matters to which my attention has been drawn by the Press. I would, therefore, simply set forth the following points: The reserve troops were

not acquainted with the handling of their weapons; the artillery did
not know how to use their guns; the Rediffs were short of officers;
over a quarter of the Nizam troops consisted of untrained men; the
premature disbandment of the old Alajlis officers (the so-called troop-
ers) was a mistake; while the firing of the Anatolian troops, who
adhered to the old system, was ineffective. There was a great shortage of officers (altogether there were, roughly, no less than 8,000
officers' posts unfilled); the placing of men in position, and their
ability when in position, were defective; and finally, the influence of
foreign instructors, both in the Army and the Navy, was suppressed.[3]

Effects of the Balkan Wars

For the Ottomans, the Balkan Wars proved a disaster of major
proportions, greater even than that associated with the defeats of
the Russo-Turkish War of 1877–8. Within the space of a year or so
the empire was deprived of the greater part of its territories in
Europe (83 per cent, including the essential hinterland of the capital, control of which was deemed essential if the city's defences and
those of the Straits were to be maintained), and the bulk of its
population (69 per cent, some four million or so in number, mainly
Christians). In the capital, where in the weeks following the collapse thousands of refugees, many suffering from typhoid and chol-
era, poured in to camp out in the city centre, mosques and schools,
violent demonstrations broke out. So extensive, indeed, was the
defeat and the collapse of morale that followed, that some observers concluded that the end of the Ottoman Empire, long predicted,
was at hand; but thanks to a supreme effort of will on the part of
the Ottoman leadership, the stubborn resistance of the Ottoman
soldiery, and the relative stability of the Asiatic parts of the empire,
largely untouched by the disasters happening in Europe, the empire survived.

The extent to which the Asiatic parts of the Ottoman Empire,
protected by sheer distance and the decentralised nature of Ottoman society, still pronounced despite the centralising policies of
the CUP, remained unaffected by the defeats inflicted in Europe
must by any standards be considered remarkable. True, in Anatolia
and Syria, where thousands of reservists were called to the colours,
restrictions imposed on freedom of movement and expression, and

---

3. Imhoff Pasha, 'A German View of the Turkish Defeat', *Fortnightly Review*, Vol.
93 (1913).

controls on prices, some disruption was caused. But for the most part the effects remained limited. In Adana and Antalya, where Pantaleon, a Greek shipping company, was forced to pull out, some interruption to trade did occur; but in Baghdad, Basra and Jeddah the effects were minimal. In Mecca a reduction in the pilgrimage trade was noted, and in Damascus, afflicted at the time by recession, freight rates rose; but in Beirut, where entrepôt trade flourished, the war had little effect. Some even remarked that the war had if anything led to an increase in trade. In Izmir, where as a result of a recent banking crisis credit was already short, some damage was done; but a series of good harvests helped to mitigate the effect. Even in Istanbul, where large-scale business, affected by increases in freight rates and the cost of insurance, suffered, business in general, it is said, carried on much as before, helped by the fact that the sea route linking Istanbul and the Black Sea remained open. As for the agricultural sector, for the most part self-sufficient, this remained almost entirely unaffected.[4]

On balance then, the social and economic effects of the Balkan Wars on the Asiatic parts of the Ottoman Empire were somewhat less than might have been expected; but it could not be expected that so profound a disaster would leave the empire unchanged. On the contrary, it soon became evident that substantial changes in the government, politics and ideology of the empire would ensue – changes which would in due course lead to a CUP seizure of power, the suppression of the remaining opposition groups, and a radical shift in the balance of Ottoman ideology, away from Ottomanism and the principle of equality on which it was supposedly based, and in favour of its great rivals, Turkism, pan-Turkism and pan-Islamism.

The Bab-i Ali coup

The most immediate effect of the Balkan Wars on the politics of the Ottoman Empire was the seizure of power carried out by the CUP in the so-called Bab-i Ali coup of 23 January 1913. At the time it was widely believed that the Bab-i Ali coup was a spontaneous action, initiated at the last moment by a group of CUP officers, led by Enver, to prevent an Ottoman surrender of Edirne, sought by the Great Powers. According to this account Kiamil Pasha had, following the cancellation of the armistice of 3 December 1912,

4. G.W. Swanson, 'A Note on the Ottoman Socio-Economic Structure and its Response to the Balkan War of 1912', *Middle Eastern Studies*, Vol. 14, No. 1 (1978).

agreed to dispatch a delegation to discuss peace at a conference to be held in London. In response to demands, put forward by the delegations representing the Balkan states at the conference, that in return for peace the Ottomans cede not only all of the conquered territories in Europe, but also the Aegean islands, the Ottoman delegation had countered with an offer to cede all of the conquered territories in Europe, except Edirne, Albania (which would become an autonomous province, ruled over by an administration to be appointed by the powers) and Macedonia (which would become an autonomous province, ruled over by a member of the Ottoman royal family). These proposals the Balkan powers had rejected out of hand. As a result Sir Edward Grey, the British foreign secretary, who chaired the conference, had proposed that the empire agree to cede all the territories lying to the west of a line running from Enos on the Aegean to the Midia on the Black Sea, a proposal which would have entailed the loss of Edirne. This proposal too the Ottomans were unwilling to accept; but they replied that they would accept it, on condition that Edirne remain part of the empire and that the territories between Edirne and the Dardanelles be formed into an independent principality, which might remain neutral and constitute a buffer zone, protecting the Straits from a possible Bulgarian attack. As a result, during the following days a rumour spread throughout the army that the government intended to accept the loss of Edirne; and on 23 January 1913 a band of disgruntled CUP officers, led by Enver, accompanied according to one account by some 40–60 people, 'mostly of the hooligan class', assembled outside the Porte, where the telephone lines had been cut and the guard suborned.[5] Enver and his companions then forced their way into the cabinet room and compelled Kiamil Pasha, the grand vizier, to resign. In the process, Nazim Pasha, the minister of war, who came out to see what the noise was, was shot (by Yakub Djemil, the noted CUP *fedai*), as were a number of guards who attempted to prevent the intrusion.[6]

It is now evident that such an interpretation of the events leading up to the Bab-i Ali coup of 23 January can no longer be sustained. Evidence has been uncovered suggesting that prior to the apparently spontaneous action undertaken by Enver and his colleagues, the CUP had already put much effort into the planning and organisation of a possible coup, the inspiration for which lay in

---

5. J. Heller, *British Policy and the Ottoman Empire* London: Frank Cass, 1983, p. 77.
6. Shaw and Shaw, *History of the Ottoman Empire and Modern Turkey*, Vol. 2, pp. 295–6.

previous events. According to this account, following the appointment of Mahmud Muhtar Pasha as grand vizier, and the formation of the Great Cabinet in 1912, the CUP had initially sought to come to an understanding with the incoming government, hoping to secure the reappointment of Mahmud Shevket Pasha as minister of war. But in this they had proved unsuccessful. On the contrary, it soon became evident that Kiamil Pasha, who in October 1912 replaced Mahmud Muhtar Pasha as grand vizier, had no intention of cooperating with the CUP. On 8 November, when *Tanin* published a report to the effect that Shevket Pasha was to be appointed inspector general, Kiamil took immediate steps to prevent the appointment and have *Tanin* suppressed. Having thus failed to reach an accommodation with Kiamil, the committee turned to Nazim Pasha, the minister of war, hoping to persuade him to continue the fight to save Edirne, which it seemed Kiamil intended to give up. To this end, it was suggested, experienced officers such as Izzet Pasha, the chief of the general staff, Enver, Djemal and Fethi might be appointed to significant posts to organise the campaign. But Nazim, like Kiamil, proved uncooperative. Thus rebuffed, the CUP then turned to Mahmud Shevket Pasha, Izzet Pasha, and other officers sympathetic to the society, raising the question of a possible coup, for which plans were drawn up. But in the end, in view of the possible effects of a coup d'état on public morale, it was agreed that no action would be taken. Nor would the CUP take action if the cabinet resigned, a development widely expected. Only following the conclusion of peace would they take action. Those responsible for the present situation would them be punished and a new government, controlled by the CUP, appointed. On no account, however, would the CUP accept a peace settlement which involved the loss of Edirne. When therefore Kiamil summoned a grand council, composed of important and responsible people, who it was believed would be expected to shoulder collective responsibility for the cession of the city, the CUP, its patience finally exhausted, decided to act. The following day, as the cabinet met at the Sublime Porte to decide its response to the collective note presented by the Great Powers, Enver and his colleagues made their move.[7]

---

7. Akşin, *Jön Türkler ve Ittihat ve Terrakhi*, pp. 225–8; H. Ertürk, *Iki Devrin Perde Arkasi* Istanbul: Pinar Yayinevi, 1964, pp. 95–8; F. Ahmad, *The Young Turks* Oxford: Clarendon Press, 1969, pp. 116–20; Y.H. Bayur, *Türk Inkilâbi Tarihi* Istanbul: Maarif Matbaasi, 1940, Vol. 2, Part 4, pp. 271 ff. The Bab-i Ali coup was seen by many, both in Istanbul and abroad, as a victory for the pro-German, and a defeat for the pro-British, faction in the Ottoman Empire.

Once again, paradoxically, following the Bab-i Ali coup the CUP did not take immediate steps to impose its authority on the government. On the contrary, still uncertain of its power, it adopted for a time a conciliatory approach. When immediately following the coup Enver went to see the sultan, he asked merely for the appointment of a 'government for all the parties'; and in the government eventually appointed, which was led by Mahmud Shevket Pasha, representatives of the CUP remained in a minority, though they did hold several important posts. On 31 January 1913, in an attempt to mobilise the nation a Committee of National Defence, similar to that set up during the Tripolitanian War, was formed, headed by the sultan. This it was hoped would succeed in uniting all parties, including the Armenian nationalist organisations, Henchak and Dashnaksutiun. At the same time the Fleet Committee, originally set up in 1909 to raise money for the purchase of ships for the navy, was reconstituted; and on 14 February a law of general amnesty was proclaimed.

The efforts made by the CUP to unite the nation proved predictably unsuccessful. In the following weeks elements within the Liberal Union, Halâskar officers and other opposition groups took a series of steps designed to secure the expulsion of the CUP from power. These included the printing of appeals to the people to rise in support of the opposition, the planning of street demonstrations against the CUP, and according to some accounts the initiation of plans to have Talaat, Mahmud Shevket Pasha, Djemal, Azmi Pasha, the police chief, Emmanuel Carassu, and a number of other leading CUP figures assassinated. But these plots, plans and stratagems were quickly discovered by the authorities, and many members of the opposition were arrested. Others, including Sabahaddin, Kiamil Pasha and Ali Kemal, the Albanian leader, tipped off by Talaat, fled abroad.

But they did not give up the struggle. On 28 May Kiamil Pasha, possibly expecting a rising to occur, similar to that of 31 March 1909, returned to Istanbul from Egypt, where he had been accused of seeking British support for a coup; but he was at once confined to his home by Djemal, now military governor of Istanbul, and later expelled from the country. Then on 15 June Mahmud Shevket Pasha was shot down by a band of assassins in Beyazit, while driving to the Porte. The effect, hardly it may be presumed that which the conspirators had intended, was dramatic. Seizing the opportunity offered for radical action, the CUP, its patience now exhausted, launched in the course of the following weeks a campaign aimed at the extinction of the opposition. The capital was placed under an immediate curfew, the assassins were ruthlessly hunted down, and civil servants and officers suspected of being sympathetic to the cause of the opposition were dismissed. Meanwhile Djemal, who had already taken the precaution of drawing up a list of suspected persons, set about arresting the leaders of the various political parties and closing down their organisations. In a series of show trials, held before a martial-law court, specially appointed, those held responsible for the assassination, either directly or indirectly, were tried and condemned to death. Others were sentenced to long periods of hard labour, or exiled to remote parts of the empire. A number of leaders of the opposition resident abroad, including Sabahaddin, Sherif Pasha, a leading diplomat, Kemal Midhat, a son of Midhat Pasha, the noted nineteenth-century reformer, and Reshit Pasha, a minister of the interior in one of Kiamil's cabinets, were condemned to death or to terms of imprisonment *in absentia*. At the same time something approaching a reign of terror was instituted, sufficient to secure for the CUP absolute control of the instruments of power throughout the period of the First World War.[8]

Following the assassination of Mahmud Shevket Pasha a new cabinet was appointed, dominated by the CUP. In the new cabinet Said Halim, a grandson of Mehmet Ali, the khedive of Egypt, and keen supporter of the CUP, was made grand vizier and Talaat minister of the interior. In January 1914, Enver, twice promoted, was made minister of war; in February Djemal was made minister of works, and later minister of marine. It was in this way that the famous triumvirate of leaders, who were to dominate the politics of the Ottoman Empire throughout the First World War, emerged.

The final victory of the CUP in the naked struggle for power which constituted Ottoman politics in the period following the Young Turk Revolution may be explained primarily in terms of its control of the army, or at least of a substantial part of it; the excellence of its organisation, compared to the almost non-existent organisation of the opposition parties; the high degree of commitment of its leaders; the size of its membership, particularly in the bureaucracy, the police and the gendarmerie; the support it received from a nascent Turkish middle class and from various artisan and labour organisations, controlled for the most part by Kara Kemal, the CUP party boss in Istanbul; and last but by no means least, the ruthlessness of the CUP *fedais*, who intimidated and even on

8. Ahmed Djemal Pasha, *Memoirs of a Turkish Statesman* New York: Arno Press, 1973, pp. 19–39; Akşin, *Jön Türkler ve Ittihat ve Terrakhi*, pp. 235–9; Ertürk, *Iki Devrin Perde Arkasi*, pp. 106–8; Ahmad, *Young Turks*, pp. 129–30.

occasion assassinated opponents of the society. In the period of the Balkan Wars, a number of *fedai* units, which had fought at the Chatalja lines, assisted in the retaking of Edirne and organised resistance in the occupied territories, in particular in eastern Thrace, were brought together by Enver to form the Teşkilati Mahsusa (special organisation), an elite force formally controlled by the minister of war. Led by Suleyman Askeri, a senior staff officer, this organisation was given the task of promoting pan-Islamism and pan-Turkism, particularly in the Islamic countries ruled by the western imperial powers; and during the First World War it was given the task of organising guerrilla forces and promoting rebellion there. But the significance of the organisation as an instrument of CUP power within the Ottoman Empire should not be underestimated, for until the end of the First World War, at least, control of the organisation, together with control of the army and the police, enabled the CUP leaders to exercise undisputed authority in most parts of the empire.[9]

Following the acquisition of absolute power in June 1913 the CUP, despite the multiple problems created by defeat in the Balkan Wars, pressed vigorously ahead with the reform programme it had earlier instituted, designed to modernise, westernise and secularise Ottoman society. Further steps were taken to modernise and reform the educational and legal systems, strengthen the position of provincial governors, reduce the rights of the *millets* and reform the tax system. At the same time the Germans were invited to send a military mission, led by General Liman von Sanders, to assist in the task of reforming and modernising the Ottoman army; and the British were invited to send a naval mission, led by Rear Admiral Limpus, to reform the navy. Vigorous steps were taken further to reduce the number of ranker officers serving in the army – it was for this reason that Enver, a keen advocate of the policy, was appointed minister of war in January 1914 – and increase the number of college-trained officers. So effective, indeed, were the reforming policies pursued by the CUP in this period that for a time, it is said, a mood of optimism prevailed. But events quickly conspired to ensure that it would not last. In the autumn of 1914 there broke out in Europe a war between the Triple Entente (Britain, France and Russia) and the Central Powers (Germany and Austria–Hungary) which in due course was to result first in the involvement of the Ottoman Empire in the war, on the side of the Central Powers, and

9. Akşin, *Jön Türkler ve Ittihat ve Terrakhi*, pp. 109–14; E.J. Zürcher, *The Unionist Factor* Leiden: E.J. Brill, 1984, pp. 114–15.

then, following the defeat of the Central Powers, in the empire's extinction.

The Triumvirate

Of the three leaders who ruled over the Ottoman Empire in the First World War, Talaat Pasha was perhaps the cleverest. According to one account a 'man of commanding presence, although of medium height, with features eloquent of resolution, high courage and tenacity of purpose', Talaat was born, in modest circumstances, in 1874, the 'son of a mother of strong character and advanced views'.[10] After teaching Turkish for a time in a Jewish school in Edirne he joined the Post Office, where in due course he was appointed chief secretary of the Directorate of Posts and Telegraphs. A founder member of the Ottoman Freedom Society, following the Young Turk Revolution he was elected deputy for Edirne.

Enver Pasha, the most charismatic of the three, short of stature but outstandingly brave, was born in Istanbul in 1881, the son of a railway official or porter. Graduating second in his class from the staff college in 1902, he was posted to the Third Army in Macedonia, where he was engaged for a time in organising the suppression of Greek and Bulgarian *komitadjis*. In 1906 he joined the CUP as member number 12, and in 1908 he participated in the Young Turk Revolution, emerging as a 'Hero of Freedom'. Following the revolution he served for a time as military attaché in Berlin (1909–11), where he is said to have acquired an admiration for the technical competence of the German army. Indeed, he is reported to have become something of an *aficionado* of all things German, keeping a protrait of Frederick the Great over his desk in his office. Like many CUP officers of his generation he served with the Action Army in 1909, and fought in the Tripolitanian War. After leading the raid on the Sublime Porte, in the Bab-i Ali coup of 23 January 1913, he was promoted first lieutenant colonel and then brigadier general, before being appointed minister of war. In 1914 he married an Ottoman princess, acquiring thereby the title Damad.

Djemal Pasha, sometimes known as Büyük (Big) Djemal, described variously as clever, efficient, ruthless, mercurial and unpredictable, was born in 1872, the son of a soldier. After graduating from the

10. Z. Charlton, 'Six Osmanli Patriots', *The Nineteenth Century*, Vol. 74 (1913), p. 1222.

War College in 1895 he was posted to the Third Army in Salonica. In 1906 he joined the CUP, and in 1908, following the Young Turk Revolution, he became a member of the central committee. After the suppression of the counter-revolution of 1909, he became military governor of Üsküdar (1909); vali of Adana (1909); and vali of Baghdad (1911). In the Balkan Wars he fought at Vize and Pinar Hisar, before retreating to the Chatalja lines, where he was appointed a member of the army inspectorate. Following the Bab-i Ali coup he was appointed military governor of Istanbul and charged with the task of preserving order in the city, a task he accomplished with his usual ruthless efficiency. Following the outbreak of the First World War, he was made military commander in Syria, where he ruled like a colonial governor; though he continued to hold the office of minister of marine, to which he had been appointed in July 1914.[11]

Rise of Turkish nationalism

A second significant effect of the defeats inflicted on the Ottoman Empire in the Balkan Wars and the loss of the extensive territories in Europe, inhabited by a majority Christian population, which those defeats entailed, was a diminution in the support given by Ottoman statesmen and intellectuals to the ideology of Ottomanism, previously seen as the essential ideological foundation of a multi-national state, and an increase in the support given to pan-Islamism, Turkism, pan-Turkism, pan-Turanism (the ideal version of the pan-Turkist ideology) and Turkish nationalism (the more practical version, later associated with Anatolianism). Pan-Islamism was of course a well-established ideology, earlier promoted by Abdul Hamid and others in the expectation that it might foster support for the Ottoman Empire among the Muslim peoples of the world and provide a useful stick with which to beat the western imperial powers. But Turkism, pan-Turkism and Turkish nationalism were ideologies of a more recent conception, originating not, as one might have expected, in the Balkans, where in the nineteenth century the virus of nationalism had spread rapidly, but in the obscure researches of mainly European scholars, and in the emergence of a sense of

11. B. Lewis, *The Emergence of Modern Turkey* Oxford: Oxford University Press, 1961, pp. 221–2; *Encyclopaedia of Islam*, new edn, Enver Pasha and Djemal Pasha London: Luzac & Co, 1965; G.W. Swanson, 'Enver Pasha: the Formative Years', *Middle Eastern Studies*, Vol. 16, No. 3 (1980).

national, cultural and ethnic identity among the Turkish-speaking inhabitants of the Tsarist Empire.

The contribution made by European scholars to the rediscovery of Turkish national identity was perhaps decisive, for it influenced not only the Ottoman Turks but also the Turkish peoples living in the Tsarist Empire. In 1832, Arthur Lumley Davids, a British scholar, published a *Grammar of the Turkish Language*, the first of its kind, containing a preliminary discourse on the history of the Turkish language and the Turkish people, whom Davids distinguished from the Tartar and Mongol peoples, with whom they had previously been associated. In 1869, Mustafa Celâleddin Pasha, a Polish exile who had converted to Islam, published *Les Turcs Anciens et Modernes*, in which he emphasised the ethnic identity of the Turkish peoples and the great contribution they had made to the development of civilisation. In 1876 Ahmed Vefik Pasha, the grandson of a Greek convert to Islam, and a keen student of Turkish customs, published the first Turkish–Ottoman dictionary. In the eighteen seventies and eighties Arminius Vambéry, a noted Hungarian Turcologist and traveller, well acquainted with the peoples of Central Asia and the Ottoman Empire, published *Das Türkenvolk* (1883) and other works, in which he endeavoured (unsuccessfully it would seem) to convince the Ottomans that they and the Central Asian Turks enjoyed a common cultural, linguistic and historical identity. In 1887 Ahmed Midhat Pasha, a leading Ottoman intellectual, published a *History of Modern Times*, in which he emphasised the Turkish ancestry of the Ottomans. Finally, in 1896 Leon Cahun, a French historian intimately acquainted with the Young Ottomans, published an *Introduction to the History of Asia*, in which he identified the Ottoman Turks not only with the Turks of Central Asia, but also with the followers of such noted figures as Yengiz Khan and Tamerlane.

Meanwhile, in the Crimea and other parts of the Russian empire, Turkish-speaking Muslims, determined to promote the cultural identity of their people and oppose the tyranny of the tsars, became active. In 1883, in the Crimea, Ismail Bey Gasprinski, a Crimean Turk, established a weekly journal in which he promoted the idea of the spiritual and linguistic unity of the Turkish peoples of the area and called for a modernisation of the educational system. About the same time Hüseyinzade Ali Bey, an Azerbaijani poet who had studied in St Petersburg and then migrated to Istanbul, wrote an immensely influential poem entitled 'Turan', calling for the unification of the Turkish peoples of the world. In 1904 Yusuf Akçuraoğlu, a Tartar born in Simbirsk (now Ulianovsk) and educated in Istanbul and Paris, published in a Cairo journal, *Türk*, an article entiled 'Three Political Systems' in which he argued that neither Ottomanism nor pan-Islamism would meet the ideological needs of the Ottoman Empire. Only pan-Turkism would fulfil that function. Finally, in 1908 Ziya Gökalp, a half-Kurdish poet and sociologist from Diarbekir in southeastern Anatolia, commenced the publication of a long series of poems and articles, which was in due course to earn for him the title 'Father of Turkish Nationalism'; though in many of his early articles he continued to promote the ideology of Ottomanism. As a result of these and other ideological influences, in the following years the idea that the Turkish-speaking peoples of the Ottoman Empire might rediscover their lost racial and national identity, and incidentally thereby save the Ottoman Empire from ruin, spread rapidly among the intellectual classes of the empire, particularly in Istanbul and Salonica, propagated in particular in a series of clubs and journals set up in the capital about that time, including *Türk Derneği* (Turkish Association) (1908), *Genç Kalemlar* (Young Writers) (1910), *Türk Yurdu* (Turkish Homeland) (1911) and *Türk Ocaği* (Turkish Hearth) (1912).[12]

A striking account of the rise of Turkism and Turkish nationalism, with particular reference to the period of the Balkan Wars, is contained in a booklet entitled *Nature and Historical Development of the Turkish National Movement*, circulated by the British war office in the closing years of the First World War. In the first chapter of this booklet, entitled 'Ottomanism and pan-Islamism', the author explains that until recently the Turks of the Ottoman Empire had regarded themselves simply as Muslims. The Anatolian peasant took the word 'Turk' to be synonymous with 'Kisilbash' (Redhead: with red fez). True, under Abdul Hamid a few Young Turks had become inspired with the spirit of Turkish nationalism, but they had made little impression on the community. The Young Turks of the CUP had for the most part remained committed to the ideology of Ottomanism, to the idea that all Ottomans, regardless of race, religion or nationality, should unite; though a minority had looked for salvation to a resurrection of pan-Islamism – the idea that the Muslim peoples of the world might unite. Following the failure of the Ottoman government to unite the various peoples of the Ottoman

12. D. Kushner, *The Rise of Turkish Nationalism* London: Frank Cass, 1977; U. Heyd, *The Foundations of Turkish Nationalism* Westport, Connecticut: Hyperion Press, 1979; N. Berkes, *The Development of Secularism in Turkey* Montreal: McGill University Press, 1964; M. Hakan Yavuz, 'Nationalism and Islam: Yusuf Akçura and Üç Tarz-i Siyaset', *Journal of Islamic Studies*, Vol. 4, No. 1 (1993).

Empire, however, evidenced by the outbreaks of rebellion in Macedonia, the Armenian provinces, Albania and the Yemen, a small group of Turks, including influential members of the CUP, had come to believe that only by promoting Turkism, pan-Turkism and Turkish nationalism could the empire be saved:

> The mainspring of the National movement [the author of the war office booklet continued] must be sought in the Branch Committee of Union and Progress in Constantinople. The Secretary of the Branch [the Central Committee was still established in Salonica] was Kemal Bey, who was one of the delegates to the Central Congress in Salonica in 1909, and showed himself on that occasion most anxious to give the first impulse to the movement in the name of his Constantinople Association. During the debates he repeatedly attempted to make his opinions heard. His words: 'Gentlemen, we must first decide upon our ultimate goal, we must be quite clear about its real object – our national progress' – fell upon deaf ears, and he was unable once to give proper expression to his ideas, being continually shouted down with cries of 'Our goal is organization and nothing else, we know our goal'. In spite of his inability to place his ideas before the congress, he got privately into touch with a quiet unassuming man, who proved to be a most energetic partisan of the national movement; this was Ziya [Gökalp] Bey, who had been sent to Salonica as a delegate from the branch committee in Diarbekr. After the congress, Ziya Bey did not return to Diarbekr, but accompanied Kemal Bey to Constantinople in order to come into closer contact and communication with his adherents.
>
> There he formed a separate Committee, which for months discussed the burning question of Turkish nationalism down to its smallest details, and finally drew up a strong carefully studied programme for the defence of their ideas. Ziya Bey was then chosen to be a member of the Central Committee, which, as we have already said, had its head-quarters in Salonica at that time. Ziya Bey took up his position with the fixed idea, which almost amounted to a monomania, of working to the end for the triumph of Turkish nationalism. This modest man, who had neither a conspicuous past to recommend him, nor an impressive demeanour, nor an eloquent tongue, nevertheless showed a curious obstinacy in clinging to his monomania, wonderful stubbornness in defending his principle, calmness in fighting his political opponents, and firmness of purpose in managing and championing his cause.
>
> He first gathered round him a group of young people who devoted themselves zealously and enthusiastically to his cause. They started a paper in Salonica called *Genj Kalemlar* (Young Writers), which from the moment of its first appearance carried on a revolutionary and offensive policy.

The *Genj Kalemlar* heralded the foundation of a new language, a new literature, and a new and purely Turkish civilization. It promised that the language should be purified of the borrowed Arabic and Persian words, opened a campaign against the expressions and ideas taken from the old literature of these two languages, and proclaimed a new literature and civilization which should be based entirely on the old Turkish traditions.

All the great and celebrated writers and poets, such as Tevfik Fikret, Halid Ziya, Abdul Hak Hamid, and others, were decried as 'Dünkiler' (old-fashioned). Such men belonged to the past, and should be relegated to oblivion.

The new literature had, however, to be made. A carefully drawn up programme for the foundation of a new language was issued, and the union 'Yeni Lisan' (New Language) was founded. This new language was to consist of purely Turkish words, and those Arabic and Persian expressions which had already become part of the Turkish vocabulary.

Nearly the whole youth of Salonica took part in this movement. The 'Yeni Lisan' group was soon followed by the 'Yeni Hayat' (New Life), who took for their organ the 'Yeni Felsefe' (New Philosophy). 'Yeni Lisan' and 'Yeni Hayat' soon amalgamated. They made sharp attacks in their papers on the youth of Constantinople, and addressed them in somewhat unflattering terms, such as 'Levantines' and 'Supbe' (coxcomb) and 'persons devoid of any ideals, who had merely taken from Western civilization a dusty veneer and manners of the demi-monde, under which they cloaked their own inanity'.

The leaders of the 'Yeni Hayat' were more or less acquainted with Western literature through those books which seemed to share their political ideals: Alfred Fouillet, Gustav Lebon, Bergson, Durkheim, Gobineau, Nietzsche, and others. They probably built up their theories from these books, as may be seen from the following extract: 'We must be ourselves, that is, we must build up our intellectual life on our national traditions, and cultivate our own talents. We must only borrow from Europe method and technique. Our whole literature, which is not Turkish in any respect, must be reformed and founded on a new basis, it must become purely national in character. Down with men such as Ahmed Midhat, who are merely blind followers, and wish to propagate a misunderstood and badly assimilated version of Western civilization!'

In this manner, the youth of Salonica encouraged and inspired each other, with loud and excited debates and bitter quarrels with every one who disagreed with them.

In Constantinople these young braggarts were simply laughed at at first, and the whole affair ridiculed, while no one even took the trouble to think of valid and logical arguments with which to ward off the Salonica attacks.

At the same time, the behaviour of the non-Turkish element in the kingdom became increasingly assertive; the other nations made no attempt to hide their own nationalism, ambitions, and narrow-minded particularism. For this reason, the Central Committee was induced to attach itself to the Turkish national movement. It is true that the · downfall of Ottomanism had not yet taken place on tactical grounds, but in reality the new movement received all possible support.

Everything was done to extend the Turkish national movement of Salonica to Constantinople, and the poet Mehmed Emin Bey was summoned, and entrusted with the mission of starting a source of propaganda for the new ideals in the capital. Mehmed Emin Bey ceased his activities after a considerable time with the conviction that the ground had been sufficiently prepared, and his place was filled by Enver Bey. This period saw the foundation of the review *Turk Yurdu*, which, under the editorship of Yusuf Akshura, soon obtained a comparatively wide circulation, and was eagerly welcomed by an enthusiastic circle of readers.

Meanwhile the Central Committee for Unity and Progress moved its head-quarters from Salonica to Constantinople. Ziya Bey and his Salonican adherents followed with the firm purpose of bringing about the outbreak of a social revolution for the 'Yeni Hayat'. The efforts of this small group of intellectual pioneers succeeded in creating a circle deeply imbued with the ideas and principles of Turkish nationalism. But the social revolution did not come. The great public, the press, and the classical writers still remained indifferent and took no notice whatever of the new movement.

But the ground was prepared, the seed sown, and it was soon to bear fruit.[13]

Whence, it may be enquired, did the author of the war office booklet acquire so profound a knowledge of the history of the rise of the Turkish movement? Not it would seem from a host of industrious intelligence agents, beavering away in the undergrowth of Ottoman society, but from a booklet entitled *Türkler Bu Muharebede ne Kazabilirler?* (What profit can the Turks gain from this war?) written by Moses Cohen (Tekin Alp) in Istanbul in 1914, or from an extended version of that work, entitled *Türkismus und Pantürkismus*, published, no doubt at the instigation of the German foreign ministry, in Weimar in 1915.[14]

---

13. Public Record Office, WO 106 63 *Nature and Historical Development of the Turkish National Movement*, Ch. 2.

14. See Berkes, *Development of Secularism in Turkey*, p. 344 note. Cohen's booklet made an immense impression on Winston Churchill and Arnold Toynbee. See W.S. Churchill *The World Crisis: The Aftermath* London: Thornton Butterworth, 1923–31, pp. 355–6; and A. Toynbee, *Turkey: A Past and a Future* London: George H. Doran, 1917.

That the account of the rise of the Turkish national movement given by Moses Cohen in the Turkish original and the German and British translations, is credible appears not to be in doubt. Ziya Gökalp and other Ottoman intellectuals did, indeed, promote pan-Turkish and Turkish nationalist ideals in such journals as *Türk Derneği, Genç Kalemlar, Türk Yurdu* and *Türk Ocaği*; but recent research has shown that the prevalence of such ideas in the journals concerned was not nearly so marked as contemporary observers and propagandists, such as Moses Cohen, may have chosen to believe. On the contrary a substantial majority of the contributors, convinced of the urgent need to defend the Ottoman state, remained committed throughout to the ideology of Ottomanism, seeing Turkism and pan-Turkism not as alternatives to Ottomanism but as vehicles for its expression. In *Türk Derneği* most of the articles advocating Turkism and pan-Turkism were written by contributors of Central Asian origin. Ottoman contributors remained for the most part firmly committed to the idea of Ottoman unity, even when promoting the reform (simplification) of the Ottoman language. In *Genç Kalemlar* the overriding concern of the contributors was not with Turkism but with Ottoman politics, history and literature. In so far as language reform was sought, it was sought in the interest of the common people. As an anonymous writer, presumed to be Ömer Seyfettin, remarked in an article, published in *Genç Kalemlar* in 1911: 'Turks, the Turanian family, who live from Scutari (Albania) to Baghdad, can protect their sovereignties and lives only through powerful and serious progress. Progress consists in diffusing knowledge, science and literature among all of us; it is a national and common language that is first necessary for diffusing these things.'[15]

In *Türk Yurdu*, the most nationalist of the journals published in this period, set up mainly by Turkish-speaking emigrés from Russia, including Yusuf Akçuraoğlu and Hüzeyinzade Ali, to promote the mutual awareness of the Turkish peoples, many articles were published advocating the promotion of Turkism; but an equal number, including articles by Ziya Gökalp and Fuat Köprülü, a noted Ottoman scholar, were published, advocating measures designed simply to preserve and defend the Ottoman state.[16]

That most Ottoman intellectuals remained, until the end of the First World War at least, committed to the ideology of Ottomanism, however interpreted, is scarcely surprising, for it could hardly be

15. M. Arai, *Turkish Nationalism in the Young Turk Era* Leiden: E.J. Brill, 1992, p. 35.
16. Ibid., Ch. 4.

expected that they would promote an ideology or ideologies predicating the destruction of the political structures of the state in which they lived. Nevertheless, the significance of the great debate concerning Turkism, pan-Turkism and Turkish nationalism, described by Moses Cohen, should not be underestimated, for in retrospect it can be seen that it portended a radical shift in the political and social consciousness of the Ottoman intelligentsia, and in due course of the Ottoman-Turkish people.

According to some accounts, the rise of Turkish nationalism in the Ottoman Empire in the years preceding the outbreak of the First World War was greatly facilitated, determined even, by a series of social and economic changes occurring in the more advanced parts of the empire at the time – changes which would in due course give rise to the creation of a Turkish-Muslim middle class and an industrial proletariat. These changes included the development of a cash economy, urbanisation and the breakdown of the traditional structures of the Ottoman state system, which had in the past succeeded to a greater or lesser extent in containing religious and national (ethnic) differences. What the rising Turkish-Muslim middle class required, so the argument goes, was a strict, stable and predictable administration, capable of providing the services required by entrepreneurs operating in a cash economy. If the Ottoman state system could not provide these services – in 1913 the annual rate of inflation reached 300 per cent – then it was inevitable that the rising middle class, supported by skilled labour and a *déracinée* intelligentsia, would look elsewhere for a solution to its problems. It would seek, in other words, the creation of a nation state, similar to those created in Europe and the Balkans in the nineteenth century.[17]

The influence of the forces that, according to this interpretation, gave rise to a genuinely indigenous form of Turkish nationalism, can perhaps be seen most clearly in the growing demands put forward at the annual congresses of the CUP, particularly in the period following the defeats inflicted on the Ottoman Empire in the Balkan Wars. At these congresses repeated demands were made for the creation of a national economy, independent of both the external controls imposed on Turkish-Muslim trade and enterprise by the Great Powers in the form of the capitulations, and of the internal restraints imposed by the evident superiority in all matters

17. K.H. Karpat, 'The Transformation of the Ottoman State', *International Journal of Middle Eastern Studies*, Vol. 3 (1972); S. Tanilli, 'Le Tournant de 1913 dans l'Histoire de l'Union et Progrès', *Varia Turcica*, Vol. 13 (1991).

concerning trade and enterprise of the Greek and Armenian merchant classes. To this end, particularly in the period following the defeats of the Balkan Wars, numerous steps were taken by the CUP to secure the abolition of the capitulations, greater protection for the economy, increased public control of economic enterprises, the creation of a national bank and the setting up of cooperatives and other types of economic enterprise, likely to shift ownership and control from the minorities to the majority population.[18]

Among the numerous intellectuals who promoted the idea of the creation of a 'national' economy – these included Moses Cohen – Alexander Helphand, the Russian Socialist, was perhaps the most extraordinary. Alexander Helphand, or 'Parvus' as he was generally known, vividly characterised by Alexander Soljenitsyn in his novel *Lenin in Zurich* (1976) as a brilliant Marxist, teacher of Trotsky, Kautsky, Liebknecht and Rosa Luxemburg, instigator of the 1905 revolution in Russia, and campaigner for the eight-hour day, was born in Beresina in 1867. Exiled to Siberia following the defeat of the 1905 revolution, he quickly escaped, making his way first to Germany and then to Turkey, where he passed the years 1910–14. Following his arrival in Istanbul, where it is said he made a fortune brokering spare parts and other equipment for the Ottoman railways and other industries, he published a series of anti-liberal and anti-imperialist articles in the Ottoman press, arguing that in order to secure their freedom and independence, now in hock to the western capitalists, the Ottomans should not cooperate with the western powers, but challenge them. They should abolish the capitulations and other external restraints on Turkish enterprise, and build a 'national' economy. Only by fighting the west would the Ottomans be able to secure the benefits of western civilisation. Moreover, so he advised Lenin, and no doubt the leaders of the CUP, the road to world Socialism lay through the reinforcement of German military power, the defeat of Russian tsarism and the break up of the Tsarist Empire. With such arguments, it may be supposed, Alexander Helphand assisted in the final destruction of whatever liberal illusions the leaders of the CUP may have still retained. He may also have played a significant part in persuading them to side with the Central Powers in the First World War. Finally, in suggesting to the German high command in the course of the war that they employ the forces of Socialist revolution and nationalism to undermine the stability of the Tsarist Empire he may have helped

18. Berkes, *Development of Secularism in Turkey*, pp. 335–7.

shape the future course not only of German and Russian but also of Ottoman history.[19]

Birth of Arab nationalism

Contemporary observers generally assumed that the Ottomanisation and Turkification policies pursued by the CUP, combined with the failure of the Ottoman government to defend the empire effectively in the Tripolitanian and Balkan Wars, gave rise to the birth of an Arab national movement, comparable to those that had played so great a part in undermining the Ottoman Empire in the Balkans in the nineteenth century. And, indeed, some evidence can be adduced in support of that contention. Already, in the preceding decade or so, Arab intellectuals in Egypt, Syria and the Lebanon had sought to promote a revival of Arab culture, the usual precursor of the rise of a national movement; and in 1905 Najib Azuri, a Syrian Catholic educated in Paris, published a book entitled *The Awakening of the Arab Nation*, calling for the establishment of an Arab state, incorporating Syria and Iraq, with an Arab caliphate located in the Hedjaz. In 1909 a group of Syrian army officers and students formed a secret society, advocating the creation of an Arab–Turkish condominium over the Ottoman Empire, similar to the Austro-Hungarian dual monarchy; and in the same year a group of students, mainly Syrians, set up al-Fatat or the Young Arab Society, in Paris. Then, in 1912, a group of Syrians living in Cairo set up an Ottoman Administrative Decentralisation Party, dedicated to securing administrative decentralisation; and a group of Lebanese established a Beirut Reform Society. About the same time Aziz Ali al Misri, an Ottoman army officer, possibly supported by the khedive of Egypt, set up al-Ahd (the Covenant), a secret society, composed of Arab army officers, supposedly committed to the acquisition of autonomy for the Arab provinces. Meanwhile a number of Arab intellectuals including such noted figures as Muhammad Abduh, an Egyptian, and Abd-al Rahman al Kawakibi, an Aleppo notable settled in Cairo, wrote widely about the political and cultural predicament facing the Arab peoples; while in the desert wastes of Arabia Arab tribes, led by such noted figures as Abd-al Aziz Ibn Saud and Sherif Husein of Mecca, continued to defend their traditional rights, manoeuvring to secure greater autonomy or independence – efforts

19. Ibid.

interpreted by the Great Powers, in particular the British, as evidence of the existence of a widespread 'Arab movement', portending the end of the Ottoman Empire. Finally, in June 1913 an Arab congress, meeting in Paris, attended by members of al-Fatat and the Ottoman Decentralisation Party, demanded a greater degree of decentralisation, the use of Arabic as an official language and local military service – demands virtually identical to those put forward in recent years by the other nationalities.[20]

That these developments indicated a change in the nature of Arab opinion regarding the place of the Arab provinces in the Ottoman Empire is not in doubt; but it may be doubted whether they constituted a movement which could as yet justly be described as an Arab national movement. Najib Azuri was, it would seem, mainly concerned to promote French interests in Syria and the Lebanon, where Christian Maronites were working for a Greater Lebanon. In any case he appears to have exercised no real influence on his community. Syrian Muslim intellectuals, such as al-Kawakibi, were at the time mainly concerned to secure the protection of Arab interests in the Ottoman Empire, and the reform of Islam, an issue of primary importance. They had little or no desire to be associated with 'Arabs' – ignorant and illiterate nomads, who lived in the desert in tents. As for al-Fatat and al-Ahd, these organisations appear to have made little or no impression on the community: Ottoman and French intelligence organisations were scarcely aware of their existence. What a majority of the delegates attending the 1913 Paris conference wanted was not Arab independence, or even for the most part autonomy, but the protection of local, often clan or family, interests threatened by the centralising policies of the CUP.[21]

Ottoman Iraq

In Iraq, as in Egypt, Syria and the Lebanon, contemporary observers were frequently inclined to detect signs of what they assumed to be the genesis of an Arab national movement. In particular they were inclined to look on Sayyid Talib al-Naqib, the 'strong man of Basra', as a proto-nationalist. But in fact, as a brief survey of his political

---

20. M.E. Yapp, *The Making of the Modern Near East* Harlow: Longman, 1987, pp. 201–11; C.E. Dawn, 'The Rise of Arabism in Syria', *Middle Eastern Studies*, Vol. 16 (1962); E. Kedourie, 'Political Parties in the Arab World', in *Arabic Political Memoirs and Other Studies* London: Frank Cass, 1974.

21. Ibid.

career indicates, he was very much the product, not of a nascent Arab national movement, but of the traditional struggle for power in which local notables in the Ottoman Empire were wont to engage.

Sayyid Talib al-Naqib was the son of Sayyid Rajab, the Naqib of Basra. Having with the aid of the sheikh of Kuwait and influential elements at court succeeded in ousting an uncooperative vali, he rapidly succeeded in building up a powerful position for himself in the Basra area, levying 'taxes' on the local population, securing control of the administration and murdering, or otherwise intimidating, his enemies and opponents. In 1904 when a newly appointed vali, not open to corruption, attempted to have him arrested, and failing that to have him expelled from the area, he went to Istanbul, where with the aid of a bribe of T.L. 5,000 he succeeded in having himself appointed a member of the state council and all evidence of his crimes expunged from the records. Following the Young Turk Revolution, fearing retribution for his crimes, he returned to Basra, having first it is said taken the precaution of setting fire to his house, in order that he might claim the insurance. In the ensuing election he succeeded in having himself elected deputy for Basra; but unable to make headway in the CUP he contacted Sadiq Bey and joined the Moderate Liberal Party, a small party later merged in the Liberal Union. In 1910 or thereabouts, unable to secure the removal of another reforming vali, he eventually secured his dismissal by having the riff-raff of Basra sign a petition calling for his continuance in office – a ruse which, it is said, persuaded Talaat of the need for the vali's replacement.

Thereafter, until the outbreak of the First World War, Sayyid Talib ruled Basra like a local warlord, intimidating his enemies, many of them members of the CUP, controlling local newspapers and even on occasion interfering in the complex politics of the Muntafik tribes of southern Iraq, who at the time were engaged in a bloody struggle for the leadership of the confederation. In the election held in 1912 for the Ottoman chamber of deputies, Sayyid Talib was again elected, this time as a candidate for the Liberal Union; and following the appointment of Kiamil Pasha as grand vizier, he helped the newly appointed vali, Ali Rida al-Rikabi, to frustrate the activities of the CUP in the area. Following the Bab-i Ali coup of 23 January 1913 and the return to power of the CUP he quickly changed tack, reaching an agreement with the local representative of the society, one condition of which was that he would refrain from political activity; but he later called a meeting of local notables at his home, at which it was decided to petition the sultan, requesting the appointment of a general council of Basra, capable of representing the area and defining its needs. At the same time he made preparations for the setting up of a Reform Society of Basra, similar to that recently established in Beirut; and in March 1913 he even organised a meeting in the palace of the sheikh of Muhammara, attended by the sheikh of Kuwait, at which it was agreed that they should demand independence or at least autonomy for Iraq. Moreover, when the enactment of the new Vilayet Law of April 1913, which greatly increased the power of the vali, threatened his position and that of the general council, which he controlled, he launched a campaign against the new law, involving the dispatch of scores of telegrams to the grand vizier and the minister of the interior in Istanbul, demanding full administrative autonomy for the province. If his demands were not met, he declared, then he would resort to force.

Faced with this threat of what amounted to open rebellion, Talaat, minister of the interior, Djemal, military governor of Istanbul, and Azmi, chief of the general security service, decided that the time, however unpropitious, had now come for action. Farid Bek, an ex-mutasarrif of the Muntafik, was asked to go to Basra and organise the elimination of Sayyid Talib and his principal supporters. Ujaymi ibn Sadun, the leader of the Muntafik, might be recruited to accomplish the task, in return for an honorary decoration and a monthly allowance. Farid Bek himself might be rewarded with the post of vali of Basra. But the plan proved unsuccessful. When Farid Bek and Ujaymi assembled their forces in the neighbourhood of Basra, Sayyid Talib responded by assembling an equivalent number of his own men; and shortly thereafter when Farid Bek and his companions were disembarking from a boat at the docks, he had Farid Bek assassinated. Following the assassination, joined now by Ujaymi, who had wisely decided to change sides, he issued a declaration, declaring that henceforth he would work to secure Arab rights; and in August he had distributed, through the Reform Society of Basra, a list of demands, calling for provincial self government, the independence of the general council, which should now be considered superior to the vali, the handing over of state lands in the area to the council, the use of Arabic for official purposes, the appointment of officials of Iraqi origin, and the expenditure of tax income in the area of its collection. Only the control of foreign policy, the making of law, the enforcement of law and order, the raising of taxes and the provision of postal and telegraph services should remain within the purview of the state. The authorities, who were accused of selling Bulgaria, Bosnia and Herzegovina and Iraqi lands to foreigners, and agreeing to Zionist plans for the purchase of Palestine, should cease from killing people and support the khalifate. If need be Arab soldiers would draw their swords and compel the government to agree to the proposed reforms.

Sayyid Talib's tactics proved effective. When further attempts to have him assassinated failed, Talaat and his colleagues were obliged to agree to a settlement which left him in effective control of Basra. In return for Ottoman recognition and support, Sayyid Talib agreed to mediate between the Porte and Abdul Aziz Ibn Saud, who had recently occupied al-Haza, and to set up a committee to raise money for the Ottoman navy. Henceforth, it was agreed, Sayyid Talib and the Ottoman government would work together for the 'happiness of our eternal state'. As a result, in the elections held in 1914, Sayyid Talib's men swept the board, and nothing more was heard of the Reform Society of Basra, which had evidently served its purpose.

Following the outbreak of the First World War, and the dispatch of a British task force to the Persian Gulf, Sayyid Talib, quick as ever to respond to changing circumstances, lost no time in approaching the government of India with offers of support in return for his appointment as sheikh or amir of Basra and the payment of a large sum of money; but the British, well aware of his duplicity, proved unresponsive. In 1915, threatened by the presence of substantial Ottoman forces in the area, he sensibly accepted the advice of Sir Percy Cox, the British resident in the Persian Gulf, and went into exile in India.[22]

22. Yapp, *Making of the Modern Near East*, pp. 211–13; E. Tauber, 'Sayyid Talib and the Young Turks in Basra', *Middle Eastern Studies*, Vol. 25 (1989).

CHAPTER FIVE

The Great Powers and the Ottoman Empire

Throughout the greater part of the nineteenth century, more particularly from the period of the first Mehmet Ali crisis of 1833
(when an Egyptian army, led by Mehmet Ali's son, Ibrahim, threatened to occupy Istanbul and bring about a complete collapse of the
empire) the Great Powers, in particular Britain, France, Russia and
the Austrian Empire, generally supported the preservation of the
Ottoman Empire. For Britain and France the Ottoman Empire was
seen as a useful bulwark, preventing the advance of Russia in the
Near and Middle East. For Russia and the Austrian Empire it was
seen as a relatively ineffective, harmless neighbour, likely to preserve a degree of stability on their southern borders. Indeed, in
1833 the Russians actually intervened to secure the survival of the
empire, dispatching a fleet to Istanbul to prevent its occupation;
and in the Treaty of Paris, which concluded the Crimean War, fought
by Britain and France to secure the integrity of the Ottoman Empire, the Great Powers agreed that henceforth the Sublime Porte
would be 'admitted to participate in the advantages of the public
law and system (concert) of Europe'. Again in the Eastern Crisis of
1876–8, when the empire was once again threatened with collapse,
Britain and France intervened to prevent the imposition by Russia
of the draconian Treaty of San Stefano (1878) on the Ottoman
Empire, clauses of which made provision for the creation of a greater
Bulgaria, incorporating territories stretching as far as the Aegean
Sea. In the Treaty of Berlin in 1878, the British and French obliged
the Russians to abandon their plans for the creation of a greater
Bulgaria and settle instead for an arrangement which, however dam-
aging it may have been for the Ottoman Empire, yet left the empire
in possession of substantial territories in Europe.

The Great Powers remained generally committed to the principle of the preservation of the Ottoman Empire until the outbreak of the First World War; but in the closing years of the nineteenth century a series of factors conspired to undermine their commitment. In particular, Abdul Hamid, outraged by Britain's occupation of Cyprus in 1878 and of Egypt in 1882, and by France's occupation of Tunis in 1881, and suspicious of the activities of those powers in Syria and Mesopotamia, where they appeared to be laying the foundations of empire, turned increasingly to the Germans, now deeply involved in the area, for support. Indeed, in order to foster that support he went out of his way to secure for the Germans a series of major economic concessions, one of the most substantial of which was for a railway line from Scutari, on the Asiatic shore of the Bosphorus, to Ankara in Anatolia, the first stage of a line later to become notorious as the Baghdad Railway. At the same time, in order to foster opposition to Russia in Central Asia and to Britain and France in North Africa and the Middle East, Abdul Hamid promoted pan-Islamism, an ideology which posed no threat to the Germans, who had not as yet established colonies in the Muslim world. For the British, French and Russians, German penetration of the Ottoman Empire, apparently encouraged by Abdul Hamid, was not to be welcomed, for it appeared to threaten their commercial and strategic interests in the area, particularly those concerning the Turkish Straits, the sea line of communications joining the Mediterranean and the Black Sea.[1]

Germany

German influence in the Ottoman Empire on the eve of the First World War was substantial; but it was by no means dominant. In 1888 the Deutsche Bank arranged a loan for the sultan, and in 1889 it played a leading part in the setting up of the Ottoman Railway Company of Anatolia. In the 1890s the German Levant Line established a shipping service between Hamburg and Istanbul; while Wankhaus, a trading company, set up a series of trading posts in the area of the Persian Gulf, and Krupp, the arms manufacturer, received substantial contracts for the supply and equipment of the

1. M.S. Anderson, *The Eastern Question* London: Macmillan, 1966; A.L. Macfie, *The Eastern Question* Harlow: Longman, 1996.

Ottoman army. In 1902–3 the Ottoman Railway Company secured a concession to build an extension of the Anatolia Railway from Konya, to which the Ankara line had been extended, to Baghdad and the Persian Gulf, with a branch line to Khanikin, a small town on the Persian border. By 1904 this line had been constructed as far as Bulgurlu at the foot of the Taurus mountains; and by 1914 it had reached Ras el Ain, some 200 miles beyond Aleppo, though tunnels through the Taurus and Amanus mountains remained incomplete. As a result of these and other developments in the decade or so preceding the First World War German economic enterprise in the Ottoman Empire expanded rapidly; though in 1914 German exports to and imports from the empire were still exceeded by those of Britain and Austria–Hungary.

German military and political influence in the Ottoman Empire generally marched hand in hand with economic investment. Already in the 1880s, German military missions, led by General Otto Köhler and Lieutenant-Colonel Baron Colmar von der Goltz, had been dispatched to reform the Ottoman army; and in 1889 and 1898 Kaiser Wilhelm II had visited the empire (travelling on a tour arranged by Messrs Thomas Cook and Co.). On the second occasion he visited Jerusalem and Damascus, where he ostentatiously proclaimed the friendship of the German people for Islam. In 1913, following the defeat of the Ottoman army in the Balkan Wars, the Germans again responded to an Ottoman request for assistance, dispatching a military mission, led by General Otto Liman von Sanders – a mission which, from the Russian point of view, appeared to place the Straits under German control.

Nor was German economic, political and military influence in the Ottoman Empire lacking in a sense of ideological support and direction. In 1886 Alois Sprenger published a book, entitled *Babylon – The Richest Land in Ancient Times*, in which he suggested that the German people colonise Asia Minor. In 1892 Carl Kaeger wrote *Asia Minor, a Field for German Colonisation*, in which he advocated the economic exploitation of the area; and about the same time the pan-German League published a book entitled *Germany's Claims to the Turkish Inheritance*.[2]

2. M. Kent, *The Great Powers and the End of the Ottoman Empire* London: George Allen and Unwin, 1984, Germany; M.L. Flaningan, 'German Eastward Expansion, Fact and Fiction: A Study in German–Ottoman Trade Relations, 1890–1914', *Journal of Central European Affairs*, Vol. 14, No. 4 (1955); W.O. Henderson, 'German Economic Penetration of the Near East, 1870–1914', *Economic History Review*, Vol. 18 (1948).

It cannot be doubted then that in the run-up to the First World War the Germans had established an influential position in the Ottoman Empire; and that they had ambitions fully to exploit the position they had won. Yet, paradoxically, when on the eve of the First World War Enver, acting in conjunction with the grand vizier, Said Halim, raised with Hans von Wangenheim, the German ambassador, the possibility that the Ottoman Empire might join in the coming war on the side of the Triple Alliance, an arrangement which would secure for Germany the closure of the Straits to the Entente Powers, the consequential isolation of Russia, and the opening of fronts against Russia in the Caucasus and Britain in Egypt, threatening British control of the Suez Canal, his approaches were initially met with a lack of enthusiasm amounting to disdain. As Wangenheim remarked:

> . . . As a member of the Triplice Turkey would have to reckon with the open hostility of Russia. The Turkish eastern frontier would be the weakest spot in the strategic dispositions of the Triplice and the natural point of attack for Russia. The Triplice Governments would doubtless hesitate to shoulder burdens for which Turkey today could make no adequate return. Even Turkey and Bulgaria as a *bloc* would scarcely be of any value to the Triplice as an ally.[3]

Whence, it may be enquired, arose this extraordinary lack of enthusiasm for an entry of the Ottoman Empire into the First World War on the side of the Central Powers? Not it would seem from German ignorance of the great advantages to be gained from Ottoman entry – these were well understood – but from a belief, prevalent in both the German general staff and the diplomatic corps at the time, that the armed forces of the Ottoman Empire, so recently defeated in the Balkan Wars, would prove incapable of fighting a modern war, and that they would therefore merely place an added burden on the resources of the Reich, certain to be stretched to breaking point in the first crucial days of the war. Not that this argument was the only one advanced against the proposal of an Ottoman–German alliance. Though relations between the CUP and the Germans, damaged by German support for Austria–Hungary in the Bosnia-Herzegovina annexation crisis and by German support for Italy and Greece on a series of issues, including Tripolitania and the Aegean islands, had improved somewhat, distrust remained profound. In particular, the Germans had good reason to expect that

3. L. Albertini, *The Origins of the War of 1914* Oxford: Oxford University Press, 1957, p. 612.

in the coming war the Ottomans would eventually side, not with the Central, but with the Entente, Powers. In May 1914 Talaat, the minister of the interior, and Izzet Pasha, an ex-minister of war, had in the course of a mission to present the sultan's greetings to the tsar at Livadia on the Black Sea (where Nicholas, as was his custom, was passing the summer months), twice raised the possibility of an alliance with Russia, which it was believed would safeguard the future of the empire, threatened with partition. Then in July, Djemal Pasha, the minister of marine, had in the course of a visit to France made in response to an invitation to observe the manoeuvres of the French fleet suggested that the empire might form an association of some kind with the Triple Entente, an association which might in due course enable the Ottomans to recover possession of the Greek islands, a principal objective of their foreign policy at the time.

In any case was it not possible – so it was argued by members of the German diplomatic and commercial establishments at the time – that the way forward for Germany in the Near and Middle East lay not in the preservation of the Ottoman Empire, but in its partition and a profitable division of the spoils. In the Wilhelmstrasse, it is said, maps of Asia Minor were prepared, showing possible spheres of interest, while negotiations regarding the future of the Baghdad Railway were allowed to founder, supposedly on the rocks of Ottoman intransigence. Russian opposition to partition might eventually be overcome by an offer of Istanbul and the Straits, in return for the creation of German colonies in Anatolia. Had not the Russians already agreed, in 1910–11, to conclude an agreement with the Germans, recognising Germany's right to continue with the construction of the Baghdad Railway, in return for German recognition of a Russian sphere of interest in northern Persia?[4]

The German decision, eventually taken on the eve of the First World War, to respond positively to Ottoman proposals regarding the possibility of an Ottoman–German alliance must be seen, therefore, not as the culmination of a long campaign, sustained by all the instruments of economic, diplomatic and military pressure, but as a sudden and unexpected development, inspired largely by the exigencies of the moment; though evidently the volte face could

4. Kent, *Great Powers and the End of the Ottoman Empire*, Germany; U. Trumpener, 'Turkey's Entry into World War I: An Assessment of Responsibilities', *Journal of Modern History*, Vol. 34, No. 4 (1962); H.S.W. Corrigan, 'German–Turkish Relations and the Outbreak of War in 1914: A Re-assessment', *Past and Present*, Vols 36–8 (1967); W.W. Gottlieb, *Studies in Secret Diplomacy* London: George Allen and Unwin, 1957, pp. 42–4.

not have been so easily accomplished had the foundations of an alliance not been so effectively laid down in earlier years.

What is perhaps most surprising of all in the strange story of Ottoman involvement in the First World War, is that it was left to Kaiser Wilhelm II to cut through the obfuscation of German diplomatic and strategic thinking and point out the evident facts of the case. On an account of Wangenheim's discussions with Enver, presented on or about 23 July 1914, the kaiser angrily minuted: 'Theoretically correct but at the present moment mistaken! Now it is a question of getting hold of every musket in the Balkans that is prepared to go off *for* Austria against the Slavs, thus a Turco-Bulgaria alliance leaning on Austria is most certainly to be agreed to!'[5] Wangenheim must respond at once, welcoming Ottoman accession to the alliance. Otherwise the empire would go over to the Franco-Russian group, and be closed to the influence of the Central Powers.

Once the change in German policy was decided on, the Germans acted with exemplary speed. On 27 July Wangenheim informed Said Halim, the grand vizier, of his government's change of heart. That night Said Halim suggested that Germany and the Ottoman Empire conclude a secret treaty, aimed at Russia. In the event of Russia intervening in a war between Austria and Serbia, then the Ottoman Empire would join Germany in defending her ally. On the following day the kaiser accepted the proposal, subject to certain conditions regarding the precise terms of the *casus foederis*, the nature of German guarantees regarding the territorial integrity of the Ottoman Empire and the appointment of German officers to command posts in the Ottoman army. And on 2 August, the day after Germany declared war on Russia, the treaty, later signed also by Austria, was concluded, subject to a proviso that 'in the present war Turkey can and will undertake some action worthy of mention against Russia'.[6]

The conclusion of an Ottoman–German treaty did not lead at once to war, for neither the Ottomans nor the Entente Powers, who were immediately informed by their agents of the existence of the treaty, were keen to provoke an immediate outbreak of hostilities. In August, when two German cruisers, the *Goeben* and the *Breslau*, running before a British flotilla in the Mediterranean, sought sanctuary in the Straits, the Entente Powers, ignoring the clear breach of international treaties concerning the closure of the Straits to

5. Albertini, *Origins of the War of 1914*, p. 612.
6. Ibid., p. 614.

foreign ships-of-war which the entry of the German ships, permitted by the Ottomans, entailed, refrained from exploiting the incident as a *casus belli*; while the Ottomans, likewise determined to remove any possible *casus belli*, proceeded to engage in an elaborate charade, involving a fictitious purchase by the Ottoman government of the German ships, which were supposedly made part of the Ottoman fleet. Not that anyone was fooled, for the German crews remained on board, under the command of a German, Admiral Souchon. Anchored in the Golden Horn, they are said to have trained their guns on the sultan's palace. Meanwhile, vigorous steps were taken by the Germans to strengthen the German position in the Ottoman Empire, particularly with regard to the defences of the Straits. Yet despite repeated German calls for action, and a mobilisation of the Ottoman army, ordered on 3 August, the Ottoman government continued to procrastinate, concerned regarding the continued neutrality of Bulgaria, whose participation in the war on the side of the Central Powers was deemed essential if the war were to be fought to a successful conclusion. (The possibility that the British might confiscate the *Sultan Osman*, a battleship being built in a British shipyard for the Ottoman navy, was also a factor affecting the Ottoman attitude.) Only in October, when Admiral Souchon, with Enver's support, sailed his fleet into the Black Sea and bombarded Odessa, Sevastopol and Novorossisk did the Ottoman Empire abandon the position of armed neutrality it had adopted and enter the war.[7]

Austria–Hungary

The interests of Austria–Hungary in the Ottoman Empire in the period immediately preceding the outbreak of the First World War, as distinct from its interest in the position in the Balkans, always vital, were limited. With regard to the Straits, Austria–Hungary wished, like the western Entente Powers, to prevent a Russian take-over; but there was little it could do to prevent one. Not that Austria–Hungary's attitude to the question was in any sense benign. On the contrary, in 1908 Alois Aehrenthal, the Austrian foreign minister, had had no hesitation in offering Alexander Isvolsky, the Russian foreign minister, support for a change in the Straits regime in a sense favourable to Russia (free passage of the Straits for Russian

---

7. A.L. Macfie, *The Straits Question, 1908–36* Salonica: Institute for Balkan Studies, 1993, Ch. 2.

warships) in return for Russian support for an Austrian annexation of Bosnia and Herzegovina – a change which, in the view of the Ottomans at least, would have placed Istanbul at the mercy of a Russian fleet. In Macedonia, Austria–Hungary cooperated willingly enough with the other Great Powers in their efforts to preserve the peace, though it remained generally sceptical regarding the likely outcome. In Albania it sought merely to prevent an Italian take-over, likely to threaten its position in the Adriatic. A scheme to link the Austro-Hungarian railway network in Bosnia with that in the Ottoman Empire, known as the Sandjack Railway project, was pursued, but it came to nothing. Nor had the Austrians any substantial territorial ambitions in the Ottoman Empire, sufficient to persuade them to seek partition. On the contrary, all they wanted was that the empire should continue to survive, in order that they might trade profitably with it: the percentage of Austro-Hungarian exports going to the Ottoman Empire rose from 3.26 in 1899 to 5.4 in 1913.

Absence of conflict, however, did not necessarily promote good relations. The Austro-Hungarian annexation of Bosnia and Herzegovina, supposedly designed to clarify the position, succeeded merely in offending the Ottomans, who had not expected so sudden and dramatic a reverse to follow the Young Turk Revolution. Austro-Hungarian support for the Albanian rebels, particularly those belonging to the Catholic church, led to Ottoman suspicion that Austria–Hungary intended to exploit the situation to its own advantage, as did Austro-Hungarian support for Bulgaria in the Balkan Wars. Following the Balkan Wars Austria–Hungary made strenuous efforts to persuade the Ottomans to join an alliance of Balkan powers, aimed at Serbia, but all to no avail. On the eve of the outbreak of the First World War, therefore, Austro-Ottoman relations were distinctly cool: suggestions that the Ottoman Empire might join the Triple Alliance were treated with the utmost reserve.[8]

Russia

For Russia, in the period immediately preceding the First World War, the preservation of the independence and integrity of the Ottoman Empire remained a primary foreign-policy objective; though her support for the Balkan League in the period of the Balkan Wars, her attempts to have the Straits opened to Russian warships, her

8. Kent, *Great Powers and the End of the Ottoman Empire*, Austria.

support for the Christian minorities, particularly the Armenians in the eastern provinces, and her dreams that Constantinople, the cradle of Russian Orthodox civilisation, might one day be liberated, tended constantly to undermine her efforts in that direction.

Russian concern regarding the nature of the regime governing the passage of the Straits, and the need to secure stability in the area, remained throughout paramount. On three separate occasions in this period Russian statesmen, convinced that only the opening of the Straits to Russian warships would enable Russia to maximise the potential of her naval establishment in the world, endeavoured to secure this objective: in the period of the Bosnia-Herzegovina annexation crisis; in the period of the Tripolitanian War; and in the period of the Balkan Wars. But on all three occasions, for want of the support of the other Great Powers, they failed. Moreover, during the Tripolitanian War, the Straits were threatened with closure on several occasions; and in April–May 1912 they were actually closed for several weeks, a closure which inflicted severe damage on the Russian economy. Again, during the Balkan Wars, the Straits were threatened with closure. As a result the Russians took vigorous steps to prevent closure, making it clear to all concerned that were a closure to occur as a result of the fighting, and were that closure to be prolonged, then they would feel compelled to take energetic action to reopen the waterway. Any attempt on the part of the Bulgarians to occupy Istanbul or the Straits would be treated as a *casus belli*.[9]

The instability of the position in the area of the Straits, created by the outbreak of the Balkan Wars, combined with the threat of a possible conflict in Europe involving the Ottoman Empire, led the Russians to undertake a fundamental reevaluation of the problem of the Straits. In a foreign office memorandum, composed in November 1912, and amended by Prince Trubetzkoy, chief of the political division, it was pointed out that while in the long run a Russian occupation of Constantinople and the Straits might adequately secure Russia's interests in the area, such an occupation could not in the present circumstances be attempted, as a Russian occupation would merely lead to a scramble for territory by the other great powers, and possibly a European war. Russia should, therefore, for the moment at least, seek merely to obtain a base on the Bosphorus, by lease or cession, and at a later date the consent

---

9. Ibid., Russia; Macfie, *Straits Question*, Ch. 1; Gottlieb, *Studies in Secret Diplomacy*, Chs 3 and 5.

of the powers to the neutralisation and demilitarisation of the Dardanelles. In this way Russia would secure the closure of the Straits against an enemy fleet, and their opening to a Russian fleet, should access to the Mediterranean be required.

This view did not go unchallenged. Prince Lieven, chief of staff of the Russian admiralty, pointed out that the creation of a Russian base in the Bosphorus (which he considered quite impractical) would not secure Russia's objectives. On the contrary, it would merely absorb prodigious amounts of men, money and materials. Russia should either appropriate the whole territory separating her from the shores of the Straits or nothing. For the time being she should build up her naval power in the Black Sea and use it to force the sultan to open the Straits to Russian warships. She should then demand the destruction of the fortifications defending the Dardanelles and the provision of anchorage rights and coaling stations in the area. Eventually she might annex the whole region.[10]

At a conference convened by Alexander Sazonov, the new foreign minister, in February 1914, the Russians once again reverted to the issue. On this occasion it was agreed that, as Russia could not in the present circumstances mount an operation likely to secure effective control of the Straits, and as she was unlikely to secure naval predominance in the Black Sea (the essential precondition for a successful campaign) until 1917, when dreadnoughts comparable in strength and size to those recently ordered by the Ottomans would be delivered, she should in the meantime put in hand measures to speed up the process of mobilisation, improve the provision of transport in the area and further strengthen the Black Sea fleet. On the strategic implications of such an operation, however, the conference could not agree. Some argued that, as any attempt to secure control of the Straits would be accompanied by a European war, Russia should initially concentrate the bulk of her forces on the western front, where the issue would be decided. Others disagreed, pointing out that victory over the Central Powers in a European war would not necessarily enable Russia to secure control of the Straits. While Russia was engaged in the west, Britain and France might move in the east. This Russia must not allow. She must herself be ready to mount an operation, should the necessity arise.[11]

10. G.B. Zotiades, 'Russia and the Question of Constantinople and the Turkish Straits during the Balkan Wars', *Balkan Studies*, Vol. 2 (1970).
11. F. Stieve, *Isvolsky and the World War* London: Allen and Unwin, 1926, Appendices 2 and 3; Macfie, *Straits Question*, pp. 42–3.

Russian concern regarding the Straits was further exacerbated in December 1913, when Liman von Sanders, the leader of the German military mission dispatched to reform the Ottoman army, was appointed commander of the First Army Corps, a command which the Russians believed secured for the Germans control of the sea passage. In the diplomatic crisis which followed, the Russians considered a number of possible responses, including a suspension of financial aid to the Ottoman Empire, a refusal to approve a proposed increase in Ottoman customs duties, and even the seizure of an Ottoman port or a portion of Ottoman territory; but eventually, for want of the support of Russia's allies, they were obliged to settle, agreeing to an arrangement whereby Liman von Sanders would be appointed, not commander of the First Army Corps, but inspector of the Ottoman army, a rank supposedly independent of a territorial command.

The threat posed to Russian interests in the Ottoman Empire by the advance of Germany was a serious one. Yet until the outbreak of the First World War, at least, the policy pursued by Sazanov remained the traditional one of seeking to build up Russian influence in the empire, whilst at the same time seeking to construct a Balkan bloc aimed at Austria–Hungary. To this end moves were made to develop trade with the Ottoman Empire, secure the appointment of a Russian delegate to the Ottoman public debt administration council, and secure, by means of subsidy or direct purchase, newspaper support. In due course, it was believed, somewhat optimistically perhaps, it might be possible for Russia to recreate the position she had secured at the time of the Treaty of Unkiar-Skelessi (1833), when she had enjoyed for a brief space not only effective control of the Straits but also something approaching hegemony in the area. Yet increasingly, as instability in the Near and Middle East mounted, elements within the Russian leadership began seriously to consider the possibility of a partition of the Ottoman Empire, a possibility which, it may be supposed, played a significant part in persuading the Russians to reject the offers of an alliance with the Ottoman Empire, tentatively put forward by Talaat at Livadia in May 1914, and surprisingly repeated (not necessarily with serious intent) by Enver in August, shortly after the conclusion of the Ottoman–German treaty.[12]

12. I.V. Bestuzhev, 'Russian Foreign Policy, February–June 1914', *Journal of Contemporary History*, Vol. 1, No. 3 (1966); Corrigan, 'German–Turkish Relations and the Outbreak of War in 1914'; F. Ahmad, 'Ottoman Armed Neutrality and Intervention, August–November 1914', *Studies in Ottoman Diplomatic History*, Vol. 4 Istanbul: Isis Press, 1990.

Russian relations with the Ottoman Empire in the period immediately preceding the First World War were by no means as bad as
they have sometimes been made to appear. The resolution in 1911
of the dispute between Russia and Germany over the construction
of the Baghdad Railway (Germany agreed to recognise a Russian
sphere of influence in northern Persia in return for the ending of
Russian opposition to the construction of the railway) did much to
relieve tension; as did the eventual resolution of the crisis provoked
by the Liman von Sanders affair. Finally, in February 1914, the
Ottomans and the Russians concluded a convention granting the
Russians a supervisory role in the implementation of a reform programme to be carried out in the Armenian provinces, an area of
Russian concern.

In the extraordinary offer of a Russo-Ottoman alliance, made by
Enver, following the conclusion of the Ottoman–German Treaty and
the outbreak of war in Europe, Enver offered to place the Ottoman
army at Russia's disposal, in return for the retrocession of the Greek
islands of Lemnos and Chios, Bulgarian territory in Thrace and
an end to the capitulations. Sazanov, seemingly unaware of the
immense issues at stake, chose to rebuff the approach. Rather he
sought, in conjunction with Edward Grey, the British foreign minister, and Théophile Delcassé, the French foreign minister, to make
it 'easy and even profitable for Turkey to remain neutral'. On 16
August the three Entente Powers joined in offering the Ottomans
guarantee of their independence and integrity, in return for a promise of Ottoman neutrality. On 22 August they repeated their offer,
provided only that the Ottoman government 'binds itself to give a
written pledge to fulfil, during the present war, all obligations arising from neutrality, and in every way to facilitate the uninterrupted
and unhindered passage of merchant vessels through the Straits'.[13]
The Ottomans, however, well aware of Russia's long-term designs
on the Straits, and of the fact that Britain and France might join
her in partitioning their empire, were not inclined to put much
faith in such guarantees.

Italy

Italy in the period preceding the First World War was primarily
concerned with the problem of resolving the difficulties created by
her occupation of Tripolitania, and the need to protect her interests

---

13. Macfie, *Straits Question*, p. 53.

in the Balkans, particularly those in Albania, threatened by both the Balkan powers and Austria–Hungary in the period of the Balkan Wars. Nevertheless she continued to harbour dreams of conquest and colonisation in Anatolia, particularly in the Antalya region; and in the spring of 1914 she succeeded in persuading the British to agree to Italian participation in the construction of a new railway in the hinterland of Izmir. But in reality her interest remained limited, scarcely sufficient to justify the dreams of further expansion in the area she harboured. In the Treaty of London, which Italy concluded with the Triple Entente Powers in April 1915, shortly before her entry into the First World War on their side, she was promised not only retention of the Dodecanese, but also 'an equitable share in the Mediterranean region adjoining the province of Adalia (Antalya), in the event of the total or partial partition of Turkey in Asia'.[14]

France

By the end of the nineteenth century France, unlike Italy, had already acquired substantial interests in the Ottoman Empire, particularly in Syria and the Lebanon. French investors held more than half of the Ottoman public debt. French governments claimed the right to protect the Catholic church. French missionaries had established a network of schools, hospitals, and other institutions, particularly in the Lebanon and the Holy Land. French railways operated on the Salonica–Istanbul, the Izmir–Cassaba and the Beirut–Damascus lines. And French enterprises were engaged in the construction of harbours, the exploitation of minerals and the business of production. In particular, French interests controlled the Régie Générale des Chemins de Fer, a company specialising in the management and construction of railways, the Imperial Ottoman Bank, nominally Anglo-French but in fact French controlled, the Société des Quais de Constantinople, the Société d'Héraclée, a mining company, the Compagnie du Gaz de Beyrouth, and the Régie des Tabacs.

German military, political and economic penetration of the Ottoman Empire caused the French as much concern as it caused the Russians. In particular they became deeply concerned regarding

---

14. Kent, *Great Powers and the End of the Ottoman Empire*, Italy; Macfie, *Straits Question*, p. 82; Gottlieb, *Studies in Secret Diplomacy*, Pt. 2.

the potential impact of the construction of the Baghdad Railway on their interests in northern Syria and Anatolia. But unable to block the project, they decided first to seek equal participation in the scheme, and then, when that proved unattainable, acting in conjunction with the British and the Russians, they sought some form of internationalisation. A complex series of negotiations followed, in the course of which the French government brought great weight to bear; but it was unable to make much headway, frustrated it would seem as much by the willingness of French financial interests involved in the project to back the company line as by German obduracy. In the end, in 1914, the French government was compelled to reach an agreement with the Germans, accepting German control of the railway, in return for German recognition of a French sphere of interest in Syria and northern Anatolia, where the French expected to construct a new rail network.

In the defence of French interests in the Ottoman Empire, the French government proved more successful. In 1903–5 vigorous steps, including the closure of the French money market to the Ottoman government, were taken to secure the survival of the Société des Quais de Constantinople, threatened by changes in government policy. In the same period even more vigorous steps were taken to protect the Société d'Héraclée. For a full year Jean Ernest Constans, the French ambassador, brought pressure to bear on the Ottoman government to satisfy the demands of the company; and in 1908 he issued an ultimatum, threatening dire consequences if the company's demands were not met. To this end, he even dispatched a contingent of French marines, on board the ambassadorial ship, to Zonguldak, where the company's principal mines were located. Only following yet another closure of the French money market to the Ottoman government was the issue finally resolved. In 1909, attacks on the Régie des Tabacs, mounted by members of the CUP, were countered by similar threats of closure.

Until the outbreak of the First World War the French remained generally committed to the preservation of the Ottoman Empire, which alone it was believed would secure French interests in the area. Nevertheless in the period following the defeat of the Ottoman Empire in the Balkan Wars, French diplomats and politicians began seriously to consider the possibility of partition. The Comité de Défense des Intérêts Français en Orient, in particular, argued that France should concentrate on developing her interests in Syria, lest a sudden partition leave her unprepared; and in 1913 a conference of French diplomats and cabinet ministers agreed that France should seek to recover railway privileges in southern Syria, previously lost. But majority opinion remained committed to the preservation of the empire. Partition would favour mainly Russia and Germany, both well established in the area. In the event of a break-up, it was unlikely that French bond holders would ever receive payment. Moreover, as Théophile Delcassé, the French ambassador at St Petersburg, pointed out, France's natural sphere of interest lay not in the Levant but in North Africa. The occupation of Syria might merely prove an unprofitable diversion.[15]

Great Britain

Great Britain's interests in the Ottoman Empire on the eve of the First World War, were if anything even more wide-ranging than those of France, for they involved strategic interests of outstanding importance. The defence of India demanded that Britain preserve its supremacy in the area of the Persian Gulf, threatened by the construction of the Baghdad Railway. The defence of Egypt and the Suez Canal, the principal route to her empire in the east, demanded that she secure control of the approaches to the Nile valley. Finally, the defence of her interests in Europe, the Near and Middle East, and even the world, demanded that she defend her interests in the area of the Straits, threatened by the advance of Germany and Russia in the area. For the British, therefore, as for the French, the preservation of the independence and integrity of the Ottoman Empire remained a major foreign-policy objective, just as it had been throughout the greater part of the nineteenth century.

What the British, in particular, feared, in the years leading up to the First World War, was that, in the event of a war breaking out in Europe, involving the Great Powers, the Ottoman Empire might form an alliance with the Central Powers. Ottoman armies, supplied and equipped by Germany and led by German officers, might then launch attacks on Britain's position in Egypt and the Persian Gulf. Meanwhile, secret agents, supported by a vigorous pan-Islamic propaganda campaign, might spark off risings among the Muslim peoples of Egypt, Afghanistan and the Indian sub-continent; while control of the Straits might enable the Central Powers to close the principal supply line linking the western Entente Powers, Britain

15. Kent, *Great Powers and the End of the Ottoman Empire*, France.

and France, with Russia. When, therefore, in August 1914, the First
World War finally broke out, the British acting in conjunction with
their Entente partners were at pains to persuade the Ottomans to
remain neutral. On 15 August Winston Churchill, the First Lord of
the Admiralty, with Grey's support, made a personal approach to
Enver, offering a territorial guarantee; and on 22 August Sir Louis
Mallet, the British ambassador, joined with his fellow ambassadors
from the Triple Entente in offering a written guarantee. Similar
offers followed, but all to no avail. On 29 October Enver dispatched
the *Goeben* and the *Breslau* into the Black Sea to attack Russian ports
and shipping, and shortly thereafter the Entente Powers found themselves in a state of war with the Ottoman Empire.[16]

Britain's financial and commercial interests in the Ottoman
Empire were by no means as extensive as her strategic interests; but
they were not insignificant. Her share in the Ottoman public debt
was about 15 per cent, and her share of investment in private enterprise 14 per cent. In Mesopotamia and the Persian Gulf, where she
had secured valuable oil concessions, she controlled two thirds of
the import–export trade. And she controlled a number of substantial
industries and institutions, including the Izmir-Aydin Railway, the
National Bank of Turkey, the Euphrates and Tigris Steam Navigation Company and the Constantinople Telephone Company.

In order to secure their interests in the area of the Persian Gulf,
the British imposed on the so-called Trucial states a series of treaties,
obliging them to acknowledge the exclusive influence of the British
government; and in 1907 they concluded with the sheikh of Kuwait
a secret agreement providing for exclusive British control of land
likely to be used as a terminus for the Baghdad Railway. Further
measures designed to limit the advance of the Baghdad Railway
followed; and in 1913–14, despite a weak negotiating position, the
British succeeded in concluding with Germany and the Ottoman
Empire a series of agreements promising that no extension of the
Baghdad Railway, from Basra to the Persian Gulf, would be permitted
to proceed without British consent. Meanwhile, in the other parts
of the Ottoman Empire, the British did what they could to secure
its survival, supporting the cause of reform in Macedonia and the
eastern provinces, and seeking a negotiated settlement of the
Tripolitanian and Balkan Wars. On the eve of the First World War,
therefore, Britain remained generally committed to the principle

16. Ibid.; Great Britain; Macfie, *Straits Question*, Ch. 2; J. Heller, *British Policy towards the Ottoman Empire* London: Frank Cass, 1983.

of the preservation of the Ottoman Empire; though just how far that commitment applied in practice remained in doubt.[17]

Uncertainty regarding the nature and extent of British support for the principle of the preservation of the Ottoman Empire has led many historians to conclude that, in the decades preceding the outbreak of the First World War, Britain's support for the principle had become merely nominal. In the period of the Crimean War – so it has been argued – when support for the principle remained strong, the British had simply 'backed the wrong horse', as Lord Salisbury once put it.[18] Thereafter, the failure of the Ottomans to implement the grandiose reform schemes, associated with the *Tanzimat*, the bankruptcy of the Ottoman state and the revulsion provoked by the Bulgarian and Armenian massacres had fatally undermined support for the empire. As a result, opinion in Britain had shifted in favour of a policy of indifference, or even of the 'bag and baggage' alternative supposedly advocated by William Gladstone, the Liberal prime minister.

In the reign of the Red Sultan, Abdul Hamid, so the argument continues, British disillusion with the Turks, once described as the gentlemen of the orient, was further exacerbated by the sultan's evident unwillingness to cooperate with the British in the defence of his empire, and by the fact that he had had the defences of the Dardanelles strengthened while leaving those of the Bosphorus neglected. In the 1890s Britain's strategic position in the Mediterranean was further diminished by the creation, in 1891, of a Franco-Russian alignment, and the conclusion, in 1894, of a Franco-Russian alliance. As a result the directors of naval and military intelligence advised that in the event of a Russian attempt on the Straits, the British Mediterranean fleet, stationed in the eastern Mediterranean specifically to prevent such a contingency, might find itself unable to proceed. The dispatch of the British Mediterranean fleet to the Straits, at the extreme end of a precarious line of communications, might leave a French fleet, based at Toulon, in undisputed control of the western Mediterranean, and possibly even of the English Channel, an unacceptable risk. Only if Britain were to receive the diplomatic and military support of the Triple Alliance powers, it was concluded, would it be possible to prevent a Russian occupation of Constantinople and the Straits.[19]

17. Ibid.
18. A. Cunningham, 'The Wrong Horse', *St. Antony's Papers*, No. 17 Oxford: Oxford University Press.
19. Macfie, *Straits Question*, pp. 24–5.

The concern of the British regarding their seeming inability to prevent a Russian seizure of Constantinople and the Straits, led Lord Salisbury, the British prime minister, to speculate from time to time about a possible partition of the Ottoman Empire. In any such partition Russia would acquire Constantinople and the Straits, and Britain Syria and Mesopotamia.[20] France might be paid off with Tripolitania and a part of Morocco and Italy with Albania. Others suggested that what was required was a shift in the emphasis of Britain's defence policy away from the Straits, in favour of Egypt and the Nile valley. But it did not, it would seem, lead to a radical reorientation, for the control of Egypt, however well established, would not in itself have resolved problems created by Britain's weak strategic position. As the directors of naval intelligence remarked in 1895:

> The power of the Russian fleet to issue from the Dardanelles at any moment, as if from their own port, within 600 miles of the Suez Canal, would give them either command of the eastern Mediterranean, or compel a superior English squadron to be kept in those waters – but not with the present advantages. . . . The transfer to Russia of the present English command in the eastern Mediterranean would mean the gradual reduction of English commerce, the *waning of English influence over the Canal and Egypt*, and the loss of touch with India through the Mediterranean. . . . The interests of the Empire, India and all Britain's eastern possessions required, that as long as England can keep it so, Russia should be vulnerable through the Black Sea – to secure this, the Dardanelles and Bosphorus must either be kept unarmed, or in the hands of Russia's foes. Once the Black Sea is a Russian lake with the Dardanelles as her safe outlet, Russian influence and power will extend through Asia and Syria, and England will be separated from India by the distance of the Cape route.[21]

Control of Egypt might, as a later report made clear, secure for Britain control of the Suez Canal and the overland route to the east. It might also secure possession of Alexandria, where a naval base might be constructed; but in a war against Russia (and possibly also France) in which Russia was enabled, by dint of her control of the Straits, to dispatch a fleet, acting in conjunction with a French fleet based at Toulon, into the eastern Mediterranean, it would not enable her to keep open the canal or maintain her communications by that route with India. Indeed, it might even add to the

20. K.M. Wilson, *British Foreign Secretaries* London: Croom Helm, 1987, p. 129.
21. K.M. Wilson, *Empire and Continent* London: Mansell Publishing, 1987, pp. 3–4.

burden of Britain's responsibility in the area, for unless heavily fortified, it was doubtful if Egypt could be effectively defended. As the director general of military intelligence remarked in 1903: 'It appears there is at the command of Great Britain no effective naval or military retort to a (Russian) *coup de main* on Constantinople.'[22]

Concern regarding the defence of India, apparently undermined by Britain's inability effectively to exercise her naval power in the eastern Mediterranean and the Black Sea, eventually led the British to abandon the policy, pursued for almost three-quarters of a century, of opposing Russia, as Sir Edward Grey, the British foreign secretary once put it, at every point, and opt instead for one of conciliation. In 1907 she concluded with her great rival in Asia a convention resolving most, if not all, of the great issues in dispute between them, in particular those concerning Persia, Afghanistan and Tibet. Only in this way, it was believed, would it be possible to halt the advance of Russia in Central Asia and prevent the collapse of British power in India, which, it was expected, the advance of Russia would in due course entail. Not that the new arrangement was unconnected with Britain's position in Europe. On the contrary, it was hoped that, in conjunction with France, with whom a similar arrangement had been made in 1904, it might now be possible to impose some restraint on the rising power of Germany.[23]

In the following years the advantages to be gained from a resolution of Britain's differences with Russia in Asia proved disappointing. The Russians continued their advance, particularly in Persia. But there was little the British could do, for a change in direction might merely persuade the Russians to abandon the entente in favour of an alliance with the Central Powers, an arrangement (effectively a resurrection of the Dreikaiserbund and precursor of the Molotov Pact) which would threaten Britain's interests not only in Asia but also in Europe. It was imperative, therefore, that Russia, the 'great counterpoise', as Sir Edward Grey put it, 'to Germany on land', be placated, and it was to this end that, in the years preceding the First World War, British policy was directed.[24]

Britain's determination to preserve at all costs her friendly relationship with Russia then became paramount; and it is in the context of that determination that Anglo-Ottoman relations in the period immediately preceding the First World War should be viewed. On the one hand the British continued to emphasise their support

22. Ibid., p. 6.
23. Ibid., Pt. 9.
24. Ibid., p. 163.

for the principle of the preservation of the Ottoman Empire. On the other hand, when pressed to do so by the Russians, they repeatedly sacrificed Ottoman (and indeed British) interests to the greater imperative. Thus in 1906, when the Russians, in the process of negotiating the 1907 convention, raised the Straits question, Grey responded that, whilst the Russians themselves must make definite proposals, Britain would respond favourably. In 1907, when the Russians once again raised the question, proposing that the Straits be opened to Russian warships whilst remaining closed to those of the non-riverain powers, Grey again responded sympathetically, though he did stress that the time was not yet ripe for a change. In 1908, when Alexander Isvolsky, the Russian foreign minister, reverted to the question, Grey, sympathetic as ever, was at pains to stress that Britain would not oppose Russia on the issue, though she would oppose what he described as a one-sided arrangement. Any new system must include an element of reciprocity, which would place belligerents on an equal footing; and it must receive prior Ottoman consent. Following those discussions, Grey, in a private letter to Isvolsky, again declared that it was not his intention to block Russian ambitions in the area of the Straits (an area of vital concern to the Ottomans). On the contrary, he wished positively to seek an arrangement which would both satisfy Russian *desiderata* and preserve Russian goodwill. At Reval, in 1908, the British, determined to maintain good relations, were at pains to accommodate Russian demands (though on that occasion some of the reforms concerning Macedonia proposed by the Russians were if anything even more favourable to the Ottomans than those proposed by the British). Following the Bulgarian declaration of independence British support for an Ottoman policy of compromise was, in part at least, inspired by a desire not to provoke the Russians, who were bent on supporting Bulgaria. Tentative approaches made by the Young Turks in 1909 and again in 1913 with regard to a possible defensive alliance with Britain were simply ignored.[25]

Other issues involving Russian interests in the Ottoman Empire provoked a similar response. In the period of the Balkan Wars, British policy was throughout influenced by a desire to remain on good terms with Russia. In the crisis provoked by the appointment of Liman von Sanders to the command of army units supposedly controlling the Straits, a question of particular concern to the Russians,

---

25. Macfie, *Straits Question*, Ch. 1; Heller, *British Policy towards the Ottoman Empire*, p. 138.

the British felt compelled to give the Russians diplomatic support. As Grey remarked, 'I do not believe that the whole thing is worth all the fuss that Sazonov makes of it, but so long as he does make a fuss it will be important and embarrassing for us, for we cannot turn our backs on Russia.'[26] Finally with regard to the Armenian question, the British bowed before Russian protests regarding the proposed reforms. So pronounced, indeed, was Britain's support for Russia in this period that Djemal, the CUP leader, wondered if the British had not already agreed on a policy of partition.[27]

Following the entry of the Ottoman Empire into the First World War, contemporary observers, particularly those in Britain and France, generally concluded that the empire was compelled to enter the war, on the side of the Central Powers, by the Germans, who had in the preceding two decades acquired so preponderant a position of influence and control that they were enabled, with the help of a pro-German CUP and army cabal led by Enver and a generous dispensation of bribes, threats and intimidation, to secure the compliance of a weak-willed and ill-informed Ottoman leadership, easily persuaded to pursue a policy contrary to the long-term interests of the empire. Nor, if a short-term view of these events is taken, need that conclusion be challenged, for the facts, in so far as they are known, appear to support it. But seen in the context of the Great Power rivalry of the period, which compelled Britain to abandon its traditional approach to the Ottoman Empire in favour of one favouring Russia, it can be argued that, in part at least, Ottoman entry into the First World War on the side of the Central Powers was a consequence of the radical shift in the nature and direction of British foreign policy which occurred in the previous quarter century or so, inspired by the advance of Russia in Asia, the probable closure, in the event of war against Russia, of the Straits against British warships and the rise of German power in Europe. That at least is what a number of well-informed Ottoman Turks, including Talaat and Djemal, believed.[28]

26. F.H. Hinsley (ed.), *British Foreign Policy under Sir Edward Grey* Cambridge: Cambridge University Press, 1977, p. 345.

27. J. Heller, 'Britain and the Armenian Question, 1912–13: A Study in Real Politik', *Middle Eastern Studies*, Vol. 16, No. 1 (1980); Djemal Pasha, *Memoirs of a Turkish Statesman* New York: Arno Press, 1973, p. 69.

28. 'The Posthumous Memoirs of Talaat Pasha', *New York Times Current History*, Vol. 15, 1921–2.

CHAPTER SIX

Entry of the Ottoman Empire into the First World War

The defeat of the Ottoman Empire in the First World War, combined with the decision of the victorious Entente Powers to partition the empire, once defeated, brought about the effective end of the empire in 1918; though the abolition of the Ottoman dynasty itself did not occur until November 1922 when, following the creation of a national movement in Anatolia and victory in a war of independence fought against the western Entente Powers and their surrogates, the Greeks, Mustafa Kemal (Atatürk), the leader of the national movement, decided on abolition. The decision of the Ottoman government to enter the First World War on the side of the Central Powers proved, therefore, to be one of the most important ever taken. Yet it was taken not by the Ottoman cabinet, acting with due deliberation, but by a cabal of Ottoman ministers, led by Enver, acting with little or no regard for constitutional propriety.

The process which led to the entry of the Ottoman Empire into the First World War began with the conclusion of the Ottoman–German treaty of 2 August 1914 (a treaty which appeared to decide the issue, but in fact did not), and ended with the dispatch on 28 October of the Ottoman fleet, under the command of Admiral Souchon, a German, into the Black Sea, with orders, issued by Enver, to attack Russian shipping and bombard the coastal towns, an action certain to lead to war. The story of these events has been told many times, and the details are clear enough; but the nature of the decision-making process which led the Ottoman leadership so to proceed remains unclear. Nevertheless enough is known of the events involved to convey an impression of

119

the process and identify some of the factors that determined its outcome.[1]

When the First World War broke out in Europe in August 1914 the Ottoman Empire was offered five possible options: (i) to enter the war immediately on the side of the Central Powers; (ii) to enter the war on the side of the Triple Entente; (iii) to offer the Central Powers moral and material support in their struggle with the Entente Powers, in particular Russia, the most dangerous of the Ottoman Empire's enemies, but remain neutral until such time as the likely outcome of the struggle had become clear; (iv) to offer the Entente Powers support, but again remain neutral until the outcome of the struggle had become clear; (v) to remain neutral throughout.

Viewed from the Ottoman point of view none of these options could be considered free from danger. Whilst it was believed that Germany, the greatest of the military powers on the continent, would in all probability prevail, the possibility of defeat remained. Nor would a victorious Germany necessarily secure the future independence of the Ottoman Empire; it might merely result in the creation of a German hegemony in the area. Immediate support for the Entente Powers, were they to prove victorious, might promise a degree of security, but in all probability it would lead merely to further losses of territory to the empire and a possible partition. Russia, intent on securing control of the Straits, might take the opportunity offered by victory in a European war to occupy the area. Such a move would inevitably lead the other Great Powers to engage in a scramble for territory, with Britain seizing Mesopotamia, France Syria and Italy southwestern Anatolia. A policy of procrastination, on the other hand, followed by eventual entry into the war, hopefully on the winning side, would, it is true, substantially reduce the risks involved, but it would not eliminate them. Moreover, such an approach, however judicious, would place at risk the substantial gains which the more ambitious of the Ottoman leaders, in particular Enver, expected to acquire as a result of Ottoman participation in what most people, both in Europe and the Near East, expected

---

1. One of the best accounts of the entry of the Ottoman Empire into the First World War is Y.T. Kurat, 'How Turkey Drifted into World War I', in K. Bourne and D.C. Watt, *Studies in International History* Harlow: Longman, 1967. Other useful accounts include A. Emin, *Turkey in the World War* New Haven, Connecticut: Yale University Press, 1930, Ch. 6; U. Trumpener, *Germany and the Ottoman Empire, 1914–1918* Princeton: Princeton University Press, 1968, Ch. 2; F. Ahmad, 'Ottoman Armed Neutrality and Intervention, August–November 1914', *Studies in Ottoman Diplomatic History*, Vol. 4 (1990); L. Albertini, *The Origins of the War* Oxford: Oxford University Press, 1957, Ch. 14.

to be a short war. Immediate support for the Central Powers in the war might secure for the Ottoman Empire the recovery of the Aegean islands, territories in eastern Anatolia and the Caucasus, previously lost to the Russians, and even Egypt and western Thrace. Support for the Entente Powers (a less likely eventuality in view of the threat posed to the empire by the advance of Russia) might also offer a recovery of the Aegean islands and western Thrace. Support for either alliance might, in the event of victory, secure an end to the capitulations, which in the eyes of most Ottomans had in the previous half century or so done so much to undermine the independence of the Ottoman Empire and hamper its economic and political development. As for a policy of complete neutrality, that too offered no guarantees of success, for victory in a European war would almost certainly encourage the victors to look for further conquests elsewhere. There were, therefore, no easy options. Of those available, an alliance with Germany, the strongest and least threatening of the Great Powers, appeared the most attractive. It is scarcely surprising, therefore, that from the beginning Enver and a number of colleagues should have decided to make that their principal objective.[2]

The decision to conclude the Ottoman–German treaty of 2 August 1914 was taken not by the whole of the Ottoman cabinet but by a faction within it, led by Enver, Talaat and Said Halim. The rest of the cabinet were kept in ignorance of the proposal, supposedly for security reasons. Djemal, when informed of the proposal, remained sceptical, but declared that in the circumstances – he had just returned from France where, according to his own account, the French had rebuffed a tentative proposal regarding a possible alliance between the Ottoman Empire and the Entente Powers – he was prepared to go along with it. Djavid, informed the day before the agreement was signed, objected strongly, insisting that it would be a fatal mistake for the Ottoman Empire to side with the Central Powers: there was no guarantee that the Central Powers would win the war, and in the event of their defeat the Ottoman Empire would disappear from the map. But there was little that he could do to reverse the process. Enver and Talaat were determined to see the business through, and there was no opposition faction capable of taking them on. Only following the conclusion of the alliance

2. Kurat, 'How Turkey Drifted into World War I'; H.S.W. Corrigan, 'German–Turkish Relations and the Outbreak of War in 1914: A Re-assessment', *Past and Present*, Vols 36–8 (1967); U. Trumpener, 'Turkey's Entry into World War I: An Assessment of Responsibilities', *Journal of Modern History*, Vol. 34, No. 4 (1962).

were the remaining members of the cabinet informed, though in all probability most of them already knew about the proposal.

Following the conclusion of the Ottoman–German treaty Enver, the most confident and ambitious member of the Ottoman cabinet, at once placed the Ottoman Empire on a war footing, a development which considerably strengthened his hand in his negotiations with his colleagues. Yet still, it seems, a majority of the cabinet opposed immediate entry, partly on the grounds that the empire was not yet prepared for war and partly on the grounds that they should wait a while and see how events developed, particularly in the Balkans, where the course adopted by Bulgaria and Romania might prove decisive in determining the outcome of events. As a result Enver and his supporters were obliged to delay entry; but they were not prevented from taking the steps necessary to prepare for war – steps which further strengthened the position of the pro-war faction in the Ottoman capital.

Among the steps taken by Enver and his colleagues, those designed to strengthen Ottoman (German) control of the Straits were perhaps the most significant. By the end of August, with the help of the Germans, Enver was enabled to assemble in the area of the Straits substantial forces and an impressive array of weaponry, more than sufficient to deter any sudden attempt the Entente Powers might make to force the sea passage. But he was not, it would seem, thereby enabled to persuade a majority of his cabinet to agree to an immediate declaration of war.[3]

In the pursuit of his strategy of reinforcing the German naval and military establishment in Istanbul and the Straits, and thereby strengthening the pro-German war faction, which he represented, Enver was assisted by a series of hasty and ill thought out actions taken by the Entente Powers, in particular the British. On or about 1 August, concerned to preserve their naval supremacy in the Mediterranean, the British informed the Ottoman ambassador in London that they intended to place an embargo on the delivery of two Ottoman warships, the *Sultan Osman* and the *Reshadiye*, presently under construction in British yards. This embargo caused immense offence in the Ottoman Empire, for the Ottoman people, both high and low alike, had voluntarily subscribed the funds needed to pay for the ships, deemed essential to the defence of the empire. On 17 August Grey, the British foreign minister, warned all the

---

3. U. Trumpener, 'German Military Aid to Turkey in 1914: A Historical Reevaluation', *Journal of Modern History*, Vol. 32 (1960); A.L. Macfie, *The Straits Question, 1908–36* Salonica: Institute for Balkan Studies, 1993, pp. 50–1.

British vessels sailing in the Black Sea not to attempt a passage of the Straits, an order later rescinded on the advice of Sir Louis Mallet, the British ambassador. On 3–4 September Mallet warned Said Halim, the grand vizier, that neither German nor Turkish warships would be permitted to emerge from the Dardanelles; and on 7 September he informed him that were the *Goeben* and the *Breslau* to venture forth, they would be treated as being German. On 20 September the British naval mission to the Ottoman Empire, led by Admiral Limpus, whose position had been made impossible by the arrival of the *Goeben* and the *Breslau*, was withdrawn. On or about 26 September, when an Ottoman torpedo boat attempted to leave the Dardanelles, it was intercepted by a British warship, an event which persuaded Enver to order the immediate closure of the Straits to all foreign shipping; and on 7 October the British informed the Ottomans that they would prevent the entry of ships carrying goods of a strategic nature, in particular coal, into the Dardanelles.[4]

The actions taken by the British indicate that they expected the Ottomans to side in the war, not with the Entente, but with the Central Powers. Yet the British did not give up hope that the Porte might be persuaded to remain neutral. As Grey remarked in a letter to Sir Francis Bertie, the British ambassador in Paris, dispatched on 15 August:

> If she [Turkey] decided to side with Germany, of course there was no help for it; but we ought not to anticipate this. If the first great battle, which was approaching in Belgium, did not go well for the Germans, it ought not to be difficult to keep Turkey neutral . . . the proper course was to make Turkey feel that, should she remain neutral, and should Germany and Austria be defeated, we would take care that the integrity of Turkish possessions as they now were would be preserved in any terms of peace affecting the Near East; but that, on the other hand, if Turkey sided with Germany and Austria and they were defeated, of course we could not answer for what might be taken from Turkey in Asia Minor.[5]

In the following weeks the British and French persisted with their efforts to persuade the Ottomans to remain neutral. But they made little or no headway, for the Ottomans remained for the most part convinced that in the event of an Entente victory Russia would

---

4. Macfie, *Straits Question*, pp. 53–4; Trumpener, 'Turkey's Entry into World War I'.
5. J. Heller, *British Policy towards the Ottoman Empire* London: Frank Cass, 1983, p. 137.

seize the opportunity offered to occupy Ottoman territory, possibly including the Straits. As Djemal Pasha is said to have remarked to Mallet on one occasion, only a cast-iron British and French guarantee to protect the Ottoman Empire against Russia would allay Ottoman fears and persuade the Ottomans to reject the advances of the Germans.[6] But this the British and the French, dependent as they were on the Russian alliance, were either unable or unwilling to give. Not that Ottoman demands were limited to such a guarantee. On the contrary, in a discussion with Mallet carried on in the third week in August, Djemal, a supposed supporter of the Entente Powers, proposed that in return for assurances of Ottoman neutrality the Ottoman Empire might be offered a defence treaty with each of the Entente Powers, the abolition of the capitulations (the Ottomans actually abolished the capitulations unilaterally on 9 September), the immediate delivery of the impounded Ottoman warships, assurances of non-intervention in the internal affairs of the empire, and the return of western Thrace in the event of Bulgaria siding with the Central Powers – concessions which, as Mallet remarked, might do much to strengthen the pro-Entente party in the empire, and enable Said Halim and Djavid to stand up to Enver and the pro-German faction.[7] Such concessions the Entente Powers were for the most part unwilling to make; but they did on several occasions in this period jointly offer the Ottomans, in return for assurances of their continued neutrality, guarantees that the independence and integrity of their empire would be preserved in any post-war peace settlement. But with regard to the survival of the empire thereafter, the issue of essential Ottoman concern, they felt unable to offer any such guarantees, for none wished to make itself a guarantor of Ottoman survival in the event of an unexpected collapse.

Throughout this period Enver remained as committed as ever to the immediate entry of the Ottoman Empire into the First World War on the side of the Central Powers. On 16 August, accompanied by his second chief of staff, Hafiz Hakki, he held a secret meeting with the leaders of the German military mission at the general headquarters. At this meeting, which was attended by Liman von Sanders, Souchon, von Kress and others, plans were discussed for a possible Ottoman landing on the Black Sea coast between Odessa and Akkerman, designed to ease Russian pressure on the Austro-Hungarian front, and for an attack on the Suez Canal, designed to

---

6. Ibid., p. 138; Ahmad, 'Ottoman Armed Neutrality and Intervention', p. 60.
7. Heller, *British Policy towards the Ottoman Empire*, p. 138.

prevent the transport of British reinforcements to the western front. Yet still a majority of the Ottoman cabinet remained unconvinced. Talaat and Halil insisted that they must first secure a Bulgarian, and possibly also a Romanian, alliance; and to this end in the third week in August they travelled to Sofia. Others pointed out that the steps taken to prepare for mobilisation of the armed forces were proving inadequate. The army needed time to recover from the losses inflicted on it during the Balkan Wars; and in any case it was woefully ill-equipped. Attempts to requisition the country's stocks of flour were threatening to create a national shortage. The country simply could not afford the costs of war. For a time such arguments proved effective: when on 14 September Enver, attempting to force the issue, authorised Souchon to conduct naval manoeuvres in the Black Sea, almost certain to lead to war, he was obliged to back down and countermand the order. But he did not give up. Later when Djavid (not for the first time) insisted on the need for financial restraint, Enver suggested that they approach the Germans with a view to obtaining credits, and when Djavid pointed out that the Germans would make Ottoman entry into the war a condition for the provision of any such credits, he insisted that they nevertheless go ahead. As a result Muhtar Pasha, the Ottoman ambassador in Berlin, was instructed to approach Zimmermann, the general secretary of the German foreign office, with a request for a loan of T.L. 5 million in gold. Djavid's prediction proved accurate: the Germans replied that the provision of any such loan would be made dependent on the immediate entry of the Ottoman Empire into the war on the side of the Central Powers; but following further discussions it was agreed that an advance of T.L. 2 million might be made available for immediate shipment, with the remainder of the loan to follow in instalments. As a result Talaat, Halil and Djemal, previously sceptical, were won over; and on 11 October Wangenheim was secretly informed that Souchon would receive orders to attack the Russian fleet in the Black Sea (the idea of a landing on the Black Sea coast, in the area of the Crimea, had been abandoned as impractical) as soon as the first payment of the loan was received. Not that the assurances given regarding the entry of the Ottoman Empire into the First World War in any way represented a formal decision of the Ottoman government to engage in the war. On the contrary, at a cabinet meeting held on 12 October, Halil declared that he had changed his mind. Might it not be wiser, he suggested, to delay entry until the following spring. Djavid, who had been kept largely in the dark regarding recent developments, threatened to resign if the Ottoman Empire entered the war on the side of the Central Powers. As for Said Halim, he appears to have been unable to make up his mind, one way or the other. In the end no formal decision was taken. It was merely agreed that military experts should be asked to report on the preparedness of the Ottoman armed forces for war.[8]

The attempts made by Djavid and a number of his colleagues to oppose the immediate entry of the Ottoman Empire into the war proved unavailing. On 16 October a first shipment of the German gold arrived in Istanbul; and on 21 October a second instalment arrived (British and Russian intelligence received immediate reports of both shipments). On the same day Enver and his chief of staff, Bronsart von Schellendorf, met to prepare a war plan. This, it was agreed, would involve an attack by the Turkish fleet on the Russian fleet in the Black Sea, and campaigns in the Caucasus and on the Egyptian front. An attack on the Russian fleet in the Black Sea would, it was believed, secure naval supremacy in that sea, while an attack on Russia in the Caucasus and Britain in Egypt would oblige both those powers to withdraw troops from the western front, or at least refrain from dispatching reinforcements there. On 25 October, at the request of the Germans, who did not wish to accept sole responsibility for the attack on the Russian fleet, Enver, who had already given Souchon verbal instructions to launch an attack, formally ordered the German admiral to 'attack the Russian fleet at a time that you find suitable'.[9] Finally, on 29 October the Turkish fleet (in effect the *Goeben* and the *Breslau*, plus a number of Ottoman torpedo boats), under the command of Admiral Souchon, bombarded Odessa and Sevastopol, laid mines in the area and sank a Russian minelayer. Following the attack Souchon, as agreed, telegraphed the general headquarters to inform the Ottoman general staff of the outbreak of hostilities, blaming the Russian fleet for provocation.

Reports of the action undertaken by the Turkish fleet in the Black Sea sparked off a major political crisis in the Ottoman capital. Said Halim ordered an immediate cessation of hostilities, and threatened to resign if his orders were not obeyed, as did four other ministers. Djavid called for the dismissal of Souchon. Mahmud Pasha, minister of public works, called urgently for a meeting of the cabinet. But once again all to no avail. Talaat refused to convene a separate

---

8. Kurat, 'How Turkey Drifted into World War I'.
9. Ibid., p. 312.

meeting of the cabinet. Rather, he convened, on 30 October, a meeting of the leaders of both the government and the CUP, the latter being a bellicose group, likely to support Souchon's action. Enver, ordered to instruct Souchon to suspend hostilities, complied, at the same time hinting broadly that his orders might safely be ignored. Moreover, at a meeting of the CUP central committee, a majority, including Halil, rejected calls for Souchon's dismissal, arguing that it would be a mistake to offend the Germans. A reversion to neutrality might result in a German bombardment of the Ottoman capital, and ultimately in a Russian seizure of the Straits. Nevertheless, as a sop to Said Halim's concerns, it was agreed that the Porte might address a note to St Petersburg, explaining that the incident had come about as a result of Russian provocation, and that the Porte would be willing to settle the matter amicably and pay compensation for the damage done. Needless to say the Ottoman note did nothing to assuage Russian anger. Sazonov replied merely that were the Porte immediately to dismiss all German officer, then it might be possible to discuss the issue further – a condition which the Ottoman government found itself either unwilling or unable to fulfil. On 31 October the Entente ambassadors left the Ottoman capital; and on 3–5 November the Entente Powers declared war. As Sir Louis Mallet, the British ambassador, remarked: 'The die had finally been cast, and the crisis we had so long feared and striven to avert had occurred.'[10]

10. Macfie, *Straits Question*, p. 54.

CHAPTER SEVEN

The Ottoman Empire in the First World War, 1914–1918

The control of the Ottoman government finally secured by the CUP in the Bab-i Ali coup of January 1913, was maintained throughout the First World War. Enver, the minister of war, remained in office until very nearly the end of the war, directing strategy and deciding military appointments. Talaat, the minister of internal affairs, continued to serve in that capacity until February 1917, when he was appointed grand vizier, in place of Said Halim. In Syria Djemal Pasha, the military governor, ruled the province as a virtual dictator. Control of the economy, particularly in Istanbul, fell to Kara Kemal, the CUP party boss in the city, and Ismail Haqqi Bey, the general director of commissariat. In the provinces party bosses of one kind or another often exercised substantial control, amounting in some cases, such as that of Rhami Bey, the vali of Izmir, to virtual autonomy. CUP control, when not exercised by individual party bosses, was exercised by committees set up to control particular aspects of the economy and the society. Thus a committee of national defence controlled the sugar, tobacco and petrol monopolies, selling supplies, frequently at grossly inflated prices, whilst an export committee or commission organised the export of wool, cotton, chrome and other raw materials to Germany and Austria–Hungary. Such committees also organised orphanages and carried out other relief work, working at times with the Red Crescent, the Turkish equivalent of the Red Cross. Monopoly control of production and exchange, together with the shortages the war produced, frequently generated massive corruption, as CUP party bosses and others exploited the opportunities offered to enrich both their party and themselves.[1]

1. F. Ahmad, 'War and Society under the Young Turks, 1908–18', in A. Hourani (ed.), *The Modern Middle East* New York: I.B. Taurus, 1993.

Surprisingly, in view of the extent of their defeat in the Balkan Wars, Ottoman armies proved remarkably effective in the First World War. Serving on five main fronts in Europe, the Dardanelles, eastern Anatolia, Palestine and Mesopotamia they fought both stubbornly and for the most part successfully in the defence of the empire. But in the end to no avail, for as the Ottomans were no doubt well aware, the fate of their empire depended not on their own efforts but on the outcome of the titanic struggle then taking place in Europe between the armies of the Central Powers and those of the Triple Entente. German victory, even if accompanied by temporary defeat in the Near and Middle East, would almost certainly secure the survival of the Ottoman Empire for some years to come, while defeat would in all probability entail the end of the empire, however many victories its forces might win in the immediate theatre of war.

The contribution made by the armies of the Ottoman Empire, it may be supposed, more than fulfilled the expectations of Kaiser Wilhelm II and the German high command, who despite initial doubts had eventually recommended the alliance. But they failed to satisfy Enver, whose ambitions were as Napoleonic as they were unrealistic. In Europe Ottoman participation in the First World War on the side of the Central Powers played a significant part in persuading Bulgaria to join the alliance in September 1915, thereby facilitating the defeat of Serbia and the containment of an Anglo-French attempt to establish a bridgehead at Salonica and secure the Entente position in the Balkans. In the Dardanelles, Ottoman forces with German support defeated an attempt, launched by the Allies in February 1915, to force the narrows, open a supply route to Russia and, if possible, knock the Ottoman Empire out of the war. In eastern Anatolia and the Caucasus, where Enver launched a major campaign in January 1915, large Russian forces were tied down throughout the greater part of the war, despite the fact that in the first weeks of the campaign the Ottoman forces suffered a major defeat at Sarikamish, losing some 80 000 men out of a total force of some 120 000. In Palestine and the Sinai desert, attacks on the Suez Canal launched in February 1915 and August 1916 by Djemal Pasha (appointed military governor of Syria in November 1914) obliged the British to keep substantial forces in the area throughout the war. In Mesopotamia, where the Ottoman army captured a substantial British force at Kut al-Amara in April 1916, the British were similarly obliged to deploy substantial forces merely to defend their strategic and other interests in the area. Finally, the involvement of the Ottoman Empire in the First World War on the side of the Central Powers enabled the Germans to spread disaffection among the Muslim peoples of the British, French, Russian and Italian empires, thereby limiting the ability of the Entente Powers, particularly the western Entente Powers, to employ troops from their imperial garrisons in the European theatre.

Europe and the Dardanelles

The contribution made by the Ottomans on the European front was not confined to support for the forces of the Central Powers and their allies, assembled in the neighbourhood of the Salonica bridgehead. In 1916, when the Austro-Hungarian front began to crack under the impact of the Brussilov offensive, the Ottoman high command dispatched three divisions to Romania and two to Galicia – a total at one point of some 100 000 troops. But it was in defeating the attempt of the western Entente Powers, Britain and France, to force the Dardanelles, first by naval power alone, attempted in February–March 1915, and then by means of a combined operation, attempted in April–December 1915, that the Ottomans were to make their greatest contribution to the war effort of the Central Powers. For by so doing they secured not only the eventual participation of Bulgaria in the war on the side of the Central Powers – Bulgaria waited patiently to see what the outcome of the struggle would be before committing herself – but also the isolation of Russia, a significant factor contributing to her later collapse into chaos and revolution.

In order to defend the Dardanelles the Ottomans assembled men and resources from every corner of the empire; though most of the heavy artillery and motor transport was supplied by the Germans. At the height of the battle, it is said, 350 000 men were assembled in the neighbourhood of the Dardanelles and the Sea of Marmara, leaving only 150 000 to face the Russians on the eastern front. Nevertheless the expectation of an Allied breakthrough was widespread in the Ottoman capital, where plans were made for the transfer of the sultan and his government to the interior, to Bursa, Eskishehir or Konya. But in the end, thanks to the extraordinary fighting spirit of the Ottoman troops, many of them of Arab extraction, the position was held. In August the Allies made a last desperate attempt to break through, but they failed to do so. As a result, in November the British war committee advised evacuation, and in

December they ordered a complete withdrawal. Following the withdrawal of the Allied forces the Second Army, consisting of the 4th, 5th and 6th Corps, was withdrawn from the area and posted to Mesopotamia and other areas threatened by the advance of British and Russian forces.[2]

Eastern Anatolia and the Caucasus

The campaign fought by the Ottoman Third Army in the eastern provinces in the opening months of the First World War proved a disaster. Following plans drawn up by Bronsart von Schellendorff, Enver's chief of staff (but opposed by Liman von Sanders), Enver responded to a Russian advance by launching a counter-attack, designed first to defeat the advancing Russian forces and then to drive them back into the Caucasus, where an anti-Russian rising might be provoked. But Russian strategy proved superior. Totally outmanoeuvred, the Ottoman forces suffered a major defeat at Sarikamish in January 1915. Further defeats followed; and in February 1916 the Russians captured Erzerum, the great fortress town defending the eastern provinces, and in April 1916 Trabzon. But in 1917 a dramatic reversal of fortune occurred, as the March revolution in Russia, rapidly followed by the October revolution, led first to a breakdown of discipline among the Russian troops and then to a total collapse. As a result in the summer of 1918 the Ottomans were enabled not only to expel the remaining Russian forces from the area but also to advance through Armenia and occupy part of Azerbaijan.

The defeat of the Ottoman Third Army at Sarikamish did not convince Enver of the need to abandon his scheme for the liberation of the Caucasus. In the spring of 1915 he dispatched an expeditionary force led by his uncle, Halil, to western Iran, which it was hoped would secure control of the area, march into Daghistan and raise the Muslim inhabitants of the region. But an Armenian rising in Van, combined with the advance of a Russian army in the area, forced a retreat.[3]

2. A.L. Macfie, *The Straits Question, 1908–36* Salonica: Institute of Balkan Studies, 1993, pp. 57–70; W.W. Gottlieb, *Studies in Secret Diplomacy during the First World War* London: George Allen and Unwin, 1957, Chs 3–5; M.T. Florinsky, 'A Page of Diplomatic History: Russian Military Leaders and the Problem of Constantinople during the First World War', *Political Science Quarterly*, Vol. 44 (1929).
3. U. Trumpener, *Germany and the Ottoman Empire, 1914–1918* Princeton: Princeton University Press, 1968, Ch. 3.

The Armenian massacres

The humiliation inflicted on the Ottoman Third Army at Sarikamish, combined with the expectation of further Russian advances and fears regarding Armenian treachery, led in 1915 to one of the greatest tragedies of the First World War, the deportation and massacre of more than half a million Armenian inhabitants of the eastern provinces. The precise motivation of the Ottoman government in ordering the deportations and instigating the massacres to which they gave rise remains in doubt; but this much is clear. In the early months of the war Armenian groups belonging to *Dashnaksutiun* and *Henchak*, based in Tiflis and other towns in the area, organised Armenian volunteer units which it was hoped would assist the Russians in their conquest of the eastern provinces and liberate the Armenian inhabitants of the area. At the same time Armenians living in Zeytun, a town in southeastern Anatolia, who had refused to be conscripted into the Ottoman army, organised a corps of volunteers designed to disrupt Ottoman lines of communication, while Armenians living abroad approached the Entente Powers with offers to raise a force of some 20 000 men, capable, if properly armed and equipped by the Entente Powers, of instigating an insurrection in Cilicia and securing control of Iskenderun (Alexandretta), a strategic port on the Syrian coast. Then in April 1915 the Armenian inhabitants of Van rose in revolt, with the result that Ottoman forces stationed in the area, convinced that they were facing a widespread Armenian uprising, began an indiscriminate massacre of Armenians; and in May, following a second Armenian uprising in Zeytun, the Porte passed a series of deportation laws authorising the removal of the Armenian population from strategic areas and their resettlement in the Euphrates valley and other areas to the south of the province of Diarbekir. In the ensuing implementation of the deportation laws, carried out by Ottoman gendarmerie units, convicts released from prison for the purpose, Kurdish tribesmen and, according to some accounts, units belonging to the special organisation, robbery, rape and murder occurred on an extensive scale. Few of the Armenian columns arrived at their destination; and even those that did were frequently exposed to further starvation and massacre.

Ottoman responsibility for the deportation and massacre of the Armenians in the eastern provinces is not in doubt. The Ottoman government ordered the deportations, certain in the circumstances to lead to widespread robbery, rape and massacre, and they took few steps to protect the deportees. But the precise extent of Ottoman culpability remains in doubt. Armenian historians and propagandists remain convinced that the deportations, far from being an accidental consequence of the situation prevailing, were the outcome of a deep-laid plot, hatched by the CUP leadership in Istanbul, designed to exploit the opportunity offered by the war to solve once and for all the problem posed to the Ottoman Empire by the existence of the Armenian minority, a potent source of conflict and Great Power intervention in the preceding quarter century or so. Turkish historians and propagandists, on the other hand, argue that the deportations instituted in 1915, in the midst of the Gallipoli campaign, which threatened the very survival of the empire, were the inevitable consequence of Armenian treachery and rebellion. It could not be expected that any responsible government, responding to such a provocation, would act otherwise. As for the unfortunate consequences of the policy of deportation, entirely unplanned and unintended, those were merely the outcome of the sickness and exhaustion suffered by the deportees on their long marches, of the attacks launched by marauding gangs of Kurds and other irresponsible elements, beyond government control, and of the poverty and deprivation suffered by all inhabitants of the area, Turk as well as Armenian, in that period. Documentary evidence, such as it is – many of the documents concerning the Armenian massacres were destroyed by the Ottoman government at the end of the First World War – would appear to support the Turkish view. Yet it is difficult, if not impossible, to escape the conclusion that, once the deportations were instituted, the Ottoman leadership, or at least elements within it, were not averse to exploiting the opportunity offered to resolve a problem that had for decades caused the empire so much difficulty. As Talaat Pasha is said on one occasion to have remarked to Henry Morgenthau, the American ambassador: 'It is no use for you to argue, we have already disposed of three-quarters of the Armenians; there are none at all left in Bitlis, Van and Erzerum. The hatred between the Turks and the Armenians is now so intense that we have got to finish with them. If we do not they will plan their revenge.'[4]

4. H. Morgenthau, *Ambassador Morgenthau's Story* Garden City, New York: Doubleday, Page & Co, 1919, pp. 337–8; Trumpener, *Germany and the Ottoman Empire*, Ch. 7; S.R. Sonyel, 'Armenian Deportations: A Re-appraisal in the Light of New Documents', *Belleten*, Vol. 36 (1972); G. Dyer, 'Turkish "Falsifiers" and the Armenian "Deceivers": Historiography and the Armenian Massacres', *Middle Eastern Studies*, Vol. 12, No. 1 (1976). Evidence that the CUP wished to destroy the Armenian inhabitants of the eastern provinces is contained in two eye-witness reports published by the Ottoman Turkish historian Ahmet Refik in *Ikdam* in 1918–19. See *Iki Komite, Iki Kital* Ankara: Kebikeç, 1914.

Contemporary observers in the Entente countries, mainly British and French, quickly concluded that the Armenian massacres were the responsibility, if not the actual work, of the German and Austrian embassies in Istanbul, and of the German military mission posted there. Such a conclusion appears unwarranted. Throughout the period of the massacres staff belonging to the embassies and the military mission made strenuous efforts to persuade the Ottoman government to abandon the murderous policies it had instituted. When in March 1915 reports of massacres and other depredations were first received in the Ottoman capital, many German and Austrian diplomats and consular officials protested. Again in April, Wangenheim, the German ambassador, directed several appeals to the Porte to prevent disorder; and on 28 April he authorised the German vice-consul in Erzerum to intervene to prevent further massacres, though he should on no account give the impression that his country intended to exercise a right of protection over the Armenian *millet*. In May Pallavicini, the Austrian ambassador in Istanbul, more passive than his German colleague, warned Talaat that persecution of the Christians would merely give the Entente Powers a stick with which to beat their enemies. But Talaat, as Pallavicini had predicted, proved unresponsive. The Porte, he declared, would proceed only against the guilty: he had no reason to suppose that women and children were being murdered. Many Muslims, as well as Armenians, had died in the recent disturbances. Shortly thereafter, in order to justify the harsh policy instituted by the Ottoman government in May, Talaat had the Porte issue a series of official reports, supposedly proving the existence of a number of Armenian plots to undermine the empire; and in June, acting in conjunction with Enver, he had the so-called 'counter-insurgency programme' intensified, ordering the closure of Armenian schools, the suppression of the Armenian press and the transfer of all 'suspect families' from the 'present centres of insurrection' to places of exile remote from the field of battle.[5] As a result, during the following weeks further reports of deportation and massacre were received by the German embassy; and on 17 June Wangenheim informed Bethmann-Hollweg, the German foreign minister, that in his opinion the Porte were now pursuing a policy designed to secure the extermination of the Armenian people. Once again Wangenheim instructed the German consuls in the eastern provinces to protest to the appropriate authorities; and in July both he

5. Trumpener, *Germany and the Ottoman Empire*, Ch. 7.

and Pallavicini protested several times against the indiscriminate measures taken. The provincial authorities, Wangenheim insisted, must be at once instructed to safeguard the lives and property of the Armenian people.

Prince zu Hohenlohe-Langenburg, who in July 1915 replaced Wangenheim as German ambassador (Wangenheim was sent home suffering from heart trouble, arteriosclerosis and a 'clearly pathological' form of nervousness) continued to protest vigorously against the Porte's Armenian policy. But once again to little or no avail. Nor did Dr Arminius Lepsius, the president of the German-Armenian Society, make any impression on the Ottoman leadership. On the contrary, on 10 August he was informed by Enver that on no account would the Porte permit him to visit the eastern provinces or organise relief work there. Clearly the Ottoman leadership intended to continue with their policy of deportation, and by implication of massacre, until the grim task was completed.

It should not be supposed that the German government could not have persuaded the Porte to abandon its policy of deportation, had it so decided. But in order to achieve that objective it would in all probability have needed to threaten a termination of the alliance. That it was not prepared to do, for as Arthur Zimmermann, state secretary at the German foreign office, explained in a letter to a German publisher in October 1915:

> Without needing any prodding from church circles, the foreign office and the imperial representative agencies in Turkey have, of their own volition, already done all that was possible by diplomatic means to mitigate the sufferings of the Armenians. To bring about a break with Turkey on account of the Armenian question we did not and do not consider appropriate. For as regrettable as it is from the Christian standpoint that innocent people, too, must suffer under the Turkish measures, the Armenians are after all less close to us than our own sons and brothers, whose sacrificial bloody struggle in France and Russia is being indirectly aided by the military help of the Turks.[6]

Syria, Palestine and the Sinai desert

The campaigns mounted by the Ottomans in January 1915 and August 1916, to secure the closure of the Suez Canal (a principal German objective), the expulsion of the British from Egypt and

6. Ibid., pp. 221–2.

possibly even the expulsion of the Italians from Tripolitania, proved as ineffective as Enver's early efforts in eastern Anatolia; though they did oblige the British to keep substantial forces in the area. From as early as August 1914 the Ottoman government dispatched agents, liberally provided with money and propaganda material, supplied for the most part by the Germans, to stir up unrest in Egypt and the North African provinces (where Enver hoped to inspire a Senussi revolt aimed not only at the Italians but also at the British in Egypt). Then in February 1915, at the instigation of the Germans, Djemal Pasha and Lieutenant Colonel Kress von Kressenstein, a member of his staff, led a force of some 20 000 men, accompanied by 11 000 camels, through the Sinai desert to launch an attack on the British forces defending the canal. But as Djemal Pasha makes clear in his memoirs, logistical problems made it impossible for them to sustain the attack. Although according to some reports a handful of Ottoman troops did manage to cross the canal, they were quickly eliminated, while the rest of the force, outgunned by the artillery of the British garrison, and by the guns of British warships anchored in the canal, were compelled to withdraw. Nor were the Ottoman agents dispatched to Egypt and Tripolitania successful in inciting widespread rebellion there; though opposition to the Italian garrison in Tripolitania did continue throughout the war.[7]

Following a second, equally unsuccessful assault on the canal, mounted by Djemal Pasha in August 1916, the Ottoman expeditionary force was once again forced to withdraw. Moreover, following the withdrawal, the British, who had by then built up a substantial garrison in Egypt, moved forward to establish a defensive position in Sinai, based on al-Arish. From that position, in the spring of 1917 they launched a series of attacks on the Ottomans. Initially unsuccessful – two attacks mounted in March and April 1917 on the Gaza front were defeated – in December they succeeded in breaking through, capturing Jerusalem. Finally, in September 1918, following an Ottoman collapse, they advanced rapidly, capturing Damascus and Aleppo.[8]

The collapse of the Ottoman position in Syria and Palestine in the closing stages of the war was, it would seem, hastened by a plan, drawn up by Enver and the Ottoman war council in the spring of 1917, to form a special army group entitled *Yildirim* (Lightning) or

7. Ibid., pp. 113–22; Djemal Pasha, *Memoirs of a Turkish Statesman* New York: Arno Press, 1973, pp. 148–51.

8. C. Falls, *Armageddon 1918* London: Weidenfeld and Nicolson, 1964.

Army Group F, which it was hoped would, under the command of General Falkenhayn, a former chief of staff of the German army, especially appointed for the purpose, march down the Euphrates and liberate Baghdad, captured by the British in March 1917. This plan many Ottoman officers, including Djemal Pasha, Halil Pasha, commander of the Sixth Army, and Mustafa Kemal Pasha, commander of the Second Army, opposed root and branch. At a meeting held in Aleppo in June 1917, Djemal Pasha pointed out that in view of the likelihood of a British attack on the Palestine front, they should first reinforce the position there:

> If we concentrate such an army in Aleppo it will be able to resist any Russian pressure on the front of the 2nd Army or oppose any advance of the English up the Tigris or Euphrates. Above all, we shall be able to force the Entente Governments to give up the idea of a landing at Adana, an eventuality we greatly fear. If the English knew we had such an army, ready to strike, at Aleppo, perhaps they would be compelled to abandon their attack, although I have not the slightest doubt that they are now preparing an offensive against the Gaza front for next autumn. In short the Baghdad scheme strikes me as dangerous.[9]

Later, at a meeting of the war council held in Istanbul, Djemal repeated his objections, pointing out the dangerous consequences which might follow from a weakening of the position in Palestine. But Enver remained unconvinced. The forces available, he insisted, were sufficient to defend the position.

Djemal Pasha's opposition to the deployment of the *Yildirim* army group on the Mesopotamian front was not well received by Enver. Shortly thereafter, for no apparent reason, Djemal was invited by the German Kaiser, Wilhelm II, to tour the western front. During his absence he was informed that, as Falkenhayn (who had apparently decided to launch an attack on the British position on the Gaza front before turning his forces eastwards, to liberate Baghdad) had decided to take the offensive in Palestine, it was considered essential that he, Falkenhayn, be placed in command of all the forces in the area. At this point Djemal Pasha, not for the first time, threatened to resign. But in the end, following further discussion, he was persuaded to stay on, remaining in command merely of the Ottoman forces, stationed to the east of the River Jordan, and in control of the civil administration.

9. Djemal Pasha, *Memoirs of a Turkish Statesman*, p. 183.

In Djemal Pasha's considered opinion, Enver's decision to form the *Yildirim* army group, under the command of Falkenhayn, and his later decision to place the German general in command of all the forces on the Palestine front, proved disastrous. Had Enver Pasha not so decided, then in Djemal's opinion the Ottoman forces in Palestine could have 'held the Gaza–Beersheba line for years, and on the day of the armistice Syria and Palestine would still have formed part of the Ottoman Empire'.[10]

That Djemal Pasha opposed a number of the policies pursued by Enver Pasha is not in doubt; but just how far his opposition went remains unclear. A curious incident, which occurred in 1915, would suggest that it was somewhat more radical than might have been supposed. In December 1915 Sazonov, the Russian foreign minister, informed Grey, the British foreign minister, that Djemal Pasha, who was believed to be friendly to the Entente, had made secret advances, by way of 'Armenian circles', offering to lead an open rebellion against the Porte, provided that he be recognised as sultan, and that the independence and integrity of Turkey in Asia, including Syria, Mesopotamia, Arabia, Armenia and Cilicia, be recognised. The loss of Istanbul and the Straits would be accepted, and steps taken, including the creation of an autonomous Armenian state governed by a Christian prince, to protect the Armenians, threatened with extinction. Were the Allies to agree to his terms, then he would at once declare the downfall of the Ottoman government and, in conjunction with the Allies, mount an expedition to secure the deposition of the sultan, seen as a 'prisoner of Germany'.[11]

Clearly such reports, passed on by 'Armenian circles' in the heat of war, should be treated with great suspicion. But the possibility that Djemal Pasha and his faction contemplated rebellion in 1915 should not be ruled out. It was well known that Djemal Pasha had established contacts with a number of wealthy Armenians – he is said to have offered the Armenian community in Syria protection in return for substantial payments – and in his memoirs he hints darkly at some such possibility. Nevertheless, it may be doubted if he would ever have undertaken so risky an adventure, particularly as he was noted for his patriotism. One way or the other, it made little difference. The proposals were not followed up by the Allies, for as the French pointed out no such arrangement was possible, as Syria and Cilicia had already been allocated, in secret

10. Ibid., p. 193.
11. Macfie, *Straits Question*, pp. 75–6; S. Akşin, *Jön Türkler ve Ittihat ve Terrakhi* Istanbul: Gerçek Yayinevi, 1980, pp. 153–5, 293.

agreements drawn up by the Entente Powers in the course of the war, to France.

Djemal's administration in Syria in the war years was both ruthless and effective. Syrian nationalists and others who engaged in anti-Ottoman activities, were simply arrested, imprisoned and on occasion executed. Not that there was any need to adopt a draconian approach. The Muslim Arab population remained for the most part loyal to the administration throughout. Indeed, the Fourth Army was recruited almost entirely from Muslim Arabs. As for the Christian and Jewish communities, which had traditionally maintained close relations with the western Entente Powers, they were in no position to engage in subversive activities: it was simply too dangerous, as the fate of the Armenians in the eastern provinces had shown.

The threat of a persecution of the Jews in Palestine, particularly the Zionist Jews, seen as disloyal, remained present throughout the war. Indeed, it may be assumed that it was only the intervention of the German and American diplomats and others, in both Istanbul and Syria, that prevented the threat from being realised. In December 1914 Djemal Pasha launched a campaign (involving the closure of Zionist organisations and deportation) against the Zionist Jews, who he believed (rightly as it turned out) were revolutionaries, working to create an independent state; and again in February 1915 he launched a similar campaign. But on both occasions, thanks to the forceful intervention of Wangenheim, Henry Morgenthau, the American ambassador in Istanbul, Talaat and others, who brought concerted pressure to bear, Djemal Pasha was obliged to desist. Thereafter Djemal Pasha, somewhat chastened, adopted for a time a more conciliatory approach, permitting sick Jewish civilians to be cared for in military hospitals and Jewish labourers employed by the army to have the Sabbath off; but the threat of further persecution remained. In March 1917, following the opening of a British offensive on the Gaza front, Djemal issued orders for the evacuation of all Jews living in the cities of Jaffa and Tel Aviv. The ensuing evacuation, in effect a deporation to the interior, caused great hardship, but once again, thanks to the forceful intervention of the German and American embassies, the worst effects of the evacuation were avoided. Agricultural workers were allowed to remain, and permission was given for the deportees to appoint watchmen to guard the properties they had left behind.[12]

---

12. I. Friedman, *Germany, Turkey and Zionism, 1897–1918* Oxford: Clarendon Press, 1977.

Mesopotamia

In Mesopotamia, to which in September 1914 the government of India, the body responsible for the execution of British policy in the area, dispatched an expeditionary force to secure control of the approaches to the Persian Gulf and the oil fields and refineries in the neighbourhood, the Ottomans won a series of spectacular victories; but in the end they suffered defeat. In November 1915 an Ottoman army, retreating before the British expeditionary force, inflicted a substantial defeat on units belonging to that force at Ctesiphon, a small town some 25 miles southeast of Baghdad. Then when the defeated force, which had suffered appalling casualties, retreated to Kut al-Amara, a mud village on the Tigris, the Ottomans, now substantially reinforced by troops dispatched by Field Marshal Colmer von der Goltz, who had just taken over command of all the Ottoman forces in the area, surrounded the village, at the same time dispatching forces to prevent the advance of British reinforcements pushing up from the south. As a result the British forces at Kut al-Amara, completely cut off, were exposed to a long and exhausting blockade, in the course of which they experienced flood, starvation and disease; and on 29 April 1916 they were forced to surrender. Following the surrender, a British delegation, which included Aubrey Herbert and T.E. Lawrence (Lawrence of Arabia), offered the Ottomans £2 million in return for the release, on parole, of the captured force. But the Ottomans, who placed a high value on the propaganda value of their victory, refused the offer. During the following weeks the British troops were marched off to prisoner of war camps in Anatolia, where most of them died; though General Charles Townshend, their commander, favoured by his captors, received considerably better treatment.

Following their victory at Kut al-Amara, the Ottomans succeeded in holding the expeditionary force dispatched by the government of India for a time, but eventually, following the arrival of substantial reinforcements, they were forced to retreat. As a result in March 1917 Baghdad was lost. Not that the Ottomans gave up the struggle. On the contrary, resistance continued until the end of the war, when the expeditionary force, following the conclusion of the Mudros Armistice, occupied Mosul.[13]

13. F.J. Moberly, *History of the Great War: The Campaign in Mesopotamia* London: HMSO, 1923–7.

Subversion in the Muslim world

The Ottoman–German war effort in the First World War was not confined to the five main fronts in the Near and Middle East. Agents belonging to *Teshkilati Mahsusa* and other organisations were sent to India, Afghanistan, Persia, the Caucasus, Arabia, Egypt, Tripolitania and even West Africa to make contact with sympathetic elements and persuade them to take action against the Entente Powers. In return for active support the Persians were offered guarantees regarding their future independence, substantial military support and a loan of 30 million marks. In Arabia new German consulates were established in Jeddah and Medina, charged with the task of winning over the Arab tribes and penetrating the Anglo-Egyptian Sudan. In Tripolitania an attempt was made to incite rebellion among the Senussi; and in Algeria and Morocco similar attempts were made to raise the Arab and Berber tribes against their French colonial masters. As a German general staff memorandum of 5 August 1914 remarked: 'Revolution in India and Egypt, and also in the Caucasus . . . is of the highest importance. The treaty with Turkey will make it possible for the (German) Foreign Office to realise this idea and to awaken the fanaticism of Islam.'[14]

Considerable resources were put into these schemes, but they proved peculiarly unsuccessful. In Persia the shah and his ministers proved unwilling to risk a confrontation with the British Empire merely in return for vague assurances of independence and limited military support, while in Afghanistan the German agents failed to make effective contact with the tribal leaders. In Egypt and the Sudan the failure of the Ottoman assault on the Suez Canal effectively ended whatever chance there might have been that the local people would rise in revolt. In Arabia, where the British were able to offer Ibn Saud, Sherif Husein and other leaders something approaching complete independence, most of the tribes remained neutral in the struggle, while Sherif Husein joined the Entente. Even in North Africa, where the prospects for subversion were greatest, little was achieved. As one commentator remarked, the actual means and personnel employed by the Central Powers and their allies in the field bore no relation to their high-flown expectations: 'they were totally inadequate, and the effect produced by them was practically nil.'[15]

14. F. Fischer, *Germany's Aims in the First World War* New York: W.W. Norton, 1967, p. 126; Trumpener, *Germany and the Ottoman Empire*, pp. 113–22.
15. Fischer, *Germany's Aims in the First World War*, p. 131.

The Arab Revolt

The ability of the Ottomans to hold their position in Syria and Palestine, and to a lesser extent in Mesopotamia, was adversely affected by the outbreak, in June 1916, of the so-called Arab Revolt. This revolt, which was led by Emir Husein, the Sherif of Mecca, and his three sons Abdullah (later king of Transjordan), Feisal (later king of Iraq) and Ali, spread rapidly among the tribes of the Hedjaz. But it made little or no impression elsewhere in the Arab provinces. No Arab unit of the Ottoman army changed sides. No significant military or political figure defected; though a handful of Syrian prisoners of war and other disaffected individuals did join the sherif's forces. No significant nationalist or other organisation emerged in Syria, capable of raising the people. As a result the uprising was confined for the most part to the Hedjaz, where Arab guerrillas, led by among others T.E. Lawrence, raided Ottoman outposts and blew up sections of the Hedjaz Railway, and to the coastal towns and villages of the Red Sea, where British naval units, operating in conjunction with Arab tribesmen, liberally supplied with British gold, secured control of the main ports, Rabegh, Yanbo, Jeddah and Akaba.[16]

The relative failure of the Arab Revolt (except as an instrument of propaganda, useful to the western imperial powers) was due to two main factors: the determined efforts made by Djemal Pasha to secure the loyalty and friendship of the Arab peoples of the empire (most of whom were in any case contemptuous of Emir Husein and his unruly Bedouin followers) and the stubborn determination of the Ottoman garrison defending Medina, never captured by the rebels. In the early years of the war Djemal Pasha, well aware of the threat which a widespread Arab uprising might pose to the survival of the Ottoman Empire, worked tirelessly to secure the support of the sultan's Arab subjects. To this end Arab civilisation, culture and language were constantly lauded, powerful tribal chiefs, such as Abdul Aziz Ibn Saud, the ruler of the Wahhabi sheikhdom of Nejd, and Ibn Rashid, the ruler of Ha'il, placated, and Arab notables, such as Abdul Kerim-el Halil (later executed) and Abdul Gani el Arisi, bought off. Not that Djemal Pasha's policy regarding the

16. D. Fromkin, *A Peace to End All Peace* Harmondsworth: Penguin Books, 1989, Ch. 28; A. Hourani, *The Emergence of the Modern Middle East* London: Macmillan, 1981, Ch. 13; E. Karsh and I. Karsh, 'Myth in the Desert, or Not the Great Arab Revolt', *Middle Eastern Studies*, Vol. 33, No. 2 (1997).

Arabs was, as we have seen, universally benevolent. On the contrary Arab nationalists accused of fomenting disaffection in Syria were ruthlessly dealt with, while leaders of the Druze and Maronite communities in the Lebanon, considered unreliable, were for a time held hostage in Jerusalem. As a result, despite the fact that in 1915 a substantial part of the Ottoman army, stationed in Syria, was withdrawn to fight in the defence of the Dardanelles, the Arab provinces held and a total collapse was averted.

Ottoman control of Medina, sustained throughout the war by a garrison of some 3,250 officers and men, led by Fahreddin Pasha, obliged Sherif Husein to keep most of his forces in the southern part of the Hedjaz until the closing stages of the war, for it was deemed inadvisable to risk the advance of substantial forces while so strong an enemy remained in the rear. The story of the defence of the city, led by Fahreddin Pasha, the 'Tiger of the Desert', has, thanks to an account of the defence later rendered by Naci Kashif Kiciman, an intelligence officer attached to Fahreddin Pasha's staff, become something of a Turkish legend.

The defence of Medina

According to Naci Kashif Kiciman's account, following the loss of Mecca and Taif, accomplished mainly by Muslim troops sent by the British from Egypt – it was not considered advisable to dispatch British or French troops – Fahreddin issued a proclamation declaring his intention to defend Medina, the 'apple of the eye of the Caliphate', to the last bullet, the last drop of blood and the last soldier:

> Until these soldiers are buried first under the rubble of Medina, and finally in a red shroud of blood and fire under the very dome of the Garden of Purity (the mausoleum of the Prophet of Islam) itself, the red flag of the Ottomans shall not be removed from the castle turrets of Medina the Radiant nor ultimately from the minarets and the green dome of the Mosque of Happiness (the mosque where the prophet's tomb is located).'[17]

Following the proclamation the defences of the city were strengthened and the bulk of the civilian population evacuated, for food was in short supply. The last substantial piece of military equipment

17. S. Tanver Wasti, 'The Defence of Medina, 1916–19', *Middle Eastern Studies*, Vol. 27, No. 4 (1991), p. 643.

was delivered to the city on 4 July 1917, when three large cannons were dragged there by buffaloes, and the last reinforcements (5 officers and 148 men) arrived on 4 March 1918. Damage caused to the Hedjaz Railway by Bedouin guerrillas and their British mentors, was for the most part quickly repaired. Nor had the garrison any difficulty in repelling the attacks launched by the sherif's forces; though an attack launched by rebel forces near Tabuk on 25 September 1917 left 22 men, women and children dead and 53 wounded. Supplies of food, now running short, were strictly rationed. In December an explosion on the railway tracks at Akhdar station, to the south of Tabuk, caused ten deaths, but the prisoners taken by the rebels were later released when Ottoman reinforcements arrived. On 16 December the birthday of the Prophet was celebrated with a recital of the *Mevlid* (a Turkish poem celebrating the birth of the Prophet), and the troops were feasted with a menu of *helva* and *pilaff* – though the food situation remained critical. In February 1918, when Fahreddin rallied forth to confront the forces of Abdullah, surrounding the city, Abdullah simply fled, leaving behind 45 camels; but in March the railway link with Damascus was finally cut. Thereafter the garrison remained isolated; but Fahreddin refused to give up. In April a freak hailstorm occurred, covering the city with white, icy hailstones. A day or two later the temperature reached 35°C in the shade. In June, when the temperature reached 47°C in the shade the rations of the officers and men were further reduced. Fortunately, in September an Ottoman unit ambushed a group of rebels near Judaa and seized two camels, five large bags of rice and two large bags of sugar; but food shortages continued, for there was not enough money in the treasury to purchase rice from the Bedouins, many of whom remained sympathetic to the Ottoman cause. To make good this deficiency Fahreddin organised a fund, to which both officers and men contributed. As a result he was enabled to buy 40 tonnes of rice from the Bedouins.

Reports of the loss of Damascus and the Mudros Armistice, which ended the Ottoman participation in the First World War, did nothing to quench Fahreddin's spirit. Ordered to surrender by Ahmed Izzet Pasha, the grand vizier and minister of war, on 6 November 1918, he refused to obey unless instructed to do so by the sultan-caliph. On 6 December he delivered the sermon for Friday prayers in the Prophet's Mosque; and in the following weeks he continued to repel Bedouin attacks on the outposts of the garrison. By then, however, as even Fahreddin had come to realise, the position was hopeless. Supplies were again running short; and both officers and men, afflicted by an epidemic of Spanish influenza and hunger, were deserting. As a result on 5 January, Fahreddin, finally defeated, ordered the closure of the special fund and resigned. Shortly thereafter, Colonel Necip Bey, his successor, concluded an agreement with Husein's son, Ali, arranging for the surrender of the city.[18]

Origins of the Arab Revolt

Credit for the instigation of the so-called Arab Revolt has been claimed by several groups and individuals. These include Arab nationalist organisations centred in Syria; members of the Arab Bureau, set up by the British in Cairo in February 1916 to foment revolt in the Arab world; Lord Kitchener, the British agent and consul general in Egypt, who first made contact with Sherif Husein in February 1914; Reginald Wingate, the British governor general of the Sudan; and Sir Henry McMahon, the British high commissioner in Egypt, who negotiated the final agreement. The actual origins of the revolt, however, appear to lie elsewhere, in the murky waters of Ottoman politics. From the beginning of the First World War, it would seem, Emir Husein, a member of the house of Hashem, descendants of the Prophet, who had been appointed sherif of Mecca by the CUP leadership following the Young Turk Revolution of 1908, had intended to remain neutral. Neutrality, if preserved, would for a time at least enable him to extort bribes and subsidies not only from the British but also from the Ottomans: shortly before the outbreak of the Arab Revolt, indeed, he succeeded in securing a grant of T.L. 50 000 in gold from the Porte, in order that he might raise and equip a force to fight the British. But in 1915 he learnt that Djemal Pasha, who had been apprised of his treacherous activities and those of his son, Feisal, by Arab nationalists arrested and interrogated in Syria, intended to have him replaced. Then, in April 1916, he learnt that Djemal intended to dispatch a specially trained force of 3,500 men, accompanied by a group of German officers, to southern Arabia, to set up a telegraph station there. Realising that Djemal Pasha would seize the opportunity offered by the passage of that force through the Hedjaz to secure his deposition, Husein at once turned to the British, with whom he was already in contact. Shortly thereafter he accepted the

18. Ibid.

heavily qualified offer of British support for an uprising, contained in letters, later known as the McMahon Correspondence, exchanged with Sir Henry McMahon, the British high commissioner in Egypt. The initial object of the Arab Revolt was, therefore, not the creation of some kind of Arab national state, as proposed in the so-called McMahon Correspondence, but the survival of the Hashemite regime. Proclamations issued by Husein in June 1916 referred not to the possible creation of an Arab state, but to the need to rid the Hedjaz of the irreligious Young Turks of the CUP, the 'heedless ones' who looked on the religion of God as 'an amusement and a sport'.[19]

Abdul Aziz Ibn Saud

The success of the Ottomans in restricting the extent of the so-called Arab Revolt owed much to the unwillingness of Abdul Aziz Ibn Saud, the ruler of Nejd, to become involved in the struggle. Not that Ibn Saud could be considered in any sense loyal to the Ottoman cause. On the contrary, in the decade or so preceding the outbreak of the First World War, following the example set by the emir of Kuwait, he had made as many as 11 overtures to the government of India and its agents, requesting protection; and in 1913, in order to compel a positive British response to his advances, he had occupied Hasa, a territory bordering the Persian Gulf, control of which the British deemed essential. But on every occasion the British response had proved negative. On no account, they had insisted, would they intervene in the internal affairs of Central Arabia. Nor would they take any action likely to undermine the integrity of the Ottoman Empire, the preservation of which remained a principal objective of their foreign policy. Following the outbreak of the First World War, however, the British, now determined to secure Arab support in their struggle with the Ottomans, changed tack, offering Ibn Saud not only recognition of his independence but also substantial financial support, if he would join the Allied side in the war. This offer Ibn Saud, fearful regarding the possible consequences of an Ottoman victory for his people, and alternatively of the possible consequences of an Ottoman return, which might be permitted by the Entente Powers following an Ottoman defeat, felt obliged to reject. But this did not mean that

19. C.E. Dawn, *From Ottomanism to Arabism* Chicago: University of Illinois Press, 1973, p. 77; Karsh and Karsh, 'Myth in the Desert'.

he was persuaded to give up his dreams of independence. On the contrary, in the following months he pursued them if anything with even greater determination. As a result in December 1915, having skilfully exploited British fears that he might actively participate in the war on the side of the Ottomans, he succeeded in obliging the British to conclude a treaty with him, guaranteeing British recognition of a Saudi state, and promising future protection. In this way he succeeded in securing his principal foreign-policy objectives without exposing himself to the risks that open participation in the war on the Allied side would have entailed.[20]

Ibn Saud's handling of his relations with the Ottomans proved equally effective. On several occasions in the decade preceding the First World War the Ottomans had dispatched forces to Nejd in order to compel his submission; and in May 1914, when war threatened, they had obliged him to conclude a treaty with the Porte, acknowledging Ottoman sovereignty in the Nejd and Hasa and promising military support in any war which might break out between the sultan and a foreign power. In return the Ottomans had offered the effective withdrawal of what remained of the Ottoman garrison in Nejd – only a token force would remain – and the appointment of Ibn Saud as vali of Nejd, a step up from the post of kaimakam of southern Nejd his father had held. From Ibn Saud's point of view, the regularisation of his relations with the Ottomans which this treaty entailed was to be welcomed. But he had no intention of engaging in hostilities against the British, whose support he wished, at some point in the future, to secure. When the call to arms came, therefore, he explained to the Ottomans that, alas, it would be impossible for him to participate in the proposed campaign, as he would of necessity have to remain in Nejd in order to defend his people against the incursions of the Rashidis. Later Ottoman demands that he participate in the war against the British in Mesopotamia and elsewhere were countered by hints that, if driven to do so, he might feel obliged to join the Hashemites in their revolt – a potent threat to the Ottomans, who feared that Saudi participation in the war on the enemy side would radically alter the balance of forces in the area.

Skilful as Ibn Saud's manoeuvrings were, however, he was unable wholly to remain untouched by the war. In a battle fought in January 1915 at Jarab, against a Rashidi force supplied and equipped by the Ottomans, he suffered a significant reverse (it was at this battle that Captain Shakespear, the British political agent in Kuwait, was killed). In a later battle, fought against the Ajman tribe of Hasa, whom the Ottomans and Rashidis had encouraged to revolt, Ibn Saud himself was seriously wounded and a brother, Sa'd, killed. Meanwhile in the Nejd discontent provoked by the war and the loss of trade that war entailed, flourished. Nevertheless, despite the weakness of his position Ibn Saud hung on, keeping Ibn Rashid at bay, promising future support to both the Ottomans and the British, and even to the Hashemites, but in fact engaging his forces in no significant operations beyond the confines of his own emirate.

It is not possible precisely to measure the extent of the support, and promises of support, offered by Ibn Saud to the British and the Ottomans in the course of the First World War, but it would appear to have been equally balanced. In the first weeks of the war he gave several promises of support to the Ottomans; but when the Ottomans sent four *ulema* to Nejd to preach holy war he had them confined to their quarters, lest their message prove too persuasive. In October 1916 or thereabouts, in order to placate the British, who had requested him to support the Hashemites, he offered to dispatch a token force of 50 men to participate in the manoeuvres of the Hashemite army; but he insisted that on no account would they be permitted to engage in hostilities. In November, he informed the British that, in order to assist them in the enforcement of their blockade of Syria and in their siege of Medina, he had detained an Ottoman envoy, Far'un, dispatched to Nejd, and seized the 700 camels he had hired there; and again in November, in order to impress the British with the extent of his support, he attended a great durbar of Arab chiefs, held in Kuwait. But when the Ottomans protested against these actions and dispatched a mission from Medina to Riyadh to discuss the issue, he not only responded by ordering a relaxation of the blockade, and the dispatch of camels to Syria and Medina to help relieve pressure on the Ottoman transport system, but also sent a delegation to Damascus to discuss relations with the Ottoman authorities there.[21]

The assistance rendered by the Saudis to the Ottoman garrison in Medina played a significant, perhaps even a decisive, part in securing the garrison's survival. At the same time Saudi neutrality, preserved throughout the war, spared the Ottomans the need to face something approaching a united Arab front in Arabia. In these

21. Ibid.

circumstances it is not surprising that Djemal Pasha in his memoirs should have felt called upon to comment favourably on the significant services rendered by Ibn Saud to the Ottoman cause in the First World War – services which, as he put it, contrasted strikingly with the treacherous behaviour of the Hashemites.[22]

Economic consequences of Ottoman participation in the First World War

The economic consequences of the participation of the Ottoman Empire in the First World War were profound. Within a matter of days the principal bourses, mostly foreign owned, closed down, as did a number of navigation companies, also foreign owned. A run on the banks, accompanied by hoarding and blackmarketeering, followed. As a result the price of many goods rose sharply; though the price of some goods, such as silk and fruit, previously exported, fell. Nor were government attempts to reestablish stability – these included the requisitioning of grain and the importation of wheat from Romania – effective. Prices continued to rise, driven upwards by shortages of supply, the conscription of the labour force – in the course of the war the Ottomans are said to have conscripted some 3 million men, of whom some 325 000 were killed in battle and 240 000 died of disease – the dispossession and ruin of the Armenian and other minorities, and efforts made by the CUP, frequently misdirected, to create a national economy. By the beginning of 1917 prices had quadrupled. By the end of 1918 they had risen twenty-five-fold.[23]

In an attempt to relieve the shortages of labour caused by conscription, the Ottoman government, in August 1916, set up a society of Muslim working women, with Enver's wife as president. This society, it was hoped, would encourage the employment of women in industry; though women aged 21 and over would be expected to marry before taking up employment. Later, in 1917, the government introduced state supervision of agricultural production and forced labour in many parts of the country. But such efforts proved once again largely ineffective. As Mustafa Kemal Pasha noted in a confidential report to Enver Pasha, dispatched in September 1917:

22. Djemal Pasha, *Memoirs of a Turkish Statesman.*
23. Ahmad, 'War and Society under the Young Turks'; A. Emin, *Turkey in the World War* New Haven, Connecticut: Yale University Press, 1930.

There are no bonds between the Government and the people. What
we call the people are composed now of women, disabled men and
children. For all alike the Government is the power which insistently
drives them to hunger and death. The administrative machinery is
devoid of authority. Public life is in full anarchy. Every new step
taken by the Government increases the general hatred the people
feel for it. All officials accept bribes, and are capable of every sort of
corruption and abuse. The machinery of justice has entirely stopped.
The police forces do not function. Economic life is breaking down
with formidable speed. Neither people nor government employees
have any confidence in the future.[24]

The result of the breakdown of the economy and government corruption was, in many areas, famine; and in Anatolia and parts of
the Arab provinces, where, according to some accounts, as many
as 1–1.5 million men had deserted, near anarchy prevailed, as
the deserters resorted to brigandage to obtain food and the other
necessities of life.

The financial position of the Ottoman state proved equally precarious. A French loan of T.L. 35 million, negotiated in April 1914,
was quickly used up. According to Djavid Bey, in August 1914 the
Ottoman state treasury contained only T.L. 92 000 in ready cash.
Civil service and army salaries were seldom paid on time; some
were not paid at all. Certainly, the German loan, delivered in October, did something to relieve the pressure, as did the fact that,
following the entry of the Ottoman Empire into the war, there was
no longer any need to pay interest on the Ottoman public debt.
But the chronic problem of financing Ottoman state expenditure,
greatly increased by the participation of the empire in the war,
remained. In the course of the war the Ottomans received further
German subsidies, amounting in total to some T.L. 250 million.
Nevertheless, by the end of the war, the Ottoman public debt,
registered at T.L. 171 million in 1914, had more than trebled.

Enver and the Germans

Djemal Pasha's opposition to the policies pursued by Enver Pasha
was, as we have seen, in part inspired by the belief that Enver had
fallen under the influence of the Germans. Ulrich Trumpener,
who has studied the issue in some detail, has concluded that little

24. Ibid., p. 262.

or no evidence can be advanced in support of this contention. Throughout the war, he suggests, German officers never exercised any command authority over the Ottoman army, except that specifically delegated to them by Enver, the deputy commander in chief; and they never decided grand strategy, except in consultation with the Ottoman high command; though with regard to the navy it has to be admitted that the Germans did exercise considerable freedom of action. Contrary to popular belief, particularly in the Entente countries, Liman von Sanders, the commander of the German military mission, played little or no part in the decision-making process that led to the entry of the Ottoman Empire into the First World War; and he failed to prevent Enver from taking the fatal decisions which led to the defeat of the Ottoman Third Army at Sarikamish, though he opposed the strategy adopted. In January 1915, when Said Halim and Wangenheim concluded a new Ottoman–German treaty, making Germany's commitment to the defence of the Ottoman Empire more specific, Enver made it clear that he would not formally renew an earlier commitment to allow the German military mission an 'effective influence' on the general direction of Ottoman military policy.[25]

Many other instances, exhibiting the determination of the Ottomans to assert their independence, may be adduced. In February 1915, when a row broke out with Enver over the deposition of the units defending the Dardanelles, Enver informed Wangenheim that Liman von Sanders's 'insubordinate attitude' made it impossible to work with him (Wangenheim believed Liman von Sanders to be on the verge of madness at the time). The kaiser should remind the chief of the military mission that he must obey the deputy Ottoman commander in chief 'unconditionally'. Later when Wangenheim and Bronsart von Schellendorff, Enver's chief of staff, conspired to have Liman von Sanders recalled, Enver, despite the difficulties he had dealing with von Sanders, intervened to prevent his recall. But in February 1916, when the Dardanelles campaign was at an end, he took a series of steps to reduce German influence; and in October 1917, when he signed a convention with the German government providing for the cooperation of the German and Ottoman armies in the post-war period, he insisted that a clause be inserted making it clear that all German officers appointed would be made subordinate to the Ottoman minister of war, and not to the head of the military mission. As Ulrich Trumpener remarked:

25. Trumpener, *Germany and the Ottoman Empire*, Chs 3 and 4.

Despite the phenomenal growth of the German military establishment in Turkey after 1915 (there were close to 25 000 officers and men belonging to the mission in the Ottoman Empire by the end of the First World War), the Ottoman armed forces remained exclusively an instrument of Turkish policy.[26]

The Ottomans were not concerned merely to secure independent control of their armed forces in the First World War. They sought also to preserve, and where possible restore, the independence, political, economic and social, of the empire. In September 1914, as we have seen, they unilaterally denounced the capitulations, a major source of discontent; and in January 1917, following lengthy negotiations, they obliged the Germans, who remained stubbornly opposed to the abolition of the capitulations, officially to acknowledge the new order. German and Austro-Hungarian attempts to secure complete control of the Ottoman economy, in particular the coal fields at Heraclea, the copper mines of Arghana Maden, the lead mines of Balia and Bulghar, the boracite mines of Bandirma and the oil fields of upper Mesopotamia, were effectively countered, mainly by Djavid, who had a shrewd understanding of the strengths and weaknesses of the German position; while proposals that all Entente enterprises be liquidated, put forward in 1917, were firmly rebuffed, though a number were sequestrated. Meanwhile Ottoman exports to Germany and Austria–Hungary, which were substantial, were paid for in cash, often at inflated prices, while imports of armaments, grain and other goods were bought on credit.[27]

In order to establish the principle of equality in their dealings with foreign powers, on which they set great store, the Ottomans succeeded in September 1916 in persuading the Germans to conclude a treaty, promising that neither Germany nor the Ottoman Empire would conclude a separate peace, without the consent of the other, as long as territory belonging to either remained in foreign hands. In any peace settlement each country would be rewarded in accordance with its 'sacrifices' and its 'efforts'.[28]

In one area of dispute alone did the Ottomans prove unsuccessful in their negotiations with the Germans. Attempts to have a number of nineteenth-century treaties, including the Paris Straits Convention of 1856 and the Treaty of Berlin of 1878, annulled

26. Ibid., pp. 104–5.
27. Ibid., Chs 8–10.
28. Ibid., p. 133.   •

failed. Though vigorously pursued by the Ottomans, on this issue the Germans stood firm, so that at the end of the First World War, substantial parts of the structure of Great Power control, imposed on the Ottoman Empire in the nineteenth century, remained (in principle at least) firmly in place.

The struggle for Transcaucasia

Following the collapse of the Russian army in the eastern provinces in the summer of 1917 and their later withdrawal from the area – provision was made in the Treaty of Brest-Litovsk of 3 March 1918 for the immediate evacuation of the Russian forces from the eastern provinces and the district of Batum, Ardahan and Kars, claimed by the Ottomans; though by then most of them had already withdrawn – the Ottomans, determined to secure control of the area, and if possible open a direct route to Turkestan, dispatched (in February 1918) an army into Transcaucasia. As a result in the following months the Ottomans found themselves engaged in an at times desperate struggle not only with Armenian and other elements opposed to their advance, but also with their German allies, who it soon transpired also harboured ambitions to secure political and economic control of the area. In the ensuing conflict German–Ottoman relations, already strained, reached a new low. Indeed, according to some accounts, they came very close to breaking point.

In the talks held by the Russians and the Germans prior to conclusion of the Armistice of Brest-Litovsk of 15 December 1917, no specific provision was made for the evacuation of Russian troops from the eastern provinces and Transcaucasia. It was merely agreed that, pending the conclusion of a peace treaty, the demarcation lines of the Russo-Turkish theatres of war in eastern Anatolia might be determined by agreements made on the spot by the local military commanders. In the event, it would seem, no such agreements were arrived at; but on 18 December 1917 a separate ceasefire agreement was concluded at Erzincan by an Ottoman delegation and representatives of a provisional government, known as the Komissariat, recently set up by Armenian, Georgian, Azerbaijani and Russian groups in Transcaucasia, pending the convocation of an all-Russian constituent assembly. But this agreement did not persuade the Ottomans to delay their advance. On 12 February 1918 an 'Army Group Caucasus', commanded by Vehib Pasha, began a general advance, supposedly with the object of protecting the Muslim inhabitants of the area, but in fact, according to Enver, with the object of securing Ottoman control of Transcaucasia, reaching the shores of the Caspian and establishing a direct connection with Turkestan.

Vehib Pasha's army group advanced rapidly. On 13 February 1918 it occupied Erzincan; on 14 April Batum; and on 24–25 April Kars, which surrendered following a fierce battle fought with Armenian elements located in the area. In May, following a short-lived armistice, and peace talks held in Batum with a delegation dispatched by the recently created independent Transcaucasian Federative Republic, the Ottoman forces occupied Alexandropol, a focal point on the rail lines running between Kars, Tiflis and Dzhulfa, a town on the Persian border. Then on 4 June the Ottomans, now supreme in the area, concluded a series of preliminary peace treaties with Georgian, Armenian and Azerbaijani delegations assembled in Batum. In the first of these treaties, concluded with the Georgians, the Ottomans secured control of the Georgian railways, restrictions on the size of the Georgian army and the withdrawal of a Georgian claim to two districts lying to the east of the Ottoman frontier of 1877, which the Ottomans intended themselves to claim in a final peace settlement. In the second, concluded with the Armenians, they secured control of the Armenian railways and a reduction in the territory of the newly created Armenian Republic. In the third, concluded with the Azerbaijanis, they acknowledged the independence of the newly created Azerbaijani Republic and promised it military and economic assistance.[29]

Further advances followed. In June a joint Ottoman–Azerbaijani task force, commanded by Enver's brother, Nuri, known as the Army of Islam, began an advance on Baku, where following a prolonged struggle for power between the Armenian and Muslim inhabitants of the city, control had passed to a council of people's commissars, mainly Bolshevik. But in July, when Nuri's task force arrived at the outskirts of the city and attempted to enter it, it proved unable to do so, for in the meantime the non-Bolshevik majority had not only ousted the Bolsheviks, but had also invited a British task force, commanded by Major-General L.C. Dunsterville, operating in northern Persia, to occupy the city and defend it against the Ottomans.

In their discussions with the Ottomans regarding the negotiation of the Treaty of Brest-Litovsk, the Germans had, after much hesitation, agreed to support Ottoman claims to the districts of Batum,

---

29. Ibid., Ch. 6; Fischer, *Germany's Aims in the First World War*, pp. 550–62.

Kars and Ardahan, lost to the Ottoman Empire in 1878. But they had no intention of allowing their allies to seize control of the whole area, which they wished to secure for themselves. Control of some kind of Transcaucasian state, constructed with Georgia at its core, would the Germans believed enable Germany not only to exploit the abundant economic resources of the area (minerals, cotton, oil), but also to build a bridge for the export of German power and influence to Persia and Central Asia. In these circumstances it is scarcely surprising that the advance of the Ottoman forces in Transcaucasia should have caused consternation in Berlin, as indeed did the intervention of the British. Immediate action followed. In May 1918 Erich Ludendorff, quartermaster general of the German high command, ordered Hans von Seeckt, recently appointed Enver's chief of staff, to use his influence with Enver to persuade him to halt the advance of the Army of Islam beyond the agreed line: the Ottomans should be instructed to employ all their available forces in the defence of their national territories, in particular Mesopotamia. At the same time a number of provisional treaties were concluded with the Georgians, according Germany extensive military and economic rights in Georgia; and in June several German infantry battalions, together with artillery units and technical staff, were dispatched to the new state from the Crimea. Moreover, on 8 June Ludendorff informed Enver Pasha of his country's unwillingness to acknowledge the treaties recently concluded by the Ottomans with the Transcaucasian states, 'without reference to Germany, Austria or Bulgaria'.[30] Were the Ottomans to persist in the pursuit of the policy they had adopted, in contravention of the treaties concluded at Brest-Litovsk, then further cooperation would become impossible. And on 4 August he ordered Seeckt to inform Enver that if the Ottoman advance on Baku were not at once halted, and the troops withdrawn to their original positions, then he would feel obliged to recommend the recall of all German officers attached to the Ottoman high command. But Ludendorff's threats proved ineffective. The Ottoman advance continued, while Enver made it clear on several occasions that were the Germans to continue in their opposition to the policy he had adopted, he would resign, a development the Germans, despite all their doubts, remained unwilling to risk.

Ludendorff's determination to prevent an Ottoman (or for that matter a British) occupation of Baku was not motivated merely by

---

30. Trumpener, *Germany and the Ottoman Empire*, p. 183.

local considerations. In a series of supplementary treaties negotiated with the Russians, initialled on 10 August but not yet signed,
the Germans had agreed not only to guarantee Russia continued
possession of Baku, but also to prevent a 'third power' (the Ottoman Empire) from occupying territories lying to the east of the
1877 Ottoman frontier. The Russians, for their part, had agreed to
guarantee the Germans substantial deliveries of oil from the Baku
oil fields. In the second half of August, therefore, Ludendorff, unable
to prevent an Ottoman advance on Baku, felt obliged to approach
the Russians, seeking their agreement to a joint German–Ottoman
occupation of the city; and when that approach proved unsuccessful – the Russians responded that while they would not oppose a
German occupation of Baku, they would on no account agree to an
Ottoman occupation of the city – he instructed Seeckt once again
to approach Enver, offering in return for an Ottoman withdrawal a
more generous aid programme and a greater share of Baku oil. At
the same time he took steps to assemble a German task force in the
Baku area. The approach to Enver proved once again unproduc-
tive; but eventually, in return for further assurances regarding Russian sovereignty in Baku and promises to secure the withdrawal of
the Ottoman army from the city, the Russians were persuaded to
give the Germans a free hand in the area.

Reports of the conclusion of the Russo-German agreement regarding Transcaucasia, which included a secret declaration confirming
that Germany would not assist the Ottomans in their Transcaucasian
venture, even if in the process the Ottomans were to come into
conflict with Russian forces, caused consternation in Istanbul. At
the same time it obliged the Ottomans to define the precise nature
of their claims in the Caucasus. In talks held in Berlin in September 1918 Talaat Pasha informed the Germans that the Ottoman
government would accept a settlement providing for the creation
of a buffer zone against Russia, made up of Azerbaijan, Armenia
and a somewhat reduced Georgia; the incorporation of Baku into
the Azerbaijani Republic; and the military organisation of the 14
million Muslim inhabitants of Turkistan, who might be employed
in the war against the British (and possibly also the Russians). In
return the Porte would agree to restrict its claims in Europe to the
return of that part of Thrace which Bulgaria had acquired in 1915.

The response of the Germans to the proposals put forward by
Talaat Pasha was not encouraging. Germany, Talaat was informed,
could not possibly recognise the independence of the Transcaucasian
republics, without first consulting the Russians. Nor would she agree

to a reduction in the size of Georgia, the incorporation of Baku into the Azerbaijani Republic and the military organisation of the Muslim peoples of Turkestan – though the Ottomans might of course take action there if they so wished, at their own expense. In the meantime they should withdraw their forces from the Baku area and leave it to the Germans to drive the British out of the city.

The firmness of the German response proved counter-productive. On 14 September the Army of Islam, now reinforced, supported by Azerbaijani auxiliaries, launched an assault on Baku, driving the British task force from the city. But it was to prove a fruitless victory. In August–September the Germans suffered a series of defeats on the western front, whilst an assault launched by the Allied expeditionary force from the Salonica bridgehead led first to the defeat of the forces of the Central Powers and their allies in the area and then to the collapse of Bulgaria and the disintegration of Austria–Hungary's southeastern front. Meanwhile, in Syria, an attack launched by the British on the Ottoman forces, now weakened not only by the formation of the *Yildirim* army group but also by the withdrawal of units dispatched by Enver to strengthen the Ottoman position in Transcaucasia, led to a complete collapse. As a result, towards the end of September Talaat, who had just returned to the Ottoman capital by way of Bulgaria, where he had been informed of the collapse on the Bulgarian front and the probable withdrawal of Bulgaria from the war, convened a meeting of the Ottoman cabinet and informed his colleagues that, in view of the isolation of the Ottoman Empire, which the fall of Bulgaria would inevitably entail, the Ottoman Empire must now consider withdrawing from the war. Shortly thereafter a proposal put forward by Talaat Pasha that the cabinet resign in order to make way for a new cabinet, more acceptable to the Entente Powers, was accepted, as was a proposal that the Ottoman Empire, acting in conjunction with the Germans and the Austrians, seek an immediate ceasefire; though Enver and Djemal both argued that the Ottoman Empire should fight on, in order to secure better terms in a final peace settlement. On 13 October, following prolonged negotiations regarding the appointment of a new cabinet, which Talaat and his colleagues insisted should contain two or three CUP ministers, Talaat resigned; and on 16 October the new cabinet, led by Izzet Pasha, a former military commander and minister of war (Talaat was successful in his efforts to secure the appointment of CUP ministers: Rauf was made minister of marine, Ali Fethi Bey minister of public works, Djavid Bey minister of finance, and Ismail Canbulat Bey minister of internal affairs; though Talaat was obliged to give an assurance that the CUP would not mount a second Bab-i Ali coup if it did not like the peace terms concluded with the Allies) confirmed that it was its intention to seek an immediate ceasefire and the convening of a peace conference. As Djavid Bey remarked in notes he made at the time, British forces were shortly expected to occupy Aleppo and Adana. They might also occupy Mosul and launch attacks on Istanbul and the Straits. On every front the forces of the Ottoman Empire were depleted: 'It is so bad you could invade the country with a handful of bandits.' There was nothing left to do but to seek a separate peace.[31]

It was commonly believed in Britain and France at the time that Enver Pasha's policy of expansion in Transcaucasia was inspired primarily by pan-Turkic motives. As a *Times* leader introducing three articles on pan-Turkism, possibly written by Arnold Toynbee, published in January 1918, put it, the 'pseudo-Turks of Salonica' looking for a new label to replace pan-Islamism had hit upon the idea of calling themselves Turanians. Armed with this new ideology, 'invented by a Salonica Jew', they intended to take advantage of the collapse of Russia to create a line of Turkish states stretching from Kazan to Chinese Turkestan.[32]

In all probability there was an element of pan-Turkic ideology in Enver Pasha's thinking. But his true motives in dispatching so powerful a force to Transcaucasia would appear to have been both more mundane and more interesting: to secure control of the abundant economic resources of the area, in particular oil; to secure control of trade routes linking Anatolia to Persia and the Crimea; to secure recognition of the borders of the Ottoman Empire in the east and if possible seize additional territory; to create a series of buffer states in the area, capable of preventing the advance of Russia; to secure control of the area as a preliminary to a campaign aimed at the recovery of Baghdad; and finally, in the later stages of the war, when defeat in the west appeared imminent, to build up a powerful concentration of forces in the east, in order to ensure that, following the probable defeat of the Central Powers and the loss of Istanbul and the Straits which such a defeat might entail, the Ottomans would be enabled to carry on the war against the Entente Powers from a secure position in the east. To this end, in the spring of 1918, Enver assembled substantial forces in the east, including

31. G. Dyer, 'The Turkish Armistice of 1918: I – The Turkish Decision for a Separate Peace, Autumn 1918', *Middle Eastern Studies*, Vol. 8, No. 2 (1972), p. 161.
32. *The Times*, 3, 5 and 7 January 1918.

several divisions, supplied and equipped by the Germans, recently returned from Romania and Galicia, where they had been used to prop up the Austro-Hungarian front; and in June he combined these forces, together with others stationed in Mesopotamia, to form an eastern armies group commanded by his uncle, Halil Pasha. By September 1918, it is said, this army incorporated more than half of the empire's forces – a concentration of resources which, as we have seen, may well have contributed to the collapse of Ottoman resistance on the Palestine front.[33]

The projection of pan-Turkism as an alternative to Ottomanism and pan-Islam was not unopposed. In June 1917 Halide Edib Hanim, a noted Ottoman woman writer and intellectual, published an article in *Vakit* which argued for a more realistic policy based on the national principle – an approach that was to acquire substantial support in the period of the war of independence:

> The forces of Pan-Turkism seek to induce us to interest ourselves in the welfare of all Mohammedan Turks, and of Turanians as well. Our young men now engaged in war are coming more and more to the conclusion that ideals do not mean anything in themselves, that they have a right to existence only as instruments to save this country. Many of its children today have the conviction that the only attractive fields of activity for them lie in their own home country, ruined and gutted as a consequence of many wars. This country has been declining in population, health, and standards of living. By the disaster of the present war the Ottoman Turks have been reduced to numbers so small that even their continued existence in our wide territories has become a matter of doubt. The occupation of the Caucasus has awakened ambitious aims. There the Turks are asking for our guidance. This is surely very charming for our national pride. We must not, forget, however, that we have not doctors enough for our provincial capitals, to say nothing of our smaller towns and villages. All our teachers would not suffice for the schools of Constantinople. Our engineers are insufficient to meet the proper needs of a single province. A mere handful of our young men will be saved from the firebrand of war. The country can be saved only if these young men remain here and decide to work uninterruptedly. Their existence will certainly be more difficult and less romantic than that of Jesus. To work in those lands outside might be very attractive, but it would be work done for an unrealizable Utopia. Races are mere theories, nations are realities. Our brothers are calling upon us because they think we may be of use to them. Do you really think they will decide

33. Dyer, 'The Turkish Armistice of 1918', pp. 148–9 and note 32.

to trust us with their destinies, if they learn the bitter truth as to the real Turkey, lying behind our small and vociferous set of visionaries? A Turkish brother who sees a village in Turkey or hears of it, cannot feel love and respect for the physician, teacher, engineer, or state official who abandons his own sick country; he will only have a feeling of distrust for him. We can give the most help to our brothers beyond our borders by concerning ourselves solely with our own home country. We should not deceive both ourselves and other people. Every Turk who carries into foreign countries his energy and capacity puts himself in the position of one robbing his own mother, his own home.[34]

34. Emin, *Turkey in the World War*, pp. 198–9. For an account of the rise of Anatolianism see F. Tachau, 'The Search for National Identity among the Turks', *Die Welt des Islams*, New Series, Vol. 8 (1962–3).

CHAPTER EIGHT

The Secret Treaties

The defeat of the Central Powers in the First World War made the destruction of the Ottoman Empire probable, but by no means inevitable. The empire might yet have survived more or less intact, had not the Entente Powers concluded in the course of the war a series of secret treaties and agreements based on the principle of partition. In making those treaties and agreements no specific decision was taken by the Entente Powers to destroy the empire, though a number of threats along those lines were made. Rather the forces leading to partition, generated more by the contingencies of war than by any pre-determined plan, became unstoppable, though by the end of the war the conditions which had inspired them had largely disappeared. Attempts of one kind or another were made to reconsider the issue, particularly in Britain; but they proved ineffective. By the end of the war the principle of partition, accompanied by a desire, not wholly hypocritical, to satisfy the national aspirations of the subject peoples, had become the bedrock of Allied policy.[1]

Constantinople and the Straits

The process by which the events of the First World War generated the secret treaties and agreements began in November 1914 when, following the entry of the Ottoman Empire into the war, the British, concerned lest the Russians withdraw forces from the western front to attempt a seizure of Constantinople (Istanbul) and the

---

1. W.W. Gottlieb, *Studies in Secret Diplomacy during the First World War* London: George Allen and Unwin, 1957; D. Fromkin, *A Peace to End All Peace* Harmondsworth: Penguin Books, 1989, Pt. 3; M.E. Yapp, *The Making of the Modern Near East* Harlow: Longman, 1987, Ch. 5.

Straits, sought Russian assurances that they would refrain from doing so. As Sir Edward Grey, the British foreign secretary, remarked
at the time, everything depended on the success of the Russian
offensive on the German front: nothing should be allowed to divert
the Russian forces from achieving their objectives in that area. Serges
Sazonov, the Russian foreign minister, acknowledged the validity of
Grey's argument, and promised that no forces would be diverted.
But at the same time he made it clear that Russia would expect to
receive from her western allies assurances regarding the complete
satisfaction of her claims with regard to the Straits. Those might
include the expulsion of the Turks from Europe, the free passage
of the Straits for Russian warships, and the acquisition by Russia of
territory on both sides of the Bosphorus, sufficient for her to guard
the entrance to the Black Sea in time of war. They might even
include the neutralisation and internationalisation of the Ottoman
capital and the annexation by Russia of the whole area.[2]

Initially the Russian claims regarding the Straits remained im-
precise, and British assurances regarding their satisfaction merely
verbal. But in March 1915, Sazonov, concerned regarding the possible consequences of the Anglo-French assault on the Dardanelles,
mounted in February, and the possible involvement of Greek forces
(the Russians particularly feared a Greek attempt to seize Constantinople) in the campaign, presented to the British and French ambassadors an aide-mémoire, demanding not only Russian possession
of the Straits but also the incorporation of Constantinople into the
Russian empire. The imperial government, Sazonov added, expected
from its allies a sympathetic response. In return Russia would be
pleased to accommodate whatever demands Britain and France
might choose to put forward regarding their *desiderata* in other
parts of the Ottoman Empire and elsewhere. Moreover, in conversations with the British and French ambassadors held shortly thereafter, he made it clear that were Britain and France to fail to support
Russia's 'national aspirations' in that area, then the consequences
might be incalculable – a threat which the British and French interpreted to mean a severing of relations with Russia's western allies
and the conclusion of a separate peace with Germany. Faced with
this dire prospect the British and French concluded that they had
no alternative but to respond positively to the Russian demands.
On 8 March, therefore, M. Paléologue, the French ambassador in

2. A.L. Macfie, *The Straits Question, 1908–36* Salonica: Institute for Balkan Studies,
1993, Ch. 2.

St Petersburg, informed Sazonov that Russia could 'rely fully on the good will of the Republic in the matter of the solution of the question of the Straits'; and on 10 March the British cabinet, at a meeting called to discuss the issue, agreed to accept the Russian claims in full, provided only that Britain and France be enabled also to realise their *desiderata* in the Ottoman Empire and elsewhere. These the Russians were informed might include the free passage of the Straits to the commerce of all nations; the establishment of Constantinople as a free port for goods in transit; the continued possession of the Holy Places in Muslim hands; and the acquisition by Britain of the neutral sphere in Persia; though a more precise definition of British *desiderata* would have to await a further consideration of the question.[3]

Not that the British, in particular, were necessarily disturbed by the Russian *démarche* regarding Constantinople and the Straits. On the contrary, they may well have welcomed it, for it was commonly believed at the time that only the promise of so rich a reward would serve to keep Russia in the war, fighting on the side of the Entente Powers. Indeed, it can be argued that the British had this fact in mind when they raised the issue in the first place. As Grey later explained to the Dardanelles Commission (a commission appointed to look into the question of Allied failures in the Dardanelles campaign), he had always contemplated, from the beginning of the war, that an arrangement would have to be made with Russia over the question of Constantinople and the Straits:

> Being in a war of this character, with these tremendous issues, with German efforts being made to separate the Allies, and with our record of having persistently fought Russia all over the world to prevent her getting an open port, and with the horrible situation of having Russia closed all through the winter, which demonstrated the need for an open port somewhere, I have always been of the opinion that we must make it clear to Russia from the very beginning that we were not going to oppose her with regard to Constantinople, and we would make an agreement with her.[4]

Or as King George V put it, in a remark dropped, apparently impromptu, into a conversation held with the Russian ambassador on 10 November 1914: 'In regard to Constantinople, it is clear that it must be yours.'[5]

3. Ibid., pp. 54–66.
4. Ibid., pp. 54–5.
5. Ibid., p. 55.

The Sykes–Picot Agreement and the McMahon Correspondence

The conclusion of the March Agreement, as it became known, forced the western Entente Powers to undertake a radical reevaluation of their *desiderata* regarding the Near and Middle East. The French rapidly concluded that in return for their recognition of a Russian acquisition of Constantinople and the Straits they would expect to secure possession of Syria, Palestine and Cilicia. The British, on the other hand, concluded that in order to protect their empire in Asia against the threat posed by the advance of Russia, now likely to be exacerbated by Russian possession of Constantinople and the Straits (or for that matter the threat posed by the advance of any other of the Great Powers), it would be necessary to establish a defensive position based on the Arab world. In order to secure that, it would be necessary to create a strategic line of defence, supported if possible by a railway, stretching from the area of the Persian Gulf (Baghdad perhaps, or Basra) to the Mediterranean (Alexandretta). As Lord Kitchener, the British secretary of state for war explained in a memorandum in March 1915:

> The area which it is here proposed to incorporate undoubtedly offers a prolonged flank to Russia for possible attack from the side of Armenia and Kurdistan, and to this extent it produces an unsatisfactory strategical situation. But it seems to be a choice of evils. It is a question of gaining definite control over the great line of communications to India, although that line is to some extent exposed to risk of being severed in time of war, or to leave that line permanently to another Great Power or Great Powers, which would thus dominate the Mediterranean terminus. It should obviously be no part of our programme to create a frontier coterminous with that of Russia; but it is to be hoped that sufficient remains of the Ottoman Empire will be left to ensure a Turkish or Armenian buffer State stretching from Anatolia to the Persian border. But, even a frontier coterminous with Russia, with all its grave drawbacks, would be preferable to a Franco-Russian domination of the line from the Gulf of Iskanderun to the Persian Gulf.[6]

Unfortunately, however, France had already staked out a claim to Syria and Palestine, a claim she was unlikely to give up. An interdepartmental committee, chaired by Sir Maurice de Bunsen, set

6. Ibid., p. 71.

up to consider British *desiderata* in Turkey in Asia in April 1915, accordingly suggested that Britain might construct a strategic line of defence and a railway from the Gulf, not to Alexandretta (Iskanderun) as hitherto envisaged, but to Haifa in Palestine. Against France, established in Syria and Cilicia, or against France and Russia (a combination which had caused the British acute anxiety in the 1880s and 1890s) such a line would in all probability be indefensible. But in the event of a conflict arising between Russia and Britain, with France remaining neutral, the line would not only be defensible but it would also have the added advantage of placing a buffer of French territory between Britain and Russia in the area.[7]

It should not be assumed that the British were at that stage necessarily committed to a policy of partition. The de Bunsen committee considered four possible solutions to the problem of the Ottoman Empire: (1) a policy of outright partition, involving the survival of only a small Ottoman state in Anatolia; (2) the preservation of the Ottoman Empire, subject to the exercise of Great Power control in zones of political and commercial influence; (3) the preservation of the Ottoman Empire in Asia as an independent state; (4) the creation of a decentralised Ottoman state in Asia, reconstructed along federal lines. Such a federal state might include five semi-autonomous units: Syria, Palestine, Armenia, Anatolia and Jazirah–Iraq. Of the four possible solutions considered the de Bunsen committee finally opted for the fourth, which they believed would best meet the needs of British imperial defence and the communities involved.[8] But by then the momentum leading to partition, all too evident in the de Bunsen analysis of the problem, had become unstoppable. In April 1915 the Italians, impressed by the ferocity of the Allied assault on the Dardanelles, and determined not to be left out should a partition of the Ottoman Empire occur, concluded with the Entente Powers the Treaty of London which promised that in the event of a total or partial partition of Turkey in Asia Italy, whose interest in the balance of power in the Mediterranean was recognised, should receive an 'equitable share of the Mediterranean region adjoining the province of Antalya'.[9] In July Sir Henry McMahon, the British high commissioner in Egypt, with

7. A.S. Klieman, 'Britain's War Aims in the Middle East in 1915', *Journal of Contemporary History*, Vol. 3, No. 3 (1968); Public Record Office, London, CAB 42/3/12 Asiatic Turkey, Report of a Committee.

8. Klieman, 'Britain's War Aims in the Middle East in 1915', p. 246.

9. Macfie, *Straits Question*, p. 82; Gottlieb, *Studies in Secret Diplomacy during the First World War*, Pt. 2.

the backing of a group of British soldiers and officials serving in Egypt, subsequently united in the Arab Bureau, opened negotiations with Sherif Husein, the emir of Mecca. These negotiations would, it was hoped, give rise in due course to a large-scale Arab revolt, an event almost certain to lead to a partition of the Ottoman Empire.[10] Finally in December 1915 Sir Mark Sykes, an assistant secretary in the British war cabinet, member of the de Bunsen committee and enthusiastic convert to the principle of partition, concluded with François Georges Picot, a French diplomat, an agreement, later known as the Sykes–Picot Agreement, delimiting the territories in which, in the event of a victorious outcome to the war and a Russian occupation of Constantinople and the Straits, Britain and France might exercise direct and indirect influence and control. In the Baghdad–Basra region of lower Iraq, Britain, it was agreed, might exercise direct control; in the Syrian littoral, France. In the remainder of the Fertile Crescent and the Syrian desert, Britain might exercise indirect control in the south, France in the north. Britain would in addition obtain control of a small enclave on the Palestinian coast, including Haifa and Acra, possible termini of a railway linking the Persian Gulf area and the Mediterranean. The rest of Palestine might be placed under an international administration. In March 1916, in order to obtain Russian consent to this scheme Sykes and Picot travelled to St Petersburg. There they concluded an agreement with Sazonov allowing Britain and France a free hand to the south of a line running from Adana to Amadia. In return Russia would acquire the *vilayets* of Van, Bitlis, Trabzon and Erzerum – acquisitions which would in due course secure for her effective control over the greater part of Anatolia.[11]

The agreement eventually concluded by Sir Henry McMahon and Sherif Husein of Mecca in October 1915 was, as we have seen, in part the outcome of contacts made by Kitchener, the British high commissioner, with Sherif Husein in September 1914, shortly before the entry of the Ottoman Empire into the First World War. Concerned to secure British control of the Muslim Holy Places and the protection of the annual pilgrimage – loss of access to Mecca and Medina might cause discontent among the king-emperor's

10. Yapp, *Making of the Modern Near East*, pp. 278–81; E. Kedourie, *England and the Middle East: The Destruction of the Ottoman Empire, 1914–1921* Brighton: Harvester Press, 1956; and *In the Anglo-Arab Labyrinth: The McMahon–Husayn Correspondence and its Interpreters, 1914–1939* Cambridge: Cambridge University Press, 1976.

11. Yapp, *Making of the Modern Near East*, pp. 277–8; M.S. Anderson, *The Great Powers and the Near East, 1774–1923* London: Edward Arnold, pp. 162–4.

Muslim subjects – in any war which might break out involving the Ottoman Empire, Kitchener then enquired of the sherif of Mecca whether in the event of the Ottoman Empire entering the war on the side of the Central Powers, the Hedjaz would be for or against Britain. At the same time he held out the prospect that Husein, a descendant of the Prophet, might assume the title of caliph, a potent symbol of Muslim authority.

Offers of British patronage and support had an undoubted appeal to Husein; but at that time he remained uncertain how to proceed. It was only later, in the summer of 1915 that, fearful that the Ottomans intended to take action against him, he decided to move. As a result, in July 1915–March 1916 he and McMahon, in a series of secret communications later known as the McMahon Correspondence, arrived at an agreement, heavily qualified, regarding the terms on which Husein and his followers would launch an insurrection – terms which, however obscure and convoluted, laid the foundations of the so-called Arab Revolt, yet another nail in the coffin of the Ottoman Empire.

According to the terms of the agreement set out in the McMahon Correspondence, following the outbreak of an Arab uprising Britain would, except in certain areas specifically mentioned, assist the Arab peoples in whatever efforts they might make to secure their independence in the territories lying between the Persian Gulf, the Indian Ocean, the Red Sea, the Mediterranean and a line running from Adana in the west to the Persian frontier in the east. At the same time she would support the creation of an Arab caliphate: the 'resumption of the Caliphate by an Arab of the true race'.[12] The areas specifically excepted by McMahon in the correspondence included the districts of Mersin and Alexandretta, parts of Syria lying to the west of the districts of Damascus, Hama, Homs and Aleppo, the *vilayets* of Baghdad and Basra, where Britain might be expected to make special administrative arrangements to safeguard her economic interests in the area, Aden and any Arab sheikdoms already in treaty relations with Britain. British assurances of support would, moreover, apply only to territories lying within frontiers 'wherein Great Britain is free to act without detriment to the interests of her ally, France'.[13]

The need to define the frontiers of a zone of French influence and control, combined with the need to respond to the probable acquisition by Russia of Constantinople and the Straits, led directly

12. Ibid., pp. 160–2; P.M. Holt, *Egypt and the Fertile Crescent, 1516–1922* Harlow: Longman, 1966, pp. 264–9.
13. Ibid., p. 266.

to the negotiation of the Sykes–Picot Agreement. In October 1915, Grey invited the French to enter into negotiations regarding the nature and extent of French claims in Syria. Initially, responsibility for the negotiations was placed in the hands of a team of foreign office, India office and war office officials, led by Sir Arthur Nicolson, permanent under-secretary at the foreign office. But when deadlock was reached, the task of negotiating an agreement was passed to Sykes.

In the talks, held in November–December, Sykes, a protégé of Kitchener, who wished to see French influence in the Near and Middle East reduced, set out as far as possible to reduce the extent of the proposed sphere of French influence and control in Syria. In particular, he set out to secure British control of Palestine and the Sinai desert, now seen as both a possible buffer zone, protecting Egypt and the Suez Canal, and the possible terminus of a railway running from the Persian Gulf area to the Mediterranean. François Picot, a keen supporter of the colonialist faction at the Quai d'Orsay and the 'Syrian Party' in French politics, on the other hand, was determined to secure French control, direct or indirect, not only of Syria but also of Palestine (for the French, as for the Ottomans, Palestine was effectively part of Syria). True, France would in other circumstances have preferred to preserve the Ottoman Empire, but partition was now inevitable. France must, therefore, realise her 'mission historique', though in view of the potential expense involved in policing the interior she might seek direct control only of the Lebanon and the Syrian littoral.[14] In the ensuing negotiations, therefore, Sykes and Picot had little or no difficulty in reaching agreement regarding the proposed British and French spheres of direct and indirect influence and control in the Lebanon and northern Syria. Indeed, to a degree the British welcomed the creation of a sphere of indirect French influence in the interior, stretching as far as Mosul, as it was believed that this would act as a barrier against the advance of Russia in the area. But on the issue of Palestine no such easy compromise was available. As a result, in the final text it was agreed that, with the exception of a small enclave on the coast incorporating Haifa and Acre, Palestine would be made the subject of an international administration, the precise nature of which would be determined only after consultation with Russia, Britain and France's other allies and the sherif of Mecca. In the spheres of indirect influence allotted to France and Britain in the

14. Fromkin, *A Peace to End All Peace*, p. 190.

interior, an independent Arab state or confederation of states might be created. The agreement reached was to come into effect only after the proclamation of an Arab revolt.[15]

The Balfour Declaration

Plans for the partition of the Ottoman Empire did not end with the conclusion of the Sykes–Picot Agreement. In 1917 at a critical moment in the war (Russia was on the point of collapse and the German submarine campaign in the Atlantic at its height), the British, hopeful that the promotion of the Zionist cause would win them the support of influential Jewish circles in Russia and America, issued, with French and American support, the so-called Balfour Declaration (Arthur Balfour was British foreign secretary at the time). This declaration promised British support for the establishment in Palestine of a national home for the Jewish people (though nothing should be done which might be considered prejudicial to the civil and religious rights of the non-Jewish communities living there) – a promise almost certain, in the event of an Allied victory, to lead to the creation of a Jewish state in Palestine.

From the British point of view the creation of a vigorous Jewish community or state in Palestine offered several advantages: it might make the need for an international administration there superfluous; it might create something like a 'buffer state' on the eastward approaches to Egypt and the Suez Canal; and in due course it might enable the British to put in place the last segment of the land bridge they intended to construct, linking Egypt and India.[16]

Unravelling of the secret treaties and agreements

No sooner had the Entente Powers concluded their elaborate and in parts inconsistent series of secret treaties and agreements than the treaties and agreements began to unravel. In April 1917 the new Russian cabinet, appointed following the March revolution, issued a declaration denouncing the policies of conquest and annexation adopted by the previous regime. In November the

15. Ibid., pp. 190–9.
16. L. Stein, *The Balfour Declaration* London: Valentine Mitchell, 1961; E. Kedourie, 'Sir Mark Sykes and Palestine, 1915–16', in *Arabic Political Memoirs and Other Studies* London: Frank Cass, 1974.

Bolsheviks, following their seizure of power, issued a decree of peace, formally renouncing Russia's claims to Constantinople and the Straits, and in December they issued a 'Proclamation to the Muslim Workers of Russia and the East', giving notice that the secret treaties concerning the seizure of Constantinople, entered into by the deposed tsar, must now be considered null and void. Henceforth, they declared, Constantinople must remain in the hands of the Muslims. In January 1918, seeking to diminish the impact of the Balfour Declaration on Arab opinion, the British, in the so-called Hogarth Message, gave assurances regarding the creation of some kind of special regime for the Muslim, Christian and Jewish Holy Places in Palestine.[17] Meanwhile President Woodrow Wilson, seeking to discover a set of principles that might form the foundation of a peace settlement, published his so-called Fourteen Points, point 12 of which suggested that the Turkish portions of the Ottoman Empire should be 'assured a secure sovereignty', while the other nationalities living under Ottoman rule 'should be assured an undoubted security of life and an absolutely unmolested opportunity of autonomous development',[18] assurances which encouraged the Greek and Armenian minorities of the empire to press claims, already established, to independence (the British had made vague promises regarding a possible Greek acquisition of western Anatolia in 1915). As for the Dardanelles, they should be permanently opened as a free passage to the ships of commerce of all nations under international guarantees.

Other qualifications of the secret treaties and agreements followed. In June 1918 Sir Reginald Wingate, the newly appointed high commissioner of Egypt, informed Husein, who had expressed concern regarding the nature of the Sykes–Picot Agreement, earlier made public by the Bolsheviks (and published in the *Manchester Guardian*), that the published documents 'did not constitute an actually concluded agreement', and that the 'subsequent outbreak and striking success of the Arab Revolt, as well as the withdrawal of Russia, had long ago created an altogether different situation'.[19] Shortly thereafter the British, in response to questions posed by seven leading Syrians living in Egypt, declared in a document known as the Declaration to the Seven that in territories which had been free and independent before the outbreak of the war, and in those liberated from Turkish rule by the actions of the Arabs themselves,

17. Holt, *Egypt and the Fertile Crescent*, p. 275.
18. A.L. Macfie, *The Eastern Question* Harlow: Longman, 1989, Doc. 27.
19. Holt, *Egypt and the Fertile Crescent*, p. 275.

the British would recognise the complete and sovereign independence of the Arabs. In the territories liberated from Turkish rule by the actions of Allied armies, on the other hand, they would seek to create governments based on the 'principle of the consent of the governed', while in territories still under Turkish rule they expected that the oppressed peoples would 'obtain their freedom and independence'.[20]

None of these statements and declarations called in question the essential principle of partition on which the secret treaties and agreements were based. But they did indicate both a shift in the balance of power in the Near and Middle East in favour of the western Entente Powers, and a willingness on the part of those powers, now joined by America, to consider the possibility of self-determination. In particular, the withdrawal of Russia from the field, combined with the military predominance of Britain in the Near and Middle East had made Britain the principal player in the area. As a result she had been enabled to promote concepts of freedom and self-determination, which many British officials believed would facilitate her task of building an Arab, and perhaps even a Turkish and Armenian bulwark against the advance of Russia (or for that matter any other of the Great Powers) in the region. Not that the significance of these developments should be exaggerated. In Iraq the Indian government and its agents, in particular Arnold Wilson, appointed civil commissioner in 1918, remained fully committed to the creation of a colonial regime. In Syria the French, who saw support for the principle of self-determination as the product of an Anglo-American conspiracy designed to deprive them of their rights there, refused to reconsider their approach. As for the Italians, whose rights established in the Treaty of London had been confirmed in a treaty concluded at St Jean de Maurienne in 1917, they remained firm in their determination to secure a fair share of any spoils which might be handed out following a partition of the Ottoman Empire; while the Greek and Armenian peoples of the Ottoman Empire continued to assert claims, already established, to independence or, in the case of the Greeks of western Anatolia, union with Greece. Paradoxically then in the closing months of the war the western Entente Powers remained committed to policies based on the principle of partition, enshrined in the Constantinople Agreement of March 1915, despite the fact that the original Russian claim to possession of the Ottoman capital and the Turkish Straits,

20. Ibid., pp. 276–7.

the origin and cause of that agreement and the policies to which it had given rise, had long since been abandoned. Great Power policy with regard to the Ottoman Empire, in other words, once shaped by considerations of long-term strategic interest, was now being driven merely by events.[21]

21. Macfie, *Straits Question*, pp. 81–5.

CHAPTER NINE

The Armistice of Mudros

Issues concerning the ultimate fate of the Ottoman Empire and its possible partition were not directly considered by either the victorous Entente Powers or the Ottomans in the negotiations leading up to the conclusion of the Armistice of Mudros of 30 October 1918. Nevertheless, the terms finally agreed on by the Allied and Ottoman delegations in the armistice negotiations, particularly those concerning the right of the Allies to occupy various parts of the empire, remain significant, for they helped shape the situation that prevailed in the post-war period, when, following the Greek occupation of Izmir in May 1919, the Turkish nationalists led by Mustafa Kemal (Atatürk) launched a war of independence which culminated in the abolition of the sultanate and the creation of a republic.

The terms imposed on the Ottoman Empire by the victorious Entente Powers in the Mudros armistice were undoubtedly severe. The Straits were to be opened to the ships of war and ships of commerce of the Entente Powers, and the forts defending the entrances to the Bosphorus and the Dardanelles occupied by Allied (but not by Greek or Italian) troops. The Ottoman army was to be demobilised, with the exception of such troops as might be required for the surveillance of frontiers and the preservation of internal order. Strategic points in the empire might, in the event of a situation arising which threatened Allied security, be occupied. All wireless, telegraph and cable stations would be placed under Allied control. Ottoman forces in northwestern Persia would be withdrawn behind the pre-war frontier, as would those in Transcaucasia, if after further consideration of the issue the Allies so decided. Garrisons stationed in the Arab provinces would be surrendered to the nearest Allied commander. All equipment, arms and ammunition, except that permitted by the Allies, would be surrendered. Finally, in the event of disorder arising in the Armenian provinces, the Allies might dispatch troops to restore order there.[1]

The course of events leading up to the conclusion of the Mudros Armistice appear in retrospect clear enough. Once made aware, in the autumn of 1918, of the true nature of the situation prevailing on the European and Asiatic fronts – Enver had been at great pains to keep his colleagues ignorant of the real position – the Ottoman government acted with alacrity. On 5 October, acting in conjunction with the German and Austrian governments, they instructed their chargé d'affaires in Madrid to request the Spanish foreign minister (whose government was looking after the interests of the Ottoman Empire in America), to pass on a note, essentially the same as notes dispatched about the same time by the German and Austrian foreign ministers, to the American secretary of state, proposing an immediate ceasefire and the convening of a peace conference on the basis of President Woodrow Wilson's Fourteen Points. And when no response was forthcoming – for some reason delivery of the Ottoman note was delayed – on or about 14 October they invited M. Marcel Savoie, a French bank director living in Istanbul, to travel to Sofia, the capital of Bulgaria, where it was hoped he would succeed in making contact with General Franchet d'Espèrey, the commander of the Entente forces in the area. But once again the Ottoman initiative proved abortive, as did other initiatives undertaken privately by the sultan, Mehmed VI Vahideddin, who had succeeded to the Ottoman throne in July 1918, and Rhami Bey, the pro-Entente vali of Aydin. Only in the second half of October, when General Charles Townshend, the commander of the British forces captured at Kut al-Amara, held prisoner on Büyükada, an island near Istanbul, was dispatched by the Ottomans to meet Admiral Calthorpe, the commander-in-chief of the British Mediterranean Fleet, anchored off Mudros, on the island of Lemnos, was contact made and an offer to open talks delivered. A swift Allied response followed. As a result, on 26 October an Ottoman delegation led by Rauf Bey, the newly appointed minister of marine, arrived in Mudros to open negotiations with a British delegation led by Admiral Calthorpe.[2]

Neither of the private initiatives undertaken by the sultan and Rhami Bey had any chance of eliciting a favourable response.

1. J.C. Hurewitz, *Diplomacy in the Near and Middle East: A Documentary Record* Princeton: D. Van Nostrand, Vol. 2, No. 18, 1956.
2. G. Dyer, 'The Turkish Armistice of 1918: I – The Turkish Decision for a Separate Peace, Autumn 1918', *Middle Eastern Studies*, Vol. 8, No. 2 (1972).

Mehmed VI Vahideddin's proposals, which were passed on to Sir Horace Rumbold, the British minister in Berne, by Boghos Nubar Pasha's agent in Switzerland, on 4 October, proved quite unrealistic, for they presupposed a willingness on the part of the British and their allies to preserve the Ottoman Empire, more or less intact; while Rhami Bey's proposals, which were passed on, at the instigation it would seem of Talaat Pasha (who wished to investigate the possibility that a new Ottoman government, effectively appointed by the CUP, might negotiate a satisfactory peace settlement) to Rear-Admiral Seymour, the commander of a British squadron sailing in the Aegean, by Karabiber, the Levantine Greek agent of Rhami Bey, proved irrelevant, for their proposers lacked all accreditation. Nevertheless, they remain of interest, for it may be supposed that they reflected the ideas and attitudes circulating in the Ottoman capital at the time. In the proposals put to Sir Horace Rumbold in Berne, the sultan suggested that, in return for certain assurances regarding the survival of the Ottoman dynasty, the sultan might agree to the granting of autonomy to Syria, Palestine, Mesopotamia and the Hedjaz, subject to the preservation of Ottoman sovereignty there; the constitutional reform of the remaining provinces of the empire, to be carried out by the British; the restoration of the Turco-Bulgarian border of 1912; and the retrocession of a number of Aegean islands, including Mitylene and Chios. In order to secure the proposed settlement British forces, acting in conjunction with a force of some 300–500 000 men recruited by the British from Ottoman deserters and prisoners of war held in Egypt, might march on Istanbul and secure the annihilation of the CUP. Following the conclusion of a satisfactory peace settlement the Ottoman Empire would form a permanent alliance with Great Britain. Rhami Bey's proposals, on the other hand, which involved a plan to eliminate German influence in Istanbul, included the preservation of Ottoman sovereignty in Istanbul and the Straits, subject to guarantees regarding the freedom of passage of the Straits for the ships of all nations; autonomy for Arabia, Mesopotamia, Syria and Armenia, subject to the preservation of Ottoman sovereignty; the retention of the 1914 frontier with Bulgaria; and the securing of Entente guarantees for the paper money of the Ottoman Empire, following a German withdrawal.

Little is known about the thinking that lay behind the proposals put forward by Sultan Mehmed VI Vahideddin and Rhami Bey, but it is evident that both expected that the British and their allies would be willing to conclude a peace treaty securing the survival of the Ottoman Empire, albeit in a decentralised form. Where they differed from one another is their attitude to the future of the CUP, for where Rhami Bey clearly expected the committee, and its control of the Ottoman government, however disguised, to continue, Sultan Mehmed VI Vahideddin looked for the complete extinction of the organisation.

General Townshend, who had in fact volunteered for the task of communicating the Ottoman offer of talks to the Allies, set out on his mission on 18 October, accompanied by Rhami Bey, the pro-Entente vali of Izmir. Travelling secretly, by steamer to Bandirma, private train to Izmir, and government tug to the islands (everyone in the area appears to have known about his mission), he arrived at Mitylene on 20 October, whence after telegraphing a report regarding the Ottoman proposal to London, he departed for Mudros. Following his arrival Calthorpe, who had in the meantime received authorisation from London to open negotiations, responded immediately to the Ottoman proposal, inviting the Ottoman government to send a delegation. The delegation, headed by Rauf Bey, arrived on 26 October.[3]

Rauf's instructions regarding the conclusion of an armistice, drawn up by the Ottoman ministries of war and foreign affairs prior to his departure, were both realistic and demanding. The Ottoman delegation, Rauf was instructed, should seek to secure Allied recognition of the battle fronts existing at the cessation of hostilities. Within those 'borders' Ottoman sovereignty should as far as possible be preserved. No Allied intervention in the government of the country should be permitted, no Allied occupation allowed; though with regard to the Straits defences and the security of the Black Sea region certain rights of inspection might be permitted. In return for these concessions the Ottomans would offer the opening of the Straits (subject to certain restrictions on the duration of passage and an exclusion of all Greek shipping) and the demobilisation of the Ottoman armed forces, with the exception of such forces as might be required to preserve internal security.[4]

Calthorpe's instructions, drawn up by the Allies early in October, when the prospect of an Ottoman approach appeared imminent, seemed if anything even more demanding; though they were in fact by no means as demanding as they appeared. First and foremost, Calthorpe was informed, he should seek to secure the opening

3. Ibid.
4. Ibid., pp. 168–9.

of the Straits to Allied shipping and access to the Black Sea; information regarding the position of minefields, torpedo tubes and other obstructions to shipping in Turkish waters; information regarding the location of mines in the Black Sea; and the release of Allied prisoners of war and other interned persons. Beyond that he might seek to secure the immediate demobilisation of the Ottoman armed forces, except for such troops as might be required for the surveillance of frontiers and the preservation of internal order; surrender of all war vessels in Turkish waters; the occupation by Allied troops of important strategic points; the free use by Allied shipping of all Turkish ports and anchorages; the use of Istanbul as a naval base; Allied occupation of the Taurus tunnel system; the withdrawal of the Turkish forces in northwestern Persia and Transcaucasia behind the pre-war Ottoman frontier; the surrender of the Ottoman garrisons in the Arab provinces; Allied control of the Ottoman railways; and Allied control of all wireless, telegraph and cable stations. Calthorpe, in other words, should seek to conclude an armistice which would enable the Allies to exercise something approaching complete control of what remained of the Ottoman Empire; but at the very least he should secure the opening of the Straits to the ships of war and ships of commerce of the Entente Powers, the essential Allied demand.[5] As the British war cabinet remarked:

> The first four conditions [those concerning the opening of the Straits] are of such paramount importance and if completely carried out will so inevitably make us master of the situation, that we do not wish to jeopardise obtaining them, and obtaining them quickly, by insisting unduly on all or any of the rest, or indeed by raising any particular one of the remaining twenty if you think it might endanger your success in getting the vital four at once.[6]

The emphasis laid by the Allies on the importance of securing the opening of the Straits to Allied shipping – an emphasis which, had the Ottoman delegation but known of it, might have considerably strengthened their hand in the coming negotiations – was mainly inspired by the conviction, widely held at the time, that control of the Straits would secure not only control of the Ottoman capital but also control of the interior. Not that concern regarding

5. British Public Records Office, ADM 116/1823, Conditions of an Armistice with Turkey arranged in order of importance.
6. G. Dyer, 'The Turkish Armistice of 1918: II – A Lost Opportunity: The Armistice Negotiations of Moudros', *Middle Eastern Studies*, Vol. 8, No. 3 (1972), p. 323.

the position of the Ottoman Empire was the only factor inspiring Allied policy with regard to the Ottoman Empire. Studies carried out by the British and French high commands in July–September 1918, had suggested that, despite recent successes, victory on the western front remained for the moment a remote possibility. Indeed, there was not even any certainty that victory would be achieved in 1919. It was therefore essential that the Allies secure the immediate withdrawal of the Ottoman Empire from the war. An immediate Ottoman withdrawal, and the opening of the Straits which that would entail, would enable the Entente Powers not only to open a new front in the Balkans but also to dispatch some half a million imperial troops, mainly Indian, to the western front. True, the defeat of the Ottoman Empire was now inevitable; but it would take British forces, advancing from Syria and Mesopotamia, many months to arrive at the Straits, while Allied forces, commanded by General Milne, advancing on Istanbul from the Macedonian front, might take almost as long. From the Allied point of view, therefore, the conclusion of an armistice securing the immediate withdrawal of the Ottoman Empire from the war and the opening of the Straits, was a matter of the utmost urgency. It was for this reason that, on 22 October, Calthorpe was instructed by the British war cabinet to proceed with the negotiation of an armistice on the basis of the proposed terms.[7]

Rauf of course had no knowledge of the urgency of the Allied position. On the contrary, he remained convinced throughout the negotiations that complete Allied victory, involving the capture of Istanbul, was imminent, and that the Ottomans had no choice but to accept the Allied armistice terms, more or less as presented. Nevertheless he presented as good a case as he could manage. Prior to the opening of the negotiations, which took place on board HMS Agamemnon, commencing on the morning of 27 October, Rauf, in a private conversation with Calthorpe, explained that the Ottoman Empire had entered the war because of Russia. Now that Russia was defeated it was possible for the Empire to revert to its traditional nineteenth-century role of acting, in cooperation with the British, as a buffer against the advance of Russia in the area. It should not, therefore, be difficult for them to reach agreement; but if the terms offered were too severe, then the Ottomans would refuse to sign and would fight to the bitter end. No one could predict what the outcome of such a struggle would be, but surely it

---

7. Ibid., pp. 313–25.

would not be to the Entente's advantage. An invasion of Thrace would in all probability spark off a rising among the minorities of Istanbul, which would be drowned in blood.[8]

Rauf's apparent willingness to cooperate with the British delegation in their search for a satisfactory set of armistice terms, albeit accompanied by a veiled threat, was no doubt welcomed by Calthorpe; but it was not in itself sufficient to resolve the contradictions inherent in the British and Ottoman positions. Those became evident, when, following the formal opening of talks, Calthorpe in his opening statement explained that the Entente Powers would insist on Ottoman acceptance of the first four clauses of the draft armistice; though some modification of the other clauses might be permitted. For as Rauf pointed out in his response, an Allied occupation of the Dardanelles forts, the principal Allied demand, would constitute an occupation of Ottoman territory, and that concession he was not authorised to make. In the ensuing discussions various solutions to this problem were offered by the Ottoman delegation, including the dismantling of the forts without an Allied occupation, their supervision by a mixed commission, and the appointment of Allied control officers to ensure that their guns would not be turned against an Allied fleet; but all to no avail. Calthorpe continued to insist on occupation: no British fleet, he declared, dare venture into the Black Sea without first securing control of the Straits defences. Otherwise, in the event of a change in government in Istanbul, it might find itself cut off in the Black Sea or the Sea of Marmara, unable to return. In the end, unable to resolve the disagreement, Rauf was obliged to offer a concession. A British and French occupation of the Dardanelles forts might be acceptable, he suggested, but on no account would the Ottomans agree to the participation of Greek or Italian forces. 'I tell you frankly,' he said, 'the English can come and secure the guns. That will not make much effect. It is sad to be beaten but it will end there. But if the Greeks or the Italians come I tell you plainly that we had better see ourselves killed properly than allow it.'[9] For the moment no final decision on the issue could be taken: he would have to seek further instructions from his government.

Further discussions followed, and substantial progress was made. In particular Rauf accepted, more or less unchanged, the Allied demands regarding the demobilisation of the Ottoman armed forces;

8. Ibid., p. 326.
9. Ibid., p. 327.

Allied control of the Ottoman wireless, telegraph and cable stations; the evacuation of Ottoman forces from northwestern Persia
and Transcaucasia; the surrender of the Ottoman garrisons in the
Arab provinces; and the surrender of arms, ammunition and equipment. But when it came to the terms involving a further Allied
occupation of Ottoman territory, in particular those concerning a
possible Allied occupation of the Taurus tunnel system, an occupation of the Armenian provinces, and the right claimed by the Allies
to occupy strategic points in the empire in the event of a situation
arising likely to threaten Allied security, he remained adamant. As
Calthorpe remarked in a telegram of 27 October, the Turks remained throughout 'firm in their opposition to any terms which
imply occupation or interference with internal affairs'.[10]

Rauf's stubbornness paid off. In the negotiation of a number of
the remaining terms he won substantial concessions. With regard to
the proposed Allied occupation of the Dardanelles forts it was agreed
that British and French troops would alone occupy the forts; though
the wording of the proposed clause would remain unchanged, so as
not to upset the Italians and the Greeks. Allied control officers
would be placed on all railways, but only in Transcaucasia would
the railways be placed under direct Allied administration. German
and Austrian troops stationed in the Ottoman Empire would be
repatriated and not, as the Allies had originally intended, be handed
over to them. But on the essential issue, the right of the Allies to
occupy Ottoman territory, previously unoccupied, Rauf was in the
end obliged to give way. For there was, Calthorpe insisted, no alternative: the proposed terms would have to be accepted, subject of
course to the agreed amendments. Any substantial change would
have to be referred back to a conference of the Allied Powers, and
that might take weeks. After further consultation with Istanbul Rauf,
who appears to have had no notion of the weakness of Calthorpe's
negotiating position, accepted virtually all of the remaining Allied
demands, including, in particular, the opening of the Straits; the
occupation of the Dardanelles forts; the free use by Allied (but not
by Greek) ships of all Ottoman ports and anchorages, including
Istanbul; and the right of the Allies to occupy strategic points in the
Ottoman Empire – terms which the Allies believed, wrongly as it
turned out, would place the whole of the Ottoman Empire under
Allied control.

10. Ibid., p. 329.

It is tempting to conclude that Rauf Bey was completely out-
witted by Calthorpe in the negotiations concerning the Mudros
armistice; and indeed there is some truth in that assertion. But in
fact Rauf's willingness to make concessions was mainly determined
not by a precise evaluation of the particular issues involved, important as those were, but by a general appreciation of the nature of
British foreign policy. As Rauf saw it the British were concerned
to secure not only control of the Straits and access to the Black
Sea, but also the preservation of a stable power in the area, capable
of opposing the advance of Russia. In his view, therefore, they
would in the future retain an interest in ensuring the survival of a
strong and independent Ottoman Empire. The Ottomans might,
therefore, accept the proposed armistice terms secure in the knowledge that in the end the British would not exploit them to their
disadvantage. It was to prove a fatal misunderstanding, for as events
were later to show the British and their allies had in fact every
intention of partitioning the Ottoman Empire, including those parts
of the empire which had remained unoccupied at the end of the
war.

CHAPTER TEN

The End of the Ottoman Empire

The defeat of the Ottoman Empire in the First World War and the expulsion of Ottoman forces from Transcaucasia and the Arab provinces which followed marked the effective end of the empire as a multi-national state, spanning vast territories and incorporating a variety of disparate peoples and cultures. But it did not necessarily entail the end of the Ottoman state and the dynasty that ruled over it. Paradoxically, this was brought about not by the victorious Entente Powers and their allies, who in drawing up their plans for a peace settlement generally accepted that an Ottoman state of some kind, however truncated, might yet be preserved in Anatolia, and possibly also in eastern Thrace, the heartlands of the empire, but by Mustafa Kemal (Atatürk) the so-called founder of modern Turkey. In November 1922 Mustafa Kemal, having in the meantime founded a national movement in Anatolia, committed not only to the preservation of a Turkish State in Anatolia and eastern Thrace, with Istanbul as its capital, but also to the preservation of the sultanate, suddenly and unexpectedly had the sultanate and by implication the Ottoman state abolished.

The challenge facing the Ottoman Turks

The situation facing the Ottoman Turks in the period immediately following the end of the First World War was dire. In Istanbul, in Galata, Pera and Scutari, Allied forces, including Indian, Senegalese and Algerian contingents, were busy establishing garrisons; whilst in the Golden Horn an Allied, mainly British, fleet lay at anchor, its guns trained on the Yildiz Palace, where cowered the sultan, Mehmed VI Vahideddin, terrified of assassination. Elsewhere in

Anatolia and eastern Thrace the Allies were at work, implementing
the terms of the armistice, occupying strategic points, destroying the
Straits defences and monitoring the disarmament of what remained
of the Ottoman army; while throughout the empire minority groups,
with substantial support from abroad, were active, preparing the
ground for independence or annexation. In Istanbul a Greek faction, mainly middle class, having engineered the fall of the patriarch, Germanos V, who doubted the viability of their schemes, was
working energetically to lay the foundations of union with Greece.
In the Pontus region of northern Anatolia, where Greek irregulars
had been engaged in fighting a guerrilla war against the Ottoman
authorities for more than a decade, Greek organisations, formed in
some cases by the new Orthodox patriarch, Dorotheos Mammelis
(a nationalist cleric who had been a staunch supporter of Greek
rights in Macedonia), were busy setting up armed bands and spreading propaganda in favour of the creation of an independent Greek
state. In Izmir, unofficially promised to the Greeks in the course of
the war – or so at least Eleutherios Venizelos, the Greek prime
minister, pretended to believe – Greek agents were active, building
up support for a possible Greek occupation. And in the eastern
provinces, in Kars, Ardahan and Batum, recently evacuated by the
Russians, Armenian bands committed to the creation of a greater
Armenia, were advancing, taking revenge on the Turks for the
massacres of Armenians they had perpetrated in the First World
War.[1]

Nor were the Ottomans in any doubt what their enemies, the
western Entente Powers, intended. As we have seen, in December
1917 the newly installed Bolshevik government in St Petersburg,
determined to expose the wicked machinations of the imperial
powers, had revealed to the world the contents of the secret treaties
and agreements concluded by the Entente Powers in the course of
the war. Just how far it was the intention of the western Entente
Powers to implement those treaties and agreements or at least those
of them that remained valid – the Constantinople Agreement of
March–April 1915 had been invalidated by the falling out of Russia,
while the St Jean de Maurienne Agreement of 1917 had been made
dependent on the consent of Russia, never obtained – in the peace
settlement they intended to impose remained to be seen. But this
much was clear. In Mesopotamia, the British, intent on creating a

1. A.L. Macfie, *Atatürk* Harlow: Longman, 1994, pp. 54–8; H.J. Psomiades, *The
Eastern Question: The Last Phase* Salonica: Institute of Balkan Studies, 1968.

strategic line of defence in the Middle East and securing the approaches to India, their greatest imperial possession, were determined to gain control. In Syria, the Lebanon and Cilicia, the French, intent on expanding their imperial interests in the area, were likewise determined to secure control; while the Italians, irrespective of the validity or otherwise of the St Jean de Maurienne Agreement, remained determined to assert their claim to a fair share in any distribution of war spoils the victorious Entente Powers might undertake. As for the remaining Ottoman territories in Anatolia, it seemed that the British and French, determined to punish the Ottomans for their participation in the First World War on the side of the Central Powers, and if possible secure strategic control of the area, intended to impose a settlement based on the principles of nationality and partition. This might include the creation of an independent Armenia and an independent or autonomous Kurdistan. Finally, with regard to the Straits, freed now from the need to consider the interests of Russia, they intended to impose a new regime based on the principles of internationalisation, neutralisation and demilitarisation, securing freedom of passage not only for ships of commerce, but also for ships of war. In this way they hoped to secure not only the freedom to exercise naval power in the area of the Black Sea, but also effective control of the Ottoman capital, which would, they believed (mistakenly as it turned out), carry with it control of the interior.

The Ottoman response

Faced with this formidable challenge to its existence, the Ottoman military and political elite responded in a variety of ways. In the Yildiz Palace, Mehmed VI Vahideddin, a man, according to one contemporary account, weak in character, highly strung and cautious to the point of timidity, convinced of the weakness of his position and determined at all costs to secure the survival of his house (the Habsburgs, Romanovs and Hohenzollerns had all recently lost their thrones) sought to ingratiate himself with the Allies, in particular the British, with whom he hoped to reestablish the relationship that had prevailed throughout the greater part of the nineteenth century, when the British had sought to preserve the Ottoman Empire as a bulwark against the advance of Russia. To this end he took immediate steps to secure the restoration of the traditional powers of the sultanate (undermined by the constitution and the

CUP dictatorship), the dissolution of the Ottoman parliament (seen as CUP, and in any case a product of the constitutional system he opposed), the complete suppression of the CUP and the arrest and trial of those held responsible for war crimes and the Armenian massacres. A commission was appointed to secure the replacement of CUP valis and other officials appointed by the previous regime. Army officers loyal to the sultanate, including many ranker officers, were promoted, and parties and organisations sympathetic to its aims and objectives supported. Finally, in March 1919 Damad Ferid Pasha, a brother-in-law of the sultan and according to all accounts a man totally committed to the extinction of the CUP, was appointed grand vizier. As a result, in the early months of 1919 something approaching a reign of terror was instituted, as leaders and functionaries of the CUP, including Emmanuel Carassu (Karasu), Rhami, Kara Kemal, Midhat Şükrü, Tevfik Rüştü, Canbolat, Fethi and scores of others were arrested and held, pending trial and execution. (Talaat, Enver and Djemal had already escaped, sailing on board a German submarine or torpedo boat to the Crimea on 1–2 November.)

The charges brought against the leaders of the CUP were not confined merely to war crimes and the Armenian massacres. The CUP leaders were also accused of executing the Bab-i Ali coup of 23 January 1913, taking the Ottoman Empire into the First World War on the side of the Central Powers, ruining the economy and engaging in war profiteering and corruption on a massive scale. In bringing these charges Mehmed VI Vahideddin clearly hoped to discredit the CUP, which though officially dissolved remained a powerful organisation. At the same time he hoped, by using the CUP as a scapegoat, to exonerate the sultanate and the Turkish people from whatever responsibility they might have incurred for the crimes committed by the Ottoman government in the period of the First World War.

In the ministry of war, on the other hand, and in the army in general, where CUP officers for the most part remained in control, many high-ranking officers, including Mustafa Kemal, recently returned from the Syrian front, convinced that the Allies had no intention of respecting the terms of the armistice and sceptical regarding the effectiveness of a policy of appeasement, were active, laying the foundations of further resistance. To this end the demobilisation of the army ordered by the Allies was delayed. Secret stocks of arms and equipment were built up, and local resistance movements established, particularly in areas threatened by Greek and Armenian armed bands. At the same time the Special Organisation

(Teshkilati Mahsusa), supposedly dissolved in October 1918, was reactivated as a secret organisation known as the General Revolutionary Organisation of the Islamic World; and at the instigation of Talaat Pasha and others, a new organisation, Karakol (Guard), was created to prepare for post-war resistance and assist in the escape of CUP officials wanted by the Allies for the war crimes they had committed in the First World War. So effective were the officers concerned in building up stocks of arms and equipment, and the secret organisations that supported them, that by the summer of 1919 they had succeeded in laying the foundations of a formidable movement of national resistance, capable of challenging the authority of the Allied Powers and their surrogates among the minorities, at least in the more remote parts of Anatolia and eastern Thrace.

Preparations to deal with the crisis generated by defeat in the First World War were by no means confined to the army and the secret organisations. In the months immediately following the end of the war a host of new political parties and societies were formed, and old ones reactivated, organised or inspired for the most part either by supporters of the CUP, supposedly dissolved in November 1918, or by those opposed to it. Political parties loyal to the aims and objectives of the CUP included the Renovation Party (Teceddüt Firkasi) and the Ottoman Liberal People's Party (Osmanli Hürriyetperver Avam Firkasi). Parties opposed to it included the Party of Freedom and Understanding (Hürriyet ve Itilâf), a successor of the Liberal Union Party of 1911. Societies and associations formed included the Ottoman Society for the Defence of Thrace – Paşaeli, set up, at the instigation of Talaat Pasha, in November 1918; the Society for the Defence of the National Rights of the Eastern Provinces, set up by leading Unionists, again probably at the instigation of Talaat Pasha, in December 1918; the Society for the Defence of Ottoman Rights in Izmir; and the Society for the Preservation of the National Rights of Trabzon. Also active at the time were the Turkish Hearth (Türk Ocaği), founded in 1911, the National Society for Instruction and Education, founded in 1916, the Society of Ottomans Professing the Principles of President Wilson, and the Friends of England.[2]

2. E.J. Zürcher, *The Unionist Factory* Leiden: E.J. Brill, 1984, Ch. 3; H. Ertürk, *Iki Devrin Perde Arkasi* Istanbul: Pinar Yayinevi, 1964, pp. 217–37; G. Jäschke, 'Beiträge zur Geschichte des Kampfes der Türkei um ihre Unabhängigkeit', *Welt des Islams*, New Series, Vol. 5, Pt. 3 (1957–8); British Public Record Office FO. 371 4141 Intelligence Report on the Committee of Union and Progress. Mehmet VI Vahideddin's policy was described as being that of 'serfüru etmek' (yielding): 'Let us raise our voice and shout, but let us not lift our hands.'

The policy pursued by Mehmed VI Vahideddin and Damad Ferid Pasha, of seeking to reestablish the authority of the sultanate and suppress all forms of opposition, in particular the CUP, proved predictably ineffective. The Allies, determined to secure the trial and punishment of those accused of war crimes and other offences, and concerned regarding the possible consequences of a complete breakdown of law and order in the Ottoman capital and the interior, did offer some limited military and financial support; but they proved unwilling to commit themselves further, seeking merely the conclusion of a satisfactory peace settlement based on the principle of partition. The army and the administration, still largely controlled by CUP officers and officials, proved generally uncooperative, unwilling to implement the policies decided on. Even the support of elements opposed to the CUP, such as the Party of Freedom and Understanding, proved counter-productive, for their repeated calls for the arrest and execution of the leaders of the CUP and others accused of war crimes, tended merely to alienate the common people, who were increasingly inclined to associate such calls with the policy of appeasement pursued by the sultan. Actual attempts, undertaken in conjunction with the Allies, in particular the British, to arrest and try those accused of war crimes proved equally unrewarding. It proved difficult to organise and staff the special courts set up to try the accused – those appointed frequently refused to serve, fearing retribution, while the ministers involved could not agree on whether the accused should be tried individually or collectively – and a number of prisoners, including Dr Reşit, the vali of Diyarbekir, were enabled to escape. When in April 1919 Kemal Bey, the former *mutasarrif vekil* of Yozgat, seen by the people as an idealist and a patriot, was convicted of carrying out orders to deport the Armenians and hanged on gallows erected in a square in Beyazit, a huge crowd gathered to witness the event, and demonstrations followed, which had to be put down by the authorities. So great, indeed, was the degree of disaffection generated by the sultan's policies, that for a time a second Bab-i Ali coup was daily expected; and in the following weeks it became difficult, if not impossible, for Mehmed VI Vahideddin to implement the programme of public executions he had decided on. Yet still he might have succeeded in securing the restoration of the power and authority of the sultanate he sought, had not the British and French, with American support, decided in May 1919 to dispatch a Greek expeditionary force to occupy Izmir (the British and French wished to preempt an Italian occupation of Izmir, expected following the landing of Italian forces in Antalya in March). For not only did this event lead to a further erosion of popular support for the sultan and his government in Istanbul, it also revealed to the Turkish people the full implications of their defeat in the First World War and the policy of partition the Allies intended to pursue.[3]

Origins of the national movement

The precise origins of the national movement – which under the leadership of Mustafa Kemal (Atatürk) was later to unite the forces of national resistance in Anatolia and eastern Thrace, challenge the authority of the sultan and his government in Istanbul, confront the occupation forces of the western Entente Powers and expel the Greek expeditionary force dispatched to occupy Izmir – remain in doubt, though numerous, generally conflicting, explanations have been offered. According to Mustafa Kemal himself, the national movement originated in Anatolia in May 1919, when following his appointment as inspector of the Third (originally Ninth) Army and his arrival in Samsun, a small town on the Black Sea coast, he and a group of like-minded colleagues, including Rauf, Ali Fuat, Refet and Kiazim Karabekir, began the laborious and at times heroic task of creating a national movement, in the interior, capable of opposing the occupation forces of the Entente Powers, and their surrogates, the Greeks, whose occupation of Izmir and the surrounding area had happened to coincide with Mustafa Kemal's own departure from Istanbul. Following the foundation of a movement based on the various societies for the defence of rights set up in Anatolia and eastern Thrace at the time and on army units loyal to the cause (congresses were held at Erzerum in July–August and at Sivas in September; at the Sivas Congress a united Society for the Defence of the Rights of Anatolia and Rumelia was set up with Mustafa Kemal as its president) Mustafa Kemal set about the task of securing the appointment of a strong government in Istanbul, willing and able, with the backing of the national movement, to negotiate a satisfactory peace settlement with the western Entente Powers. Other more mundane accounts would seek the origin of the movement in the organisation of the numerous defence of rights associations set up in Anatolia and eastern Thrace at the time; in preparatory work

3. Ertürk, *Iki Devrin Perde Arkasi*, pp. 297–301; S. Akşin, *Istanbul Hükümetleri ve Milli Mücadele* Istanbul: Cem Yayinevi, 1992, pp. 37–47, 149–55, 197–201.

understaken by Enver Pasha and others in the closing stages of the war; in the work of Karakol and the other secret organisations set up in the last weeks in the war; and in the organisation, by Rauf and others, of the irregular forces that sprang up in western Anatolia, following the Greek invasion.

Many of the defence of rights associations set up in Anatolia and eastern Thrace were, it would seem, established at the instigation of Talaat Pasha, who expected that, in the period following the conclusion of peace, the Ottoman Muslim peoples of Anatolia and eastern Thrace might be enabled, like their counterparts in the minority communities, to make claims based on the principle of self-determination contained in President Woodrow Wilson's Fourteen Points. The preparatory work undertaken by Enver Pasha and others in the closing stages of the war included the dispatch of substantial forces, well equipped and supplied, withdrawn from the Galician and Moldavian fronts, to Transcaucasia, where it was expected the Turks, defeated in the west, might be enabled to carry on the 'second phase' of the war against the Entente Powers that Enver envisaged might take place in the east. The forces located in Transcaucasia were later withdrawn to Erzerum, where, under the command of Kiazim Karabekir, they were to form the backbone of the national forces in the area. As for the work of Karakol, it was later discovered, to Mustafa Kemal's supposed surprise, that its agents had actually organised a conspiracy to take over control of the Ottoman army in Anatolia. In these circumstances it would seem sensible to conclude that the national movement that emerged in Anatolia in 1919 was the outcome, not of the actions of Mustafa Kemal alone, but of a complex series of events; though the part played by Mustafa Kemal in uniting the forces at work and providing the movement that emerged with a coherent strategy cannot be gainsaid.[4]

The national struggle

Leadership of the national movement, established at the congresses of Erzerum and Sivas, enabled Mustafa Kemal rapidly to secure control of the greater part of both the army and the civil administration in Anatolia and eastern Thrace. As a result in the autumn of

---

4. Zürcher, *The Unionist Factor* Ch. 3; Mustafa Kemal, *A Speech Delivered by Ghazi Mustafa Kemal* Leipzig: Koehler, 1929, Pt. 1; Akşin, *Istanbul Hükümetleri ve Milli Mücadele*, pp. 296–7.

1919 he was enabled to secure first the downfall of the Ottoman government, led by Damad Ferid Pasha, and then the appointment of a new government supposedly committed to the aims and objectives of the national movement, as set out in manifestoes issued at Erzerum and Sivas and in a list of aims and objectives, known as the National Pact, drafted in Ankara, to which Mustafa Kemal transferred the representative committee (in effect the executive committee) of the Society for the Defence of the Rights of Anatolia and Rumelia in December 1919. The aims and objectives of the National Pact, which were adopted by the Ottoman chamber of deputies, convened in Istanbul in January 1920, included the preservation of an independent Ottoman state ruled by an Ottoman sultan-caliph, in those parts of the empire, inhabited by an Ottoman Muslim majority, that had remained unoccupied by Allied forces at the conclusion of the Mudros armistice; the determination of the future of the Arab provinces, occupied by Allied forces, at the time of the armistice, by a free plebiscite of their populations; the determination of the juridical status of western Thrace by a free vote of the peoples concerned; the determination of the status of the three *sancaks* (Kars, Ardahan and Batum) by a similar process; the opening of the Straits to the commerce and traffic of the world, provided only that the security of Istanbul be assured; the provision of guarantees regarding the protection of the minorities; and the abolition of all restrictions previously imposed by the Great Powers on the future development, political, economic and social, of the Ottoman state.

Mustafa Kemal's strategy of securing the appointment of a new government in Istanbul capable of negotiating a satisfactory peace settlement with the victorious Entente Powers, though initially successful, proved in the end disappointing. In March 1920 the Allies, concerned regarding their inability to impose their authority in the interior – in February a massacre of Armenians had occurred at Marash in Cilicia – ordered a formal occupation of Istanbul (the previous occupation had been informal) and at the same time they ordered the arrest and transportation to Malta of some 170 nationalist deputies, officials and intellectuals resident in the city. But the Allied action, which was accompanied by a threat that if resistance were to continue the Ottomans would risk losing possession of their capital, far from undermining the national movement, served merely to strengthen it. Following the Allied occupation of Istanbul, the chamber of deputies (known henceforth as the grand national assembly) reconvened in Ankara, where Mustafa Kemal and the representative committee had awaited the outcome of events. It was from the relative security of that vantage point that, in the period of civil war and national struggle that followed, Mustafa Kemal, with the more or less constant support of the Ottoman army units stationed in Anatolia, the grand national assembly and the majority of the Turkish Muslim population of the area, including the Kurds, was enabled to defeat the so-called army of the caliphate, sent against him by the sultan, Mehmed VI Vahideddin; establish what rapidly became in effect an independent government and administration in the interior; confront and even on occasion fight the occupation forces of the Entente Powers; and finally, following a series of indecisive battles fought against the Greeks, culminating in the battle of Sakarya (August–September 1921), drive the Greek expeditionary forces out of Anatolia (August–September 1922). Moreover, following a prolonged crisis known as the Chanak Affair, in the course of which war between the Allies and the nationalists constantly threatened – the crisis was finally resolved by the conclusion on 11 October 1922 of the Armistice of Mudania, which conceded most of the nationalist demands – he was enabled to conclude with the western Entente Powers, and the other powers concerned, a treaty of peace, signed at Lausanne on 24 July 1923, securing the greater part of the aims and objectives of the national movement, as set out in the National Pact.[5]

It should not be supposed that the commitment of the nationalists to the aims and objectives of their movement, as set out in the Erzerum and Sivas manifestoes and the National Pact, was in any sense absolute; though under the leadership of Mustafa Kemal it did for the most part remain firm. From time to time alternative scenarios were considered, including in particular one put forward by Refet Pasha, minister of defence in the Ankara government, in conversations held at Inebolu in 1921 with one Major Henry, an English businessman with a penchant for diplomacy. In his conversations with Major Henry, Refet Pasha, according to the British records, suggested that the Ankara regime, despite their present distrust of the British, might yet be persuaded to reach an accommodation with them. As he understood it, it was the intention of the British to create in southern Asia Minor and Arabia a series of

5. Macfie, *Atatürk*, Chs 4–7; Mustafa Kemal, *Speech*, Pt. 1; M. Goloğlu, *Milli Mücadele Tarihi, Erzerum Kongresi* Ankara: Nüve Matbaasi, 1968; and *Milli Mücadele Tarihi, Sivas Kongresi* Ankara: Başnur Matbaasi (1969); P.K. Jensen, 'The Greco-Turkish War, 1920–1922', *International Journal of Middle Eastern Studies*, Vol. 10 (1979); S. Selek, *Anadolu Ihtilâli* Istanbul: Burçak Yayinevi, 1966.

dependencies in order to link up Britain's possessions in Africa and India. This plan they had begun to implement before the First World War, by setting up, in conjunction with the Russians, zones of influence in Persia. The war had now created an opportunity to complete the links in that chain. In Palestine, for which they had secured a mandate, the British had set up a home for the Jews. In order to protect the Jews from the Arabs, with whom they had previously lived in peace, they had now created the state of Transjordan, under the kingship of a scion of Mecca (Sherif Husein's son, Adullah). Finally, in Iraq they had created an independent state, with Feisal as king, the last link in the Cape–Colombo chain. Nor was that all. Throughout the nineteenth century, in order to impose a limit on pan-Slavic expansion to the south, they had sought to secure the preservation of a strong Turkey, within fixed frontiers. Now more than ever Britain's vital interest lay in preventing the Russians or the Slavs from reaching Constantinople (Istanbul), the Mediterranean and India. The best and cheapest way of doing this was to revert to Britain's former policy of preserving an inviolable Turkey. Once that fundamental truth was recognised then every remaining question would be settled automatically. Was it not in Britain's interest to place Turkey in sole control of the Straits, and to secure Turkish possession of Thrace, the breastwork for the defence of the Straits? Was not any attempt to employ the Greeks instead of the Turks (Lloyd George's policy) certain to fail, for the Greek population in Thrace was not sufficient to carry such a burden? Britain should therefore let Turkey live, much as she had used to, as her friend and her ally. The Turks might then join with the Arabs (who would be united in an independent Arab state, with its own national assembly) to form a dual or federal state, protected by the British. In this way Britain would succeed in maintaining her influence in Mesopotamia and the Gulf without the immense expenditure direct intervention would entail. The creation of this duality and the recognition of the fact that England was with Turkey would 'have an immediate effect among all Mohammedan peoples, and states, more especially those on the northwest frontiers of India'. Peace could be assured there and once again a bulwark would be erected against the continuing advance of the Slavs towards the south.[6]

6. *British Documents on Atatürk*, Ankara: Türk Tarih Kurumu, 1973–84, Vol. 4, Nos 46–7.

It is difficult to tell how far Refet's proposals reflected opinion in Ankara. No doubt a settlement along the lines he proposed would have proved popular in many quarters; but it may be doubted if it would have received majority support, as it would have involved an unacceptable degree of British tutelage and in any case challenged the central thesis of the National Pact. One way or the other it made little difference, for the British had no intention of responding to Refet's unofficial approaches, which they interpreted merely as an attempt on the part of the nationalists to drive a wedge between Britain and her allies.

Response of the sultanate

Throughout the period of national struggle the sultan, Mehmed VI Vahideddin, and his government in Istanbul, despite occasional attempts at compromise, remained generally opposed to the national movement and its leaders, whom Mehmed VI Vahideddin characterised variously as mere brigands, men without any real stake in the country, revolutionaries and reincarnations of the old CUP (Mustafa Kemal was described as a Macedonian revolutionary of unknown origin). Thus on 8 June 1919, at the behest of the British high commissioner, who was concerned regarding the potential effects of the programme of agitation and incitement initiated by Mustafa Kemal and his colleagues in the interior, the minister of war dispatched a telegram ordering Mustafa Kemal's return; and on 23 June, when this order was ignored, Ali Kemal, the newly appointed minister of the interior, again ordered Mustafa Kemal's recall, at the same time giving instructions that no government servant should be permitted to enter into communication with him. On 2 July the sultan's chief secretary dispatched a telegram requesting his resignation, and on 7 July he was declared a rebel and stripped of his rank and decorations. At the same time posters were issued declaring the errant general to be a rebel and a traitor, and steps taken to secure his arrest and possibly also his assassination.[7]

Further steps against the nationalist movement and its leaders followed. In September, when Mustafa Kemal ordered a nationalist

---

7. M. Aktepe, 'Atatürk 'e Dair Bazi Belgeler', *Belleten*, Vol. 32 (1968), pp. 449–51; Jäschke, 'Beiträge zur Geschichte des Kampfes der Türkei um ihre Unabhängigkeit', Pt. 5; Mustafa Kemal, *Speech*, pp. 37–40.

take-over of the civil administration in Anatolia and eastern Thrace, isolating the government in Istanbul, the grand vizier, Damad Ferid Pasha, sought, unsuccessfully as it turned out on this occasion, to secure the permission of the Allied high commissioners to dispatch a force of some 2,000 troops into the interior to hold back the nationalists and if possible suppress them. In January 1920, when the newly elected chamber of deputies assembled in Istanbul (and not in Ankara as Mustafa Kemal had desired), Mehmed VI Vahideddin at once approached the nationalist delegates, hoping to win them over to a policy of appeasement; and in February he had a circular issued, pointing out that henceforth the chamber of deputies should be considered the only body representing the nation: any such claims made elsewhere should be considered illegal. Finally, in March, following the Allied occupation of Istanbul and the arrest of some 170 or so nationalist deputies, intellectuals and other unreliable elements, he had Damad Ferid Pasha, once again reappointed as grand vizier following his dismissal in October, launch a campaign, backed by the Allied Powers, aimed at the complete extinction of the national movement and the forces loyal to it.

The assault launched on the national movement by the Army of the Caliphate and other anti-nationalist elements proved formidable; but in the end, thanks to the loyalty and determination of the national forces, in particular the irregular units led by such noted guerrilla leaders as Cherkes Ethem, Ibrahim Bey, Yörük Ali and Mehmet Effe, the Army of the Caliphate was defeated and the authority of the Ankara regime sustained.[8]

The Treaty of Sèvres

The struggle between the national forces and the Army of the Caliphate and its supporters, in effect a civil war, lasted for more than six months. A significant factor determining the outcome of the struggle may well have been the publication in May 1920 of the peace treaty, proposed by the Allies, later signed by a representative of the Ottoman government at Sèvres. The terms of the treaty, drawn up by the Allies in a series of meetings and conferences

---

8. Macfie, *Atatürk*, Ch. 5; Mustafa Kemal, *Speech*, pp. 371–423; Selek, *Anadolu Ihtilali*, Pt. 1, pp. 351–9; H. Edib, *The Turkish Ordeal* London: John Murray, 1928, pp. 143–4.

culminating in a conference held at San Remo in April, were, as Sir Horace Rumbold, the British high commissioner in Istanbul and others frequently remarked, harsh in the extreme. In the area of Constantinople and the Straits, a Straits zone would be created, garrisoned by Allied troops and administered by a Straits commission, responsible for securing freedom of passage not only to ships of commerce, as heretofore, but also ships of war, a key Allied demand; though nominal Turkish sovereignty would be preserved in the zone. Eastern Thrace, up to the Chatalya lines, would pass to Greece, as would the Izmir region of western Anatolia, subject to a proviso that after five years a plebiscite would be held to determine the final outcome. In the Armenian provinces an independent Armenian state would be created, and in the Kurdish provinces an independent or autonomous Kurdish state. Syria and Mesopotamia would be recognised as independent states, subject to the proviso that administrative advice and assistance might be rendered to them by a mandatory, until such time as they might be enabled to stand alone. As for the administration of Palestine, that would also be placed in the hands of a mandatory, which would be made responsible for the implementation of the Balfour Declaration.[9]

The humiliating provisions contained in the Treaty of Sèvres did not complete the catalogue of injuries which the Entente Powers intended to inflict on the Ottoman Empire. In a separate agreement, known as the Tripartite Agreement, also concluded at Sèvres, Britain, France and Italy agreed that Anatolia would be divided into three spheres, British, French and Italian, in which each power would exercise exclusive rights of commercial exploitation and influence.[10]

Faced with the prospect of so draconian a settlement, which would have reduced the Ottoman Empire to a rump state, controlled by the western Entente Powers, occupying merely Istanbul and a part of Anatolia, it is scarcely surprising that the Turkish-speaking Muslims of Anatolia and eastern Thrace, when apprised of the situation, should for the most part have decided to back, not the sultan and his government, who wished to contest the issue in the council chambers of Europe, but Mustafa Kemal and the nationalists, who were prepared to contest it if need be on the field of battle. Not that the nationalists sought war with the western Entente Powers.

9. J.C. Hurewitz, *Diplomacy in the Near and Middle East: A Documentary Record* Princeton: D. Van Nostrand, Vol. 2, No. 31 (1956).
10. Ibid., No. 32.

On the contrary, they were at pains throughout to avoid conflict, sending delegates, when invited to do so, to a conference convened by the Allies in London (February–March 1921).

It should not be supposed that Damad Ferid Pasha and his colleagues in the Ottoman government in Istanbul found the proposed peace treaty any more acceptable than did the nationalists in Anatolia. On the contrary, from the beginning they made it clear to the Allied high commissioners that they were deeply concerned regarding the intentions of the Allies; and on receiving a copy of the proposed terms Damad Ferid Pasha at once launched a diplomatic campaign aimed at their mitigation. In particular he objected to the proposed terms regarding the future of the Straits, eastern Thrace and the eastern provinces. The proposed settlement, he urged (borrowing perhaps the language of the National Pact), should be revised in such a way that it would leave the Ottoman state in possession of those parts of the empire that were inhabited by an Ottoman Muslim majority. As for the Straits, the creation of a Straits zone, garrisoned by Allied troops, would place a 'sovereign state' between the sultan and his territories in Asia. Might not the freedom of the Straits, the principal Allied objective, be effectively secured by an Allied occupation of the approaches to the Dardanelles alone, and by the maintenance at sea, in the Dardanelles and the Sea of Marmara, of a sufficient number of Allied naval units?[11]

In a written account of his government's observations on the draft treaty, presented to the Allies at the Paris peace conference in June 1920, Damad Ferid Pasha repeated his objections. The proposed settlement, he declared forthrightly, amounted to the dismemberment not only of the Ottoman Empire but also of the Turkish nation. The mutilated corpse of the Ottoman Empire would be stripped of virtually all of its attributes as a sovereign state, both internal and external. Yet at the same time, it was expected that it would remain responsible for the execution of the treaty and the fulfilment of international obligations. Even in Istanbul the rump Turkish state would not be her own mistress: 'Side by side with His Imperial Majesty the Sultan and the Turkish government (sometimes even above them) a "Commission of the Straits" would reign over the Bosphorus, the Sea of Marmora and the Dardanelles.'[12] As for the military occupation authority, in reality there would be three military authorities, each representing its national authority. Far from

11. Ibid., No. 23; A.L. Macfie, *The Straits Question, 1908–36* Salonica: Institute for Balkan Studies, 1993, pp. 119–20.

12. Macfie, *Straits Question*, p. 119.

assuring the internationalisation of the Straits, the regime proposed would merely facilitate their nationalisation by another state.

Argument alone, however, was unlikely to persuade the Allies to change course. Nor had Damad Ferid Pasha and his colleagues any other means of persuasion at their disposal: in Istanbul and the surrounding area they remained dependent on the forces of the occupying powers for what little power they continued to exercise: and in the interior the nationalists had deprived them of all effective control. Accordingly, they concluded that they had no choice (short of an outright abdication of responsibility) but to continue with the policy of appeasement they had originally decided on; and on 10 August 1920 they concluded the Treaty of Sèvres.

Abolition of the sultanate

The actual occasion, selected (according to his own account) by Mustafa Kemal, for the abolition of the sultanate and the formal dissolution of the empire that abolition entailed, was the receipt in October 1922 of an invitation from the Allies to both the Istanbul and Ankara governments to send delegations to the peace conference shortly to be convened in Lausanne. Faced then with the urgent need to resolve the problems inherent in the existence of a dual system of government in what remained of the Ottoman Empire, he decided to opt, not for an abolition of the provisional administration set up in Anatolia by the nationalists, as advocated by Tevfik Pasha, the new grand vizier, and others, but for the abolition of the Ottoman sultanate and the administration which supported it. As a result, on 30 October, eschewing all suggestions, put forward by many of his supporters, that he opt instead for the creation of a constitutional monarchy, the solution effectively provided for in the Law of Fundamental Organisation, enacted by the grand national assembly in January 1921, he had a motion introduced in the grand national assembly declaring that the Ottoman Empire must now be considered dead, and that a new Turkish nation, enjoying absolute sovereignty, had taken its place. And on 1 November he had a motion introduced, making provision for the separation of the sultanate and the caliphate, and the immediate abolition of the former.[13] But when a joint committee made up of

13. B. Lewis, *The Emergence of Modern Turkey* Oxford: Oxford University Press, 1961, pp. 251–6.

members of the constitutional, judicial and *Sheriat* committees, appointed to look into the issue met the same evening, it quickly transpired that majority opinion, traditionally conservative, was opposed to the proposed changes, which were deemed to be in contravention of Muslim law and tradition. Thus thwarted, Mustafa Kemal, who had observed the proceedings of the committee from a corner of the room, concluded that, if he were to succeed in securing his principal objective, the abolition of the sultanate, action of a more decisive kind would be required. Casting aside all pretence of constitutional propriety, therefore, he climbed on to a bench and declared in a loud voice:

> 'Gentlemen, neither the sovereignty nor the right to govern can be transferred by one person to anybody else by an academic debate. Sovereignty is acquired by force, by power and by violence. It was by violence that the sons of Osman acquired the power to rule over the Turkish nation and to maintain their rule for more than six centuries. It is now the nation that revolts against these usurpers, puts them in their right place and actually carries on their sovereignty. This is an actual fact. It is no longer a question of knowing whether we want to leave this sovereignty in the hands of the nation or not. It is simply a question of stating an actuality, something which is already an accomplished fact and which must be accepted unconditionally as such. And this must be done at any price. If those who are assembled here, the Assembly and everybody else, would find this quite natural, it would be very appropriate from my point of view. Conversely, the reality will nevertheless be manifested in the necessary form, but in that event it is possible that some heads will be cut off.'

The impact of his intervention was, as he later remarked, considerable. 'Pardon me', responded Hodja Mustafa Efendi, deputy of Angora, 'we had regarded the question in another light. Now we are informed.' What happened then is, perhaps, best described in Mustafa Kemal's own words:

> 'The draft Act was quickly drawn up and was read on the same day in the second sitting of the Assembly.
>
> Following a motion to proceed to nominal voting, I mounted the tribune and declared: "This procedure is useless. I believe that the High Assembly will unanimously adopt the principles which are destined to preserve the independence of the nation and the country for all time."
>
> Shouts were raised: "Vote!" "Vote!" Finally, the chairman put the motion to the vote and declared: "It is unanimously agreed to." One

single voice was heard declaring: "I am against it," but this was drowned in cries of "Silence!"

In this way, Gentlemen, the curtain fell on the last act of the overthrow and breakdown of the Ottoman Monarchy.'[14]

According to his own later account, given in the great six-day speech he delivered to a congress of the Republican People's Party in October 1927 (in effect a history of the national struggle later published as *Speech*) Mustafa Kemal claims that from the beginning of the national struggle, and even before, he and a number of his colleagues had contemplated the abolition of the sultanate and the caliphate and the creation of a 'New Turkish State', in effect a republic. But in the circumstances prevailing at the time they had been compelled to proceed slowly, 'by stages', lest they upset the people, traditionally conservative.[15] Nor is there any reason to doubt Mustafa Kemal's personal commitment to radical reform. According to Ali Fuat Cebesoy, a fellow student of Mustafa Kemal's at the War College and later leader of the national movement, he had as early as 1907 argued in favour of the creation of a Turkish nation state, incorporating Anatolia, eastern and western Thrace, the Aegean islands approximate to the coast, Aleppo and Mosul.[16] In October 1918, he had remarked to Ali Fuat that radical action of some kind would be required if the Ottoman nation were to be saved from disaster. And in August 1919 he is said to have informed Mazhar Mufit, an old friend, that, from the moment of his first arrival in Samsun in May 1919, he had envisaged that the possible outcome of the struggle in which they were engaged was the creation of a republic.[17] But that such forecasts and predictions indicated anything more than a keen understanding of the forces at work in the empire and a predilection for prophecy may be doubted, for throughout the period of the First World War and its aftermath, until the period of the civil war at least, he appears to have concentrated all his efforts on securing, not the creation of a republic, but the salvation of the Ottoman Empire and the dynasty that ruled over it. Thus throughout the First World War, along with colleagues such as Djemal Pasha, Ali Fuat, Refet, and Ismet, he fought to defend the Arab provinces against the assault mounted by the Entente

14. Mustafa Kemal, *Speech*, p. 578.
15. Ibid., pp. 17–18.
16. Ali Fuat Cebesoy, *Sinif Arkadaşim Atatürk* Istanbul: Inkilâp, 1981; A. Mango, 'Turkey in Winter', *Middle Eastern Studies*, Vol. 31, No. 3 (1995), p. 634.
17. G. Jäschke, 'Auf dem Wege zur Türkischen Republik', *Welt des Islams*, New Series, Vol. 5 (1958), p. 209.

Powers; and in the period immediately following the end of the war he sought initially to secure not a posting to eastern Anatolia, where the prospect of establishing an independent republic beckoned, but office in the Ottoman government, which he believed, if properly led, might yet succeed in saving the empire, or at least a substantial part of it.[18]

Nor did any essential change occur in Mustafa Kemal's approach following his posting to Anatolia. In manifestoes issued at the Congresses of Erzerum and Sivas, and in the National Pact, which he played a significant part in drafting, it was made abundantly clear that the principal objective of the national movement was the salvation of the Ottoman motherland and the preservation of the sultanate and the caliphate. In a telegram dispatched on 11 September 1919, he informed the grand vizier that the nation had no confidence in the sultan's ministers but only in the sultan himself; and in a public declaration issued shortly thereafter he announced that the Congress of Sivas intended to break off relations with the Ottoman government which, although the congress had never ceased to prove, in a legal and legitimate manner its unfailing fidelity to the padishah-caliph, had interposed itself between the nation and its sovereign.[19] In a telegram dispatched to the army corps commanders and other state officials on the eve of the opening of the grand national assembly in Ankara in April 1920, he declared forthrightly that it was the intention of the assembly to secure the 'independence of our country and the deliverance of the seat of the Caliphate and the Sultanate' from the hands of the country's enemies.[20] Finally, in a motion proposing the setting up of a provisional administration, presented to the newly convened grand national assembly, Mustafa Kemal made it clear that, as soon as the sultan-caliph was delivered from all pressure and coercion, he would be enabled to take his place 'within the frame of the legislative principles which will be determined by the Assembly'.[21]

It can of course be argued, as Mustafa Kemal himself later asserted, that such declarations were mere formalities – deceptions made necessary by the contingencies of the moment. But it may be doubted whether a leader bent on the abolition of the sultanate and the creation of a republic could have brought himself to communicate the following message to the sultan, dispatched by the grand national assembly on 26 May 1920:

18. Macfie, *Atatürk*, p. 60.
19. Mustafa Kemal, *Speech*, pp. 121–5.
20. Ibid., pp. 372–4.
21. Ibid., p. 380.

We have met on this occasion in a Great National Assembly in order to study the situation which has arisen owing to the occupation of Constantinople and the tragic events which followed and with the object of ensuring the defence of the rights of the Sultan and our National independence. The deputies have come from every part of ANATOLIA that is not under foreign invasion and have been elected with full powers by the Nation. They have regarded it as their duty of fidelity and obedience to submit certain matters to Your Imperial Presence in accordance with a decision which they have unanimously adopted.

Our Padishah. You are well acquainted with the story of the dream which was dreamed by Sultan OSMAN, the founder of the Sultanate, on a night which is famous and beloved in the annals of our National history. The memory of this dream has been handed down from one generation to another. Of the Holy Tree which spread its shadows over three continents and under which an Islamic world of a hundred million was sheltered, only the great trunk remains shorn of all its branches. This trunk is ANATOLIA and its roots which strike deep, are embedded in our hearts. When our great ancestors conquered and occupied the tracts of RUMELIA which are a world in themselves, they obtained their armies from the soil of ANATOLIA. In order to find means of protecting the main lines of communication with distant countries, they again referred to ANATOLIA and established settlements from that country at the most important points. Compact masses of this people extended as far as BOSNIA, HERTZEGOVINA and the MOREA. They were brought down to the Gulf of BASRA. They were established here and there on the roads leading to PALESTINE and SYRIA.

Our Padishah. For the honour and the maintenance of the illustrious seat of the Caliphate the people of ANATOLIA have for centuries regarded it as their most sacred duty to sacrifice their lives on battlefields far away from their hearths and homes. ANATOLIA has been emptied and has been brought to a state of ruin. But whatever suffering and misery has been endured for the enhancement of the majesty and power of the Sultan over his dominions, it was regarded as a favour bestowed upon it. That land is surrounded by the graves of innumerable martyrs fallen for the Faith in battle, which extend from the interior of HUNGARY to the deserts of the YEMEN, and from the CAUCASUS to BASRA. Again it is old ANATOLIA that is now engaged in a new Holy War for the sake of her freedom and liberty.

Illustrious Padishah! When on all sides the banners of ISLAM were suffering defeat, they came and collected together in the direction of ANATOLIA, and in these parts they sought their last refuge. Upon the invasion of SMYRNA you know how the most prosperous and cultivated part of the country was completely ruined by fire, plunder and massacre. After this barbarous incursion had been made, which was not supported by right, and which aimed at reducing your people in this, their last home, to a state of slavery, you personally communicated to the press of the world the bitter feelings which it had aroused in your heart. The occupation of SMYRNA came after the others. Against this condition of affairs what was a nation able to do which had for thousands of years brought Sultans to the most magnificent thrones in the world? Seeing that the Sultan was prevented from, and deprived of the right of, employing his armies as a result of a miserable war, the nation itself took up arms and hastened to the areas that were the object of attack in order to save the faith and the national honour.

Our Padishah! For thirty years the heroes of Islam in the CAUCASUS, both men and women, put up a defence against an enemy a hundred times stronger than themselves. Since twenty years ALGERIA is living under a luckless regime. For ten years unfortunate MOROCCO has refused to recognise a French Occupation and will not surrender its arms. In TRIPOLI a handful of heroes are engaged in the same struggle. To-day the Islamic World finds itself on all sides deprived of its arms. Your Great Nation, which has risen up in order to throw off the yoke of oppression and treachery, has, for over one thousand one hundred years, since the time of the ABBASID, & FATIMITE Caliphate, and since that of the SELJOUK Turks, waged a holy war for the sake of liberty, independence and religion. Your Nation which is the standard-bearer of ASIA and of Islam, and which enjoys a world-wide reputation, does not expect its life to be saved through the mercy of thirsty enemies.

Your Majesty! There are traitors who are continuously working to deceive the people and to interpret our national defence to Your Imperial Presence as being in the nature of a rebellion. These persons wish to plunge the nation into civil war and thus open the road for enemy conquests. For, whichever side is victorious or vanquished, both alike are your subjects. All are in the same degree your faithful children. We cannot abandon our national defence until the enemy standards are withdrawn from our paternal homes. The religious edifices in Constantinople, each of which constitutes an imposing evidence of the love for the Faith of a great Sultan, are surrounded by enemy soldiers. We are obliged to continue our holy struggle until the impure feet of these men are removed from our national soil. God is on the side of your children who are protecting their mothers' homes and are striving for the honour and independence of the Sovereign-Khalif. It is a thousand times preferable to live under the modest and unfortunate rule of our own administration than to enjoy the ease and enjoyment which are the price of foreign slavery.

Our Padishah! Our hearts are full of feelings of fidelity and hommage we are attached to your throne by closer bands than ever before. The first words at our Assembly were expressions of fidelity to our Khalif and Padishah. The last words will be to the same effect, and we submit the above with all humility and respect.[22]

In the light of these and other assertions of loyalty, not all quite so fulsome, it is not surprising that in the period of the war of independence it was widely believed in Anatolia that the national movement had been created at the behest of Sultan Mehmed VI Vahideddin, the 'beloved Caliph and Ruler of the World'.[23] Nor is it surprising that it was still possible for a peasant, questioned in 1920, to refer to Mustafa Kemal as a 'loyal servant of the Sultan'.[24]

Historians have generally accepted Mustafa Kemal's assertion that he had, from the beginning of the national struggle, and even before, contemplated the abolition of the sultanate and the caliphate; and that, in order to secure those objectives, he had throughout concealed his intentions, working surreptitiously to attain his ends. Such may, indeed, be the case; but it would seem more likely that the idea of abolishing the sultanate, as a practical proposition at least, was conceived only in the course of the war of independence. In the period immediately following the end of the First World War Mustafa Kemal, it is said, at one point contemplated a flight to Anatolia, accompanied by a prince of the royal house. In July 1920 he actually invited the prince regent, Abdul Medjid, to come to Ankara to join the movement of national resistance, an invitation Abdul Medjid, after serious consideration, declined. In October 1921, an unofficial representative of the nationalist movement in Istanbul named Hamid Bey felt able to assure representatives of the government that, following the conclusion of peace, no action would be taken against the sultanate, with whom the nationalists had no quarrel. Even in September 1922, following the defeat of the Greek expeditionary forces in the west, the most that Mustafa Kemal appeared willing to contemplate, in an interview with G. Ward Price, a British journalist, was the deposition of the sultan, Mehmed VI Vahideddin, considered a traitor, and his replacement by Abdul Medjid, the prince regent.[25] Not that in the period of the war of independence Mustafa Kemal avoided all reference to a possible abolition of the sultanate. In telegrams dispatched to the grand

22. *British Documents on Atatürk*, Vol. 2, No. 35.

23. G. Jäschke, 'Die Nichtabdankung des Sultans Mehmed VI', *Welt des Islams*, New Series, Vol. 11 (1967–8).

24. G. Jäschke, 'The Moral Decline of the Ottoman Dynasty', *Welt des Islams*, New Series, Vol. 4 (1955–6), p. 12.

25. *Daily Mail* 15 September 1922; G. Jäschke, 'Mustafa Kemal und Abdülmecid', *Welt des Islams*, New Series, Vol. 2 (1952–3).

vizier, Tevfik Pasha, in January 1921, following the enactment of the Law of Fundamental Organisation, he pointed out that as the grand national assembly had been established, by the Law of Fundamental Organisation, as the only independent and sovereign power, it alone was entitled to negotiate the terms of a peace settlement with the Allies. In these circumstances it might be considered desirable for the sultan to issue a public declaration recognising the authority of the grand national assembly as the only institution capable of expressing the national will. In the event of the sultan agreeing, then the assembly would at once take over full responsibility for the administration of the country, while any such institutions functioning in Istanbul would cease to exist. In the budget of the grand national assembly provision would be made for all such expenditure as might be connected with the civil list. But were the sultan to refuse to agree, then 'the position of His Majesty, the occupant of the Throne of the Sultans, and the dignity of the Caliphate, would run the risk of being shaken'.[26]

Michael Finefrock, an American historian, in a thesis presented in 1976, goes even further, arguing, on the basis of documents published in the supplementary volumes of *Speech* and elsewhere, that Mustafa Kemal's decision to abolish the sultanate was entirely spontaneous, the product of a series of accidents and misunderstandings arising out of the failure of Hamid Bey, the nationalist representative in Istanbul, to pass on a message dispatched by Mustafa Kemal to Tevfik Pasha, the grand vizier, in October 1922. According to this interpretation, when on 17 October Tevfik Pasha approached Mustafa Kemal, suggesting that they dispatch a joint delegation to the coming peace conference, Mustafa Kemal replied immediately, rejecting the invitation. But Mustafa Kemal's reply, sent by way of Hamid Bey, was, for one reason or another, not delivered. As a result on 29 October Tevfik Pasha sent a second invitation to Ankara, worded in the elaborate and overblown language traditionally employed by the Ottoman Sultanate, giving the impression that the Istanbul government not only intended to assert its right to send a delegation to attend the peace conference, but also to continue to represent the country thereafter. Thus alerted to what they believed to be a serious threat to the absolute sovereignty of the grand national assembly, as defined in the Law of Fundamental Organisation of January 1921, members of the assembly, led by Hoca Rasih, the deputy for Antalya, Feyzi Pasha, the deputy for Diarbekir, and Husein Avni, the deputy for Erzerum, launched a series of violent attacks on the sultan, accusing him of presumption, pride, arrogance and illegality. At the same time Riza Nur, the deputy for Sinop, concerned lest the grand vizier's response give Turkey's enemies the impression that two government systems existed in the empire, drew up a resolution, signed by 81 deputies, including Mustafa Kemal – Riza Nur claims that he met Mustafa Kemal by chance in a corridor of the assembly building – proposing that the Ottoman Empire, along with its autocratic system of government, be henceforth considered extinct. Sovereignty now belonged to the grand national assembly, and the Turkish nation which elected it; though the grand national assembly would rescue the office of the caliphate, now held prisoner by its enemies. In the ensuing debate Riza Nur's resolution received wide-ranging support, including that of a number of the principal leaders of the national movement, including Kiazim Karabekir, Rauf, Ali Fuat and Ismet; but at the instigation of a number of conservative clerics, who feared that, deprived of the support of the sultanate, the caliphate would be left powerless, the issue was passed to the joint committee for further consideration. It was at the meeting of this committee, held in the evening of 1 November, that Mustafa Kemal, now persuaded of the urgent need for action, made his dramatic intervention. As a result, in the early hours of 2 November the motion, somewhat revised by the constitutional committee to secure the support of the opposition deputies, was passed by acclamation.[27]

Finefrock's contention that the abolition of the sultanate was the product, not of a carefully worked out scheme, executed by Mustafa Kemal with his usual foresight and thoroughness, but of a spontaneous outburst of anger, provoked in the national assembly by what appeared to be the grand vizier's arrogance and presumption, clearly deserves serious consideration; though it may be doubted whether Mustafa Kemal would have permitted the introduction of so radical a reform without sharing in its inception. One way or the other there is no doubt that once the opportunity of abolishing the sultanate arose it was exploited by Mustafa Kemal with enthusiasm. At a meeting of the national assembly held on 1 November, he delivered a long speech outlining the history of the caliphate and proving that the Turkish people had the right to separate that institution from the sultanate. And throughout he exerted himself to secure

27. M.M. Finefrock, 'From Sultanate to Republic: Mustafa Kemal Atatürk and the Structure of Turkish Politics 1922–1924'. Ph.D. dissertation, Princeton, New Jersey, 1976.

the passing of Riza Nur's motion. For like many members of the assembly he harboured a profound hatred of the sultan and his advisers, forged in the furnace of the civil war, when the sultan, with the support of the Allies, had treacherously (in his view) dispatched the so-called Army of the Caliphate to secure the destruction of the national movement. Not that hatred of the sultan and his advisers was the only factor motivating Mustafa Kemal's support for abolition. Other considerations, equally important from Mustafa Kemal's point of view, affected his decision. These included, as we have seen, the need to unite the administrative system of the state, divided in the period of national struggle; the need to present a united front to the Allies at the forthcoming peace conference; and a fear that the sultanate, however reduced in power and influence, might yet provide a focal point for those opposed, on both political and personal grounds, to his own leadership (and no doubt later reform) of the state.

The abolition of the sultanate was not the only substantial reform of the Turkish state structure undertaken by Mustafa Kemal in this period. On 13 October 1923, following the victory of his newly formed People's Party in elections held in June, and the opening of a new session of the grand national assembly, he had a clause added to the constitution making Ankara the seat of government, and by implication the capital, of the new Turkey. On 29 October, following a carefully engineered crisis in the national assembly, he had a republic, the logical form of government, as he put it, implied by the abolition of the sultanate, declared. And in March 1924, following a series of leaks and other indications of a coming change, he had the caliphate, a focal point of reaction, abolished.

Had Abdul Medjid, the prince regent, felt able to respond to Mustafa Kemal's invitation to join him in Anatolia, communicated by Yümnü, a former adjutant to the prince, in July 1920, then it is possible that he would have succeeded in saving the Ottoman Sultanate, whose reputation would have been immeasurably enhanced thereby. But concern expressed by Abdul Medjid's advisers regarding the probable impact on the reputation of the Ottoman dynasty of his participation in the national struggle, seen at the time as a rebellion, together with the strong opposition of his father, prevented him from so doing, despite the fact that an Italian ship, specially chartered, lay at anchor off Büyükdere, awaiting his departure. Later in March 1921 Abdul Medjid's son, Omer Faruk, along with his teacher, Asim, made a similar attempt to escape to Ankara, but by then the civil war, which as Mustafa Kemal later remarked might have been prevented by the dispatch of a member of the Ottoman royal family to Anatolia, had occurred and the die had been cast. Omer Faruk's approach was, therefore, rebuffed. When he arrived in Inebolu in April he was politely advised that his presence in Ankara was not required, as he had come without an invitation.[28]

The moment of Abdul Medjid's proposed departure for Ankara was by no means the first occasion on which he had displayed sympathy and support for the nationalists. A man of retiring disposition, fond of poetry and painting, he had earlier attempted to influence Allied policy, approaching the Allied heads of state with requests that they bring pressure to bear on their ministers to moderate their policies, and writing articles in the press criticising the Ottoman government, which he believed was incapable of dealing with the situation. As a result he had become popular with the nationalists, many of whom would have welcomed his election to the sultanate in place of Mehmed VI Vahideddin.

The Treaty of Lausanne

In the Treaty of Lausanne, concluded following long and tortuous negotiations between the Allies and the Turkish nationalists on 24 July 1923, the remaining issues regarding the residue of the Ottoman estate were finally resolved and, as Mustafa Kemal later put it, 'centuries-old accounts' regulated. In Europe eastern Thrace, including Edirne and Karaağaç (ceded by Greece in return for the cancellation of a Turkish claim for reparations) was recognised as belonging to the new Turkish state, as was the whole of Anatolia, including Cilicia and the eastern provinces. With regard to the Straits, an issue of primary importance to the Great Powers, in particular Britain, France and Russia, it was agreed that, subject to certain restrictions, agreed by the powers, they would henceforth remain open, not only to ships of commerce, as heretofore, but also to ships of war; and that the sea passage would be administered by an international commission; while the area approximate to the Straits would be demilitarised. As for Mosul, claimed by the Turks, it was agreed that for the moment the issue would be set aside.

---

28. Ertürk, *Iki Devrin Perde Arkasi*, pp. 304–5; Jäschke, 'Mustafa Kemal und Abdülmecid'.

Further negotiation, and a possible adjudication by the League of Nations, would decide its fate. (In 1926 Mosul was allotted by the League of Nations to Iraq.) Finally, with regard to the capitulations, they would be abolished. Henceforth, as Mustafa Kemal later remarked, the world would be required to recognise the absolute sovereignty and complete independence of the Turkish nation.[29]

29. H. Nicolson, *Curzon: The Last Phase* London: Constable, 1937, Chs 10 and 11; A.L. Macfie, 'The Straits Question. The Conference of Lausanne', *Middle Eastern Studies*, Vol. 15 (1979); Mustafa Kemal, *Speech*, pp. 585–7, 608–42.

CHAPTER ELEVEN

The Peace Settlement and the Minorities

The Greeks

The Greek attempt, in the period of the First World War and its aftermath, to realise the *Megali Idea* (great idea) in Anatolia and Thrace proved for the Greek Orthodox inhabitants of the Ottoman Empire a disaster of major proportions, leading first to harrassment and persecution, and then, following the defeat of the Greek expeditionary forces in Anatolia, to a mass exodus, shortly followed by the deportation of those remaining. That exodus, more or less accomplished by the time of the Mudania armistice of 11 October 1922, was formally completed by an exchange of populations, agreed by the Greek and Turkish delegations at the Lausanne conference; though in a protocol attached to the Treaty of Lausanne, which set out the terms of the agreement, the Greek Orthodox inhabitants of Istanbul and the Muslim inhabitants of western Thrace were exempted from the arrangement.[1]

The exchange of populations provided for in the protocol attached to the Treaty of Lausanne was not a consequence merely of the participation of Greece in the First World War on the side of the Entente Powers. Already, in the period of the Balkan Wars, the CUP had proposed to the Greeks that an exchange of populations might take place, similar to one arranged by the Ottomans with the Bulgarians in the Treaty of Constantinople of 29 September 1913. At the same time, in order to persuade the Greek government of the need for some such arrangement, they had begun to expel the Orthodox inhabitants of western Anatolia and eastern Thrace; and

1. H.J. Psomiades, *The Eastern Question: The Last Phase* Salonica: Institute of Balkan Studies, 1968.

they had even threatened that, in the event of a Greek failure to conclude a satisfactory agreement regarding the future of the Aegean islands, then in dispute, they might expel the whole of the Orthodox population of the area. As a result in May 1914 Venizelos, the Greek prime minister, felt obliged to accept an Ottoman proposal, put forward by Galib Kemali (Söylemezoğlu), the Ottoman minister in Athens, that an arrangement be made for an exchange of populations, provided only that the emigration be voluntary, and that proper arrangements be made for the evaluation and liquidation of the property of the emigrants. In June 1914 a mixed commission was appointed to arrange the proposed exchange; but the work of the commission was cut short by the outbreak of the First World War.[2]

At the Paris peace conference, and in the weeks following the Greek occupation of Izmir, Venizelos raised once again the possibility of a population exchange in Anatolia, which he believed would alone save the Orthodox minority from extinction. But at that time no agreement was arrived at. Only following the expulsion of the Greek expeditionary forces from Anatolia in September 1922, by which time the majority of the Greek inhabitants of Anatolia had already departed, did it become possible to arrive at an understanding. The possibility was then raised by among others Dr Fridtjof Nansen, the League of Nations official appointed to look into the question. In the negotiations which followed it quickly emerged that many of the Greeks involved would have preferred a voluntary arrangement, but the Turks, who were intent on nation building, would have none of it. Not that, from the point of view of the Greeks, at least, it made much difference, for as Venizelos later remarked: 'The expulsion of the Asia Minor population has not been a consequence of the Exchange Accord, but had been already an accomplished fact, – in it I merely received the consent of Turkey to move the Turkish Muslims from Greece in order to help to reestablish the Greek refugees.'[3] In the final text of the agreement, provision was made for an exchange of Turkish nationals of the Greek Orthodox religion established in Turkish territory, except those established in Constantinople before 30 October 1918 (the date of the Mudros armistice) and of Greek nationals of the Muslim religion, except those established in western Thrace. As a result, paradoxically, as many authors have pointed out, in addition to those

2. S. Akgün, 'Turkish Greek Population Exchange with a Selection from American Documents', *Turkish Review of Balkan Studies*, Vol. 1 (1993).

3. Psomiades, *Eastern Question*, p. 65.

correctly identified, large numbers of Greek-speaking Turks were dispatched from Turkey to Greece in exchange for a similar number of Turkish-speaking Greeks, dispatched from Greece to Turkey.[4]

The Greek and Turkish governments, with the support and assistance of a mixed commission, provided for in the protocol attached to the Lausanne Treaty, lost no time in implementing the agreement arrived at. Between 1923 and 1925 more than 188 000 Greek Orthodox Turkish nationals were transferred from Turkey to Greece, and more than 355 000 Muslims from Greece to Turkey. The intractable problem of liquidating the property of the refugees and paying compensation took somewhat longer. Only in 1930, when Venizelos and Mustafa Kemal concluded the Convention of Ankara, was the issue finally resolved.

The Kurds

For the Kurds, who in the preceding half century or so had failed to develop a mature sense of national identity, capable of supporting a claim to independence or autonomy, the settlement arrived at at Lausanne proved initially disappointing and ultimately disastrous. In Turkey and Iraq (and also in Iran, where a substantial number of Kurds lived) the settlement left them exposed as a minority, deprived to a greater or lesser extent of political, social and cultural rights; and in due course it opened the way to exploitation and oppression, and even, under Saddam Hussein, a later ruler of Iraq, to genocide. Nor can it be argued that the British, the people mainly concerned, were unaware of the realities of the situation prevailing. As Lord Curzon, the British foreign minister, responsible for negotiating the Treaty of Lausanne, at one point remarked: 'The whole of our information shows that the Kurds, with their own independent history, customs, manners and character, ought to be an autonomous race.'[5] But the imperatives of empire, and the urgent need for a settlement with the Turks, prevailed, and the Kurdish provinces, with the exception of Mosul, which was left for a later adjudication by the League of Nations, were partitioned.

---

4. B. Lewis, *The Emergence of Modern Turkey* Oxford: Oxford Universtiy Press, 1961, pp. 348–9.
5. D. McDowall, *A Modern History of the Kurds* New York: J.B. Tauris, 1996, p. 142. Sir Percy Cox, the British high commissioner in Iraq, would have wished to offer the Kurds military and political support against the Turks, but his proposals were rejected by Winston Churchill, the minister concerned.

Kurdish national identity in the period of the First World War, though underdeveloped, was by no means non-existent. In the period of Young Turk government that preceded the war most Kurds supported the policy of decentralisation promoted by the Liberal Union Party, in the expectation that that would enable them to secure a degree of autonomy in the Kurdish provinces; and in 1908, a group of educated Kurds resident in Istanbul formed a Society for the Rise and Progress of Kurdistan. Other groups formed societies for the promotion of education in the Kurdish provinces, and published journals promoting ideas of mutual aid and progress; and in 1910 a group of Kurds resident in Istanbul, many the sons of Kurdish notables whose power was threatened by the centralising policies of the Young Turk regime, formed a Kurdish Hope Society. At the same time Hamidiye chiefs and religious sheikhs, many supporters of the failed counter-revolution of April 1909, set up secret societies opposed to the centralising and secularist policies of the CUP; while sheikhs Abd al Salam of Barzan and Nur Muhammed of Dohuk organised a petition, demanding for the five administrative districts of Bahdinan the adoption of Kurdish as an official language, the appointment of Kurdish speaking officials, exemption from the *corvée*, the expenditure of taxation raised locally for local purposes, and the administration of the law in accordance with the *Sheriat*. So extensive, indeed, did the opposition of the Kurdish notables, religious sheikhs, *aghas* and others become, that in 1913 the Ottoman government felt obliged to modify its policies, abandoning its attempt to impose central control, and reconstituting the old Hamidiya cavalry, earlier disbanded, under a new name, the Tribal Light Cavalry.[6]

That such changes of policy did much to reduce the risk of an uprising is not in doubt; but they did not remove it. In January 1914 Sheikh Abd al Salam of Barzan, having formed (possibly with Russian backing) an alliance with Sheikh Taha of Nihri and Abd al Razzaq Badr Khan, rose in revolt; and in March Mullah Salim and an alliance of sheikhs in the Khizan district rose, calling for the withdrawal of atheist officials and the restoration of the *Sheriat*. Following the dispatch of Ottoman troops to the area both revolts quickly petered out, for the rebels, considered by the townsfolk as mere riff-raff, lacked both a coherent ideology and an effective strategy; but they nonetheless caused the Ottoman authorities considerable concern.

---

6. McDowall, *A Modern History of the Kurds*, Chs 5 and 6.

In the First World War the Kurds remained generally loyal to the Ottomans, fighting in their armies and assisting in the extermination of the Armenians. Indeed, a majority of the troops serving on the eastern front were, it is said, of Kurdish extraction. Not that their loyal service was invariably appreciated. According to David McDowall, whose *Modern History of the Kurds* was published in 1996, in 1917 the Ottoman government took steps, under cover of the scorched-earth policy they were then enforcing, to secure a dispersal of the Kurdish inhabitants of the areas concerned, in order that in the post-war period they might be more easily absorbed by the Turkish majority.[7]

The Kurdish sense of national identity, previously inchoate, received a substantial boost as a result of the defeat of the Ottoman Empire in the First World War. In May 1917 a group of Kurdish notables, meeting in Sulaymania, proposed the creation of a provisional Kurdish government; and in 1918 Sheikh Abd al Qadir and the leading Badr Khans reconstituted a Society for the Rise of Kurdistan. In January 1919 a Committee of Kurdish Independence led by Suraya Badr Khan issued in Cairo an appeal to the British for support in establishing a Kurdish state; and in April Sheikh Taha of Nihri approached the British authorities in Baghdad, proposing the creation of a united Kurdistan. Other proposals of this sort followed; and it is possible that a Kurdish state of some kind, however unstable, might have been created, had the Allies, in particular the British and the French, been prepared to throw their weight behind the project, but it rapidly transpired that the British, grossly overstretched elsewhere, had no intention of so doing, while the French, committed, initially at least, to the possession of Cilicia, saw a united Kurdistan as a threat to their position in the area.

Whatever small possibility there might have been that the Kurds would succeed in the period following the end of the First World War in securing their independence or autonomy – a majority of the tribes remained throughout either loyal to the Ottomans or totally indifferent to the issue – vanished with the rise of the Turkish national movement in Anatolia. Following the establishment of their movement, the nationalists mounted an immediate propaganda campaign, emphasising the dangers which the creation of an independent Armenia would pose to the Kurds. At the same time they pointed out the threat which Allied control of Istanbul posed to the survival of the caliphate, an institution with which the Kurds,

7. Ibid., pp. 105–6.

as good Muslims, generally identified. As a result by the end of 1919, at least 70 Kurdish tribes and a substantial number of urban notables had declared for the nationalists. Nor did the publication of the Treaty of Sèvres, which promised both the Armenians and the Kurds either independence or autonomy, sway the balance; though in the summer of 1920 the Alevi Kurds of Dersim and Kharput, traditionally opposed to government control of any kind, rose in revolt, causing the nationalists some concern. In June 1921 nationalist forces occupied Rawanduz, on the border with Iraq, and in October the French, overextended in Syria, concluded an agreement with the nationalists, acknowledging Turkish possession of Cilicia. In August–September 1921 the nationalist forces in western Anatolia, following a series of desperate battles, inflicted a severe defeat on the Greek expeditionary forces at Sakarya; and in September 1922 they swept the Greek forces out of the sub-continent. As a result, at Lausanne, a treaty of peace was concluded, incorporating the greater part of the Kurdish provinces, but not Mosul, into the new Turkish state.[8]

The Armenians

For the Armenian inhabitants of the eastern provinces – those few that had survived – and Transcaucasia, where more than 400 000 refugees had sought sanctuary, the settlement arrived at at Lausanne marked merely the last act of the tragedy enacted in the period of the First World War. Allied promises regarding the creation of an independent or autonomous Armenian state, made in the closing stages of the war and in the period immediately following, raised among the Armenians expectations which, as events were soon to prove, the Allies were neither able nor willing to fulfil. As a result, squeezed between the growing power of the Turkish nationalist forces in Anatolia and the advancing Bolshevik forces in Transcaucasia, the Armenians found themselves once again trapped, the victims on this occasion, not only of massacre and war, but also of Great Power duplicity, self-delusion and betrayal.[9]

8. R. Olson, *The Emergence of Kurdish Nationalism and the Sheikh Said Rebellion* Austin, Texas: University of Texas Press, 1989; and 'The Churchill–Cox Correspondence regarding the Creation of the State of Iraq', *International Journal of Turkish Studies*, Vol. 5, Nos 1 and 2 (1990–1).

9. A. Nassibian, *Britain and the Armenian Question* London: Croom Helm, 1985; C.J. Walker, *Armenia* London: Routledge, 1980.

Allied assurances regarding the creation of an Armenian state in eastern Anatolia were nothing if not fulsome. In a speech given at the Guildhall in November 1916, H.H. Asquith, the British prime minister, had declared that Britain was 'resolved to liberate the Armenians from the Turkish yoke and to restore them to the religious and political freedom they deserve and of which they have been so long deprived'. In a speech given at the Central Hall, Westminster, in January 1918, Lloyd George, who in December 1916 had succeeded H.H. Asquith as prime minister, had declared that 'while we do not challenge the maintenance of the Turkish Empire in the homelands of the Turkish race, with its capital at Constantinople, the passage between the Mediterranean and the Black Sea being internationalised and neutralised, Arabia, Armenia, Mesopotamia, Syria, and Palestine are in our judgement entitled to a recognition of their separate national conditions'.[10] And in his Fourteen Points Woodrow Wilson had declared that all nations subject to Turkish rule would be assured an 'undoubted security of life and an absolutely unmolested opportunity of autonomous development'.[11] Nor in the period immediately following the end of the war did the Allies in any way retract the assurances they had given. On the contrary they frequently repeated them; and in the numerous drafts of a peace treaty considered by the Allies, and in the final treaty itself, a provision for the creation of an independent Armenian state, incorporating the eastern provinces, was invariably included. In these circumstances it is not surprising that, in arguing the Armenian case at the Paris peace conference in February 1919, Boghos Nubar, the leader of the Armenian delegation, was encouraged to claim not only the Armenian Republic of the Caucasus, recently established, but also the seven Ottoman *vilayets* of Van, Bitlis, Diyarbekir, Harput, Sivas, Erzerum and Trabzon, the four Cicilian *sancaks* of Marash, Kozan, Cebel Bereket and Adana, and the port of Iskenderun (Alexandretta) – all areas, according to the Armenian view of history, traditionally inhabited by Armenians.

Unfortunately for the Armenians, however, the numerous Allied protestations of support for an independent or autonomous Armenian state, incorporated in the various Allied declarations and in the Treaty of Sèvres, found no reflection in the realm of reality. Already, in the Mudros armistice, the Allies had failed to make adequate provision for the demobilisation of the Ottoman army,

---

10. Nassibian, *Britain and the Armenian Question*, p. 176; British Public Records Office, WO 106 1415 British Statements.

11. A.L. Macfie, *The Eastern Question* Harlow: Longman, 1989, Document 27.

particularly in the eastern provinces and Transcaucasia; though a clause providing for an Allied occupation of the Armenian provinces, in the event of disorder arising there, had been included. As a result, in the province of Kars, Yakup Şevki Pasha's Ninth Army, which incorporated units, well equipped and supplied, dispatched to the east by Enver Pasha following the withdrawal of Ottoman forces from the Galician and Moldavian fronts, was permitted to remain for some months in possession, thereby enabling the Muslim inhabitants of the province to set up a Muslim national council capable, with the assistance of Turco-Tartar armed bands, of intimidating the Armenian inhabitants of the area, and preventing the return of Armenian refugees to their homelands. Later the Allies did secure the withdrawal of the Ottoman Ninth Army to Erzerum, where, redesignated as the Fifteenth Army Corps, it became the backbone of nationalist resistance in the east; but they proved incapable of securing effective control of the area. Moreover, in January 1919 the British, grossly overstretched elsewhere, felt obliged to initiate a withdrawal of their forces from Transcaucasia, a process completed, following the evacuation of Batum, in the autumn. As a result, Allied policy regarding the eastern provinces became increasingly one characterised by pretence; though an attempt was made, following the massacre of Armenians perpetrated in Marash in February 1920, to recover control by carrying out an occupation of Istanbul, seen as a pledge of Ottoman good behaviour – an approach which, as we have seen, proved counter-productive. Nor were Allied attempts to persuade one or other of the Great Powers to accept a mandate for the proposed Armenian state successful. As Georges Clemenceau, the French premier, remarked at a meeting of the supreme council held in August 1919, the French could do nothing, the Italians could do nothing, the British could do nothing, and even the Americans (who at one point had appeared likely to accept the offer) could do nothing. Later attempts to persuade the League of Nations to take up the burden proved equally ineffective. As the secretary general of the organisation remarked, the League was not a state: it had no armies to execute its policies. By the summer of 1920, therefore, it had become all too evident to those concerned that the western Entente Powers had no intention of implementing the policy regarding the Armenian provinces they had so frequently espoused.

The actual task of destroying the last vestiges of the Armenian dream of independence was left to the Turkish nationalists. On 26

April 1920, Mustafa Kemal determined to scotch any attempt the Armenians might make, in conjunction with their Allied mentors, to establish an Armenian state in the eastern provinces, and concerned regarding the threat posed by the advance of Bolshevik forces in Transcaucasia, dispatched a letter (drafted for the most part by Kiazim Karabekir, the commander of the Fifteenth Army Corps, in Erzerum) to the Bolshevik government in Moscow, making it clear that the nationalists would welcome Soviet aid in their struggle with the imperial powers and their surrogates, provided only that the Soviets would agree to recognise the complete independence of Turkey. Should they agree to act together, then the nationalists might abandon Georgia and Azerbaijan to the Soviets, while the Soviets, for their part, might allow the nationalists to suppress what was referred to as the 'Imperialist Armenian Government'. And shortly thereafter, he dispatched a nationalist delegation, led by Bekir Sami Bey, foreign minister in the Ankara government, to Moscow to negotiate directly with the Bolsheviks, now seen as the rising power in the east.

The Soviet response to Mustafa Kemal's letter, dispatched on 2 June, proved discouraging. Whilst apparently welcoming the nationalist proposals and promising support for the aims and objectives set out in the National Pact, the Soviets in their reply gave what Mustafa Kemal and his colleagues considered to be an undue emphasis to nationalist assurances regarding the rights of the minority peoples. The Soviet government hoped, Chicherin, the Soviet foreign minister remarked, that the frontiers between Turkey, on the one side, and Armenia and Persia, on the other, would be established by negotiation, possibly with the Soviets acting as mediators. Despite all their assurances to the contrary, therefore, Mustafa Kemal and his colleagues concluded that the Russians intended merely to encourage the establishment of a series of independent states on the borderlands of Russia, in the expectation that in due course those states might once more be absorbed into the Russian empire.

Turkish suspicions regarding the intentions of the Soviets were further confirmed when talks opened between the nationalist delegation and Soviet officials in Moscow. When Bekir Sami and his colleagues insisted on the need to open a route through the independent republics of Armenia and Georgia, in order that a supply line might be opened to Anatolia, the Soviets prevaricated. Not only did they declare that they were too weak themselves to open the road, they also insisted that the Turks should not undertake the task. Later, however, they changed tack, quickly agreeing the main clauses of a draft treaty promising the nationalists aid and support on a substantial scale. Having thus whetted the appetite of the Turkish delegation, they then informed them that the actual signature of the treaty, and the dispatch of the promised aid, would be made dependent on the nationalists agreeing to the cession of extensive territories in eastern Anatolia to the Armenians. On being informed of these developments, Mustafa Kemal, already concerned regarding an Armenian occupation of Olti, a district rich in coal on the pre-war Russo-Turkish border, decided to act. He accordingly informed the Soviets that on no account would he agree to cede territory in eastern Anatolia; and at the same time he ordered the forces of Kiazim Karabekir in the east to advance and occupy Kars and other territories claimed by Turkey in the area. His gamble paid off. Urgent appeals for help, dispatched by the Armenians to the Allied Powers and the League of Nations, remained unanswered; though Admiral de Robeck, the British high commissioner in Istanbul, did make arrangements for the dispatch of 1,000 tons of fuel oil, for use on the Armenian railways. As a result the Turkish national forces were enabled to advance rapidly, capturing Sarikamish and Kars, while in the north Bolshevik forces, taking advantage of the opportunity offered, advanced on the Dilijan front. In December 1920 the defeated Armenians were obliged to conclude with the Turks the Treaty of Gümrü (Alexandropol), establishing agreed frontiers, favourable to the Turks. According to the terms of this treaty the Armenian state would henceforth be entitled to enlist only 1,500 troops, equipped with 20 machine guns and 8 cannon; and it would be obliged to accept inspection by a Turkish political agent, based in Erivan. It would, in other words, be reduced to the status of a protectorate. Not that in the end the conditions imposed on the Armenian state proved very significant. In the following weeks Bolshevik forces, advancing rapidly, occupied the greater part of Armenia, including Erivan. And in March 1921 the Turkish nationalists and the Russians concluded the Treaty of Moscow, which allocated Kars and Ardahan (but not Batum) to Turkey in return for assurances, given by the nationalists, that in any conference regarding the Straits convened by the littoral powers (or presumably others) Turkey would support a resolution of the Straits question in a sense favourable to Russia.[12]

12. H. Bayur, 'Birinci Genel Savaştan Sonra Yapilan Bariş Antlaşmalarimiz', *Belleten*, Vol. 30 (1966); Walker, *Armenia*, Ch. 8, Nassibian, *Britain and the Armenian Question*, Chs 4 and 5.

The Arab provinces

SYRIA

In the Arab provinces the settlement eventually arrived at proved, from the point of view of the British and French at least, to be very much along the lines envisaged in the Sykes–Picot Agreement. In Syria, the Lebanon and Palestine, following the victory of the Allied forces, predominantly British, the British commander, General Allenby, at once established an occupied enemy territory administration, divided into three zones: a western zone (OETW, originally OET North), consisting of the Syrian littoral, where it was expected that France would undertake the administration; an eastern zone (OETE), consisting of the interior of Syria and Transjordan, where it was expected that Feisal, the third son of Emir Husein, the sherif of Mecca, would undertake the administration; and a southern zone (OETS), consisting of Palestine, west of the Jordan, where following an agreement concluded by Lloyd George, the British prime minister, and Georges Clemenceau, the French premier, in December 1918, it was agreed that Britain would not only undertake the administration but also acquire ultimate control. Then in September 1919, following a prolonged period of uncertainty, inspired in part by what the French saw as British prevarication, and in part by an American attempt to implement the principle of self-determination embodied in the Fourteen Points (in June–July 1919 President Woodrow Wilson dispatched a commission of enquiry to Syria to investigate the hopes and expectations of the local populations) the British and French concluded an agreement providing for the evacuation of the British garrison in OETW and their replacement by a French garrison. And in April 1920, at the Conference of San Remo, they agreed that, in accordance with the provisions of the recently established League of Nations – the League had made provisions for the recognition of the existence of independent nations, 'subject to the rendering of administrative advice and assistance by a Mandatory', to be appointed by the League – France should be awarded a mandate for Syria and Britain mandates for Palestine and Mesopotamia.[13]

The French did not for long remain content with the system of direct and indirect influence and control envisaged for Syria in the

13. P.M. Holt, *Egypt and the Fertile Crescent, 1516–1922* Harlow: Longman, 1966, Ch. 20; M. Yapp, *The Making of the Modern Near East* Harlow: Longman, 1987, pp. 322–7; Macfie, *The Eastern Question*, Ch. 10.

Sykes–Picot Agreement. In July 1920, as Arab resistance, promoted by Emir Feisal and his supporters, for the most part local notables, mounted, both in OETW and OETE – on 7 March 1920 a Syrian national congress claimed independence for the whole of Syria, including Palestine and the Lebanon, and elected Feisal king – they dispatched a substantial force under the command of General Gouraud into the interior which, after a battle (little more than a skirmish) at Khan Maysalun, quickly occupied Damascus and placed the whole area under a common administration.

MESOPOTAMIA

In Mesopotamia, where in the closing stages of the First World War the British had established a quasi-colonial administration, staffed for the most part by British officials, – in 1920, of the holders of senior administrative posts 507 were British, 7 Indian and 20 Arab – the British eventually decided (against the advice, it must be said, of Arnold Wilson, the acting high commissioner, a keen advocate of the British colonial system of government) to seek the creation of a unitary Arab state, ruled over by an Arab king but subject to British tutelage. The territory of this state would stretch from the northern boundary of the Mosul *vilayet*, acquired by Britain in the Anglo-French agreement of December 1918, to the Persian Gulf.

The creation of a unitary Arab state in Iraq, subject to British control, was not accomplished without difficulty. Throughout the spring and summer of 1920 Arab unrest among the tribes of the middle and lower Euphrates mounted, inspired in part by propaganda put out by Syrian nationalists based in Damascus – on 8 March 1920 Iraqi nationalists in Damascus had Sherif Husein's eldest son, Abdullah, proclaimed King of Iraq – and in part by Shiite opposition to infidel rule. Then in July insurrection broke out on a considerable scale, engulfing almost one-third of Iraq; though not for the most part the principal towns, the lower Tigris area and the Kurdish provinces. As a result implementation of British policy was for a time delayed; but in November 1920, following the suppression of the insurrection, which required the dispatch of substantial forces and an expenditure of £40 million, Sir Percy Cox, who in October had replaced Wilson as acting high commissioner, succeeded in persuading a number of Iraqi notables, including Sayyid Talib of Basra and Jafa Pasha al Askari, to form an interim government, led by Said Abd al-Rahman al Gaylani, naqib of Baghdad; and on 11 July 1921 the council of state was persuaded to pass a unanimous resolution declaring Feisal, recently expelled from Damascus, king. Finally, in October 1922 an Anglo-Iraq treaty was concluded, providing for a substantial degree of self-government; though foreign policy, defence and finance were to remain under British control.

The British decision to opt in Iraq for the installation of Feisal as king, adopted at a conference convened by Winston Churchill, the British secretary of state for the colonies, in Cairo in March 1921, was by no means a foregone conclusion. Numerous other solutions to the problems of government created by the eviction of the Ottomans were considered. These included the creation of a republic, the return of Sayyid Talib, the so-called strong man of Basra, the installation of the Aga Khan as king, and even the installation of Abdullah, Sherif Husein's eldest son. But in the end Emir Feisal, considered the most amenable of Husein's sons, was selected.[14]

PALESTINE

Arab discontent also found expression in Palestine. Provoked by the unwillingness of the Allies to admit the claims of the Syrian nationalists for the complete independence of Syria, including Palestine, presented by Emir Feisal at the Paris peace conference in January 1919, and by Jewish demands for unrestricted immigration, also presented by a Zionist delegation at the conference, militant Palestinian Arabs formed liberation societies, organised conferences and, on occasion, attacked Jewish settlements and communities. Following the decision of the supreme council to grant Britain a mandate for Palestine, taken at the San Remo conference in April 1920, these attacks increased both in frequency and intensity, as they did again when in July 1920 the British established a civil administration, headed by a Jewish high commissioner, Sir Herbert Samuel. Nor did British attempts to placate the Palestinian Arabs, which included a tightening of Jewish immigration controls following a riot in 1928, and the appointment of Palestinian Arab notables to advisory and legislative councils, succeed in reducing tension; though later British attempts to form alliances with leading Palestine families did to some extent succeed in reestablishing stability.

14. Holt, *Egypt and the Fertile Crescent*, Ch. 20; A. Vinogradov, 'The 1920 Revolt in Iraq Reconsidered: The Role of Tribes in National Politics', *Middle Eastern Studies*, Vol. 3 (1972); A. Wilson, *Mesopotamia, 1917–20* Oxford: Oxford University Press, 1931; Olson, 'The Churchill–Cox Correspondence regarding the Creation of the State of Iraq'.

Throughout, the Palestinian Arabs, with few exceptions, refused to acknowledge either the legality of the mandatory regime or the equal rights accorded to the Jewish settlers. As a result in 1929 disturbances broke out in Jerusalem, sparked off, it is said, by a dispute regarding Jewish rights to worship at the Western or Wailing Wall, the first of a series of major disturbances and riots that were in due course to give rise to that most intractable of problems, the Palestine question.[15]

Palestinian Arab opposition to Jewish immigration in Palestine did not at that time find a reflection in the Hashemite camp. In May 1918 Chaim Weizmann, the Zionist leader, met Emir Feisal in Palestine to discuss the question; and in January 1919 the two men agreed not only that Palestine should be excluded from any proposed settlement involving the creation of an Arab state in the area, but also that the Zionist programme, or at least a part of it, might be implemented there. In return Weizmann promised economic assistance to the proposed Arab state and respect for the basic rights of the Palestinian Arabs. Not that Feisal's commitment to the implementation of the Zionist programme was necessarily unqualified, for it was made dependent on the creation of an independent Arab state, an unlikely development.[16]

TRANSJORDAN

The installation of a British administration in Palestine did not complete the Allied task of creating a new order in the Arab provinces. In November 1920 Sherif Husein's eldest son, Abdullah, arrived in Transjordan, accompanied by some 500 bedouin tribesmen, intent, it is said, on opposing a French conquest of Syria. As a result the French, concerned regarding the threat posed to their position in Syria, requested their British ally to take action against Abdullah; and the British, seizing the opportunity offered to secure strategic control of the interior without the expense which direct British control might entail, responded by offering Abdullah the governorship of Transjordan, together with a substantial subsidy, on condition merely that he abandon whatever plans he might have had to oppose the French, and restore order in the area. This offer Abdullah, reportedly none too keen to engage the French in battle, accepted gratefully; and in due course the arrangement, initially

15. D. Fromkin, *A Peace to End All Peace* Harmondsworth: Penguin Books, 1989, Chs 50 and 58.
16. Ibid.

intended to be merely temporary, became permanent. In this inconsequential way was the emirate of Transjordan, later Jordan, created.[17]

ARABIA

In the period of the peace settlement in the Near and Middle East Abdul Aziz Ibn Saud, the emir of Nejd, acted throughout with great caution, refraining from attempting a conquest of the Gulf states and the Hedjaz lest a policy of expansion result in a confrontation with the British, now the predominant power in the area. Thereafter British (and later American) protection continued to secure the survival of the Gulf states; but with regard to the Hedjaz declining British interest in the area enabled Ibn Saud, in 1924, to undertake its conquest. Taking advantage of Sherif Husein's increasing alienation from the British – against British advice he insisted on declaring himself caliph – and of his failure to conclude with the British a treaty guaranteeing his independence – the McMahon Correspondence consisted merely of notes and letters – Ibn Saud then moved quickly to secure control of the emirate. Already, in 1919, a Saudi force had proved its superiority by eliminating a five-thousand-strong Sherifian force at Khurma. In 1924, in order to test out the strength of a possible British reaction, he occupied Taif; and then, in 1925, finally persuaded that the British would not intervene to secure the survival of their wartime ally, he moved to complete the conquest of the emirate.[18]

Saudi claims to the possession of the Hedjaz dated back as far as the 1800s, when a Wahhabi force had conquered Mecca and Medina; but Ibn Saud's grievances against the Hashemites were of more recent origin. In 1910 a dispute had broken out between the Saudis and the Hashemites over the allegiance of the Utaiba, a tribe inhabiting a strategic territory on the borderlands of the two emirates. Shortly thereafter a sherifian force had captured Ibn Saud's brother, Sa'd. In return for his release, Ibn Saud had been obliged, not only to pay an annual tribute of £1,000, but also to acknowledge Ottoman sovereignty. Such a humiliation was more than sufficient to justify further conflict, but other considerations too played a part in shaping Ibn Saud's thinking. In the period of the Arab Revolt Sherif Husein's repeated claims to the title of 'King of the

17. Yapp, *Making of the Modern Near East*, pp. 330–1.
18. J. Goldberg, *The Foreign Policy of Saudi Arabia* Cambridge, Massachusetts: Harvard University Press, 1986.

Arabs' had convinced him that Hashemite ambitions in Arabia would ultimately prove incompatible with the security and survival of the Saudi state. Initially, in order to secure the support of the British, who sought a Saudi–Hashemite alliance against the Ottomans, he pretended to a degree of cooperation. But in 1924, when circumstances proved more favourable, he moved quickly to eliminate his rival.[19]

19. Ibid.

CHAPTER TWELVE

The End of the Committee of Union and Progress

The end of the CUP, officially dissolved in November 1918, but in fact preserved, first in the form of a political party, the Renovation Party (Teceddüd Firkasi), and then as a loose network of individual members, groups and organisations, including Karakol and the General Revolutionary Organisation of the Islamic World (both successor organisations of Teşkilati Mahsusa), came in 1926. Mustafa Kemal (Atatürk), recently elected president of the republic, seizing the opportunity offered by an outbreak of rebellion in the Kurdish provinces (the outbreak led to the passing of a draconian law for the maintenance of public order, which gave the president extraordinary powers) and by the discovery of a plot to secure his assassination organised by discontented elements opposed to his regime, then took decisive action to suppress the remaining elements of the organisation and eliminate its leadership.[1]

The business of eliminating the remaining elements of the CUP was carried out with ruthless speed and efficiency. In the week or so following the discovery of the plot more than 100 supposed suspects were arrested, including not only the principal leaders of the CUP but also the leaders of the Progressive Republican Party, an opposition party organised by leaders of the national movement and others critical of the despotic powers increasingly exercised by Mustafa Kemal. In the show trials which followed, held at Izmir and Ankara, little mercy was shown. Along with the conspirators and their associates, a dozen or so in number, many former leaders of the CUP, including Dr Nazim, the grand old man of the Unionist Movement and a former minister of education, Djavid Bey, a former

---

1. A.L. Macfie, *Atatürk* Harlow: Longman, 1994, Ch. 9; E.J. Zürcher, *The Unionist Factor* Leiden: E.J. Brill, 1984; and 'The Last Phase in the History of the Committee of Union and Progress, 1923–1924', *Varia Turcica*, Vol. 13 (1991).

minister of finance, *Yenibahçeli* Nail, a Unionist *fedai*, and Ismail Canbolat, a founder member of the organisation, were condemned to death and executed, as were a number of deputies belonging to the Progressive Republican Party. Other CUP and Progressive Republican Party leaders, including Rauf, convicted *in absentia* (he happened to be abroad at the time) were sentenced to long periods of imprisonment. As for Kiazim Karabekir, Ali Fuat and Refet, all heroes of the war of independence, Mustafa Kemal, fearful of the reaction that their execution or imprisonment might provoke in the army, was in the end persuaded to relent, but it was made clear to all concerned that they would not in the future be permitted to engage in Turkish politics. Meanwhile Kara Kemal, the Unionist party boss, who had escaped arrest, finally cornered, chose to commit suicide rather than surrender.[2]

Before concluding its business at the show trials the Ankara court, on the instructions of Mustafa Kemal, ordered that all funds and property belonging to the CUP be transferred to the state (a similar order, made by Mehmed VI Vahideddin, had not it seems been acted on).

In the show trials, the leaders of the CUP and the Progressive Republican Party were accused, not only of complicity in the plot to assassinate Mustafa Kemal, but also of a catalogue of other crimes, including responsibility for procuring the entry of the Ottoman Empire into the First World War on the side of the Central Powers, profiteering on a massive scale in the war, living in luxury and debauchery while Turkish soldiers were fighting in the field against a superior enemy, concluding the supposedly disastrous Armistice of Mudros, and seeking in the period of the war of independence to secure, in conjunction with Enver Pasha, a CUP take-over of the government of the grand national assembly in Ankara.[3]

The purpose of the wide-ranging catalogue of charges brought against the accused in the show trials of 1926 – little or no evidence was adduced to prove the charges: the guilt of the accused was simply assumed – was essentially twofold: to justify suppression of the opposition elements associated with the CUP and the Progressive Republican Party, and to establish the absolute power of the new Kemalist regime. A third purpose, less evident, but nonetheless significant, was the distancing of the new regime (itself the product of the CUP organisations and networks established in the

2. Zürcher, *Unionist Factor*, Ch. 6.
3. British Public Records Office, FO 424 265 Nos 15 and 16, enclosures.

previous decade) from the CUP which, as in the time of Mehmed VI Vahideddin, could conveniently be blamed for the multiple failures of the previous regime.

For the triumvirate of CUP leaders, who in the last days of the war had fled the Ottoman capital, fate proved if anything even more exacting. Enver Pasha, as ever energetic and ambitious, was killed in August 1922, leading *Basmachi* (bandit or free men) guerrillas fighting a Bolshevik force in the neighbourhood of Baljuwan, just north of the Afghan border, in Central Asia. Talaat was assassinated by an Armenian, Soghomon Tehlirian, on a street corner in Berlin in March 1921. Djemal was assassinated, also by Armenian terrorists, in Tiflis, the Georgian capital, in July 1922. To the end all three continued to work energetically for the attainment of their political objectives, Talaat mainly in Berlin, Enver in Moscow and Central Asia, and Djemal in Afghanistan. Whereas Talaat and Djemal, following a period of uncertainty, came eventually to accept the leadership of Mustafa Kemal, and the national movement he and his supporter had founded in Anatolia, Enver appears never to have done so. On the contrary, until very nearly the end of his life, he remained committed, not only to a restoration of the CUP, but also to a recovery of the power he had wielded as leader of the organisation in the war years.

Enver

Following his arrival in the Crimea Enver, unlike Talaat and Djemal, who made immediately for Berlin, set out by ship for Transcaucasia, where he hoped to make contact with the Turkish forces stationed in the area. There he hoped to set up a provisional government and carry on what he had once referred to as the 'second phase' in the war, which he believed would continue in the east following defeat in the west. But shipwreck, ill health and reports of the demobilisation of Turkish forces in Transcausasia obliged him to change direction, and travel instead by train to Berlin, the focal point of expatriate Turkish resistance to the Entente Powers.

In Berlin, where he took up residence in Babelsberg, and quickly made contact with Turkish, Volga and Crimean Tartar communities resident there, Enver was in due course introduced to Karl Radek, the noted Communist agitator and publicist, incarcerated at the time in Moabit prison, whose release it is said he later helped to secure. Persuaded by him of the advantages to be gained from the

formation of an Islamic Bolshevik alliance, in April 1919 or thereabouts, with the support and approval of Hans von Seeckt, a German general who during the war had held the post of chief of the
Ottoman general staff and who like Radek saw the advantages to be
gained from cooperation with the Soviets, he then set out to travel
by plane to Moscow, where after an incredible series of accidents,
setbacks and adventures, including a series of air crashes and a
period of imprisonment, he arrived in the summer of 1920.

In Moscow Enver, quick to respond to the new ideological cli-
mate, made immediate contact with a number of Bolshevik leaders,
including Trotsky and Chicherin, who not surprisingly proved somewhat suspicious of their new-found ally. Nevertheless they encouraged him to attend the great anti-imperialist Congress of the Peoples
of the East, being organised by the Bolsheviks at the time in Baku.
This he did; but his reception at the congress proved less than
cordial. Failing to understand the significance of the ten-minute
rule, it is said, he was barracked, and stormed out of the hall;
though he did later send a lengthy address to the congress, which
was read out on his behalf by a delegate. Not that he would necessarily have found it easy to identify with the aspirations of the more
extreme of the Bolshevik delegates attending the congress. At the
time, it would seem, he aimed merely to secure a synthesis of Bolshevik, nationalist and pan-Islamic ideas, sufficient to support the
formation of an anti-imperialist alliance: he had no desire to see
Bolshevik revolution, as such, exported to the Islamic world. To
this end, in conjunction with Turkish colleagues resident in Baku,
he set about drawing up a fully fledged political programme, *Mesaî*
(Labour), which it was hoped might attract the support of the so-
called Green Army and other anti-imperialist, radical and socialist
parties and groups, for the most part opposed to the leadership
and policies of Mustafa Kemal, organising at the time in Anatolia.
Later Enver had copies of *Mesaî* printed and distributed in Anatolia;
but to little effect.[4]

4. Yamauchi M., *The Green Crescent under the Red Star: Enver Pasha in Soviet Russia
1919–1922* Tokyo: Institute for the Study of the Languages and Cultures of Asia and
Africa, 1991; S.R. Sonyel, 'Mustafa Kemal and Enver in Conflict, 1919–22', *Middle
Eastern Studies*, Vol. 25, No. 4 (1989); and 'Enver Pasha and the Basmaji Movement
in Central Asia', *Middle Eastern Studies*, Vol. 26, No. 1 (1990); M.B. Olcott, 'The
Basmachi or Freemen's Revolt in Turkestan, 1918–24', *Soviet Studies*, Vol. 33, No. 3
(1981). Shortly before the armistice Enver, it is said, had a substantial sum of money
(some T.L. 700 000), weapons and ammunition sent to Azerbaijan, in preparation
for the second phase of the war, which he believed would follow defeat in the west.
It should be remembered that it was in the second phase of the Balkan Wars that
the Turks recovered Edirne.

Following the conclusion of the Baku congress Enver returned to Moscow and thence to Berlin, where with seemingly undiminished enthusiasm he set about organising a Union of Islamic Revolutionary Societies, supposedly representative of all the anti-imperialist groups in the Islamic world, but in fact incorporating only a handful of members, mainly CUP. Following the convening of a congress, thinly attended, Enver once again returned to Moscow, where he not only organised a second congress of members of the new Union, but also established a People's Soviet Party, committed to a programme even more radical than that contained in *Mesaî*. He then travelled to Batum, from which vantage point, it is believed, he hoped to execute a plan, long cherished, of entering Anatolia at the head of a volunteer force, locally recruited, and in the event of Mustafa Kemal suffering a decisive defeat at the hands of the Greeks, taking over the leadership of the national movement there. In Batum, Enver organised yet another congress of his Islamic Union, now significantly renamed the Party of Union and Progress. But all to no avail. In September, the nationalist forces in Anatolia inflicted a decisive defeat on the Greeks at Sakarya, a victory which not only secured the survival of the national movement, as organised by Mustafa Kemal and his supporters, but also made Mustafa Kemal's own position, as leader of the movement and commander-in-chief of the nationalist army, invincible. Not that in any case there was much chance that Enver's plan would have succeeded. In recent weeks Mustafa Kemal, well informed by his agents of the ambitions of his rival, had taken the precaution of having unreliable officers stationed in the east removed, supporters of Enver arrested or otherwise dealt with, and reinforcements dispatched. Were Enver to appear in eastern Anatolia, it was made clear, then he would be arrested.

Enver's failure at Batum did not mark the end of his remarkable career. Now fully convinced, by the decisive nature of the nationalist victory in Anatolia, of the impossibility of his making a successful comeback in Ottoman politics, and increasingly convinced of the duplicitous nature of Bolshevik policy – Enver's inability to organise a volunteer force in Transcaucasia was, it would seem, in part due to Soviet obstruction; the Soviets had no desire to see the forces of pan-Islamism and pan-Turkism strengthened in the area – in October 1921 or thereabouts he decided to abandon his search for an Islamic–Bolshevik alliance and opt instead for participation in the *Basmachi* revolt then taking place in eastern Bukhara. Travelling from Moscow – where his suspicions regarding the duplicitous nature of Soviet policy had been fully confirmed by amongst others a disaffected private secretary of Chicherin, who informed him of the true position – he first visited Bukhara and then, assuming the grandiose titles of commander-in-chief of all the armies of Islam, son-in-law of the caliph and representative of the Prophet, he placed himself at the head of the *Basmachi* rebels. In an ultimatum to the Soviet government he declared that it was the 'unshakeable will of the people of Bukhara, Turkestan and Kiva' to secure a 'free and independent life'; and in a letter to Amanullah Khan, the king of Afghanistan, he declared that it was his intention to create a 'confederation of the eastern Islamic governments' and 'put an end to Russian rule' in Central Asia.[5] But once again all to no avail. Though for a time he did make a significant impact on the struggle, commanding large forces in the field and inflicting defeats on the Bolshevik forces in the area, he proved unable to unite the various beys, emirs and other leaders opposed to the Soviets. Nor did the ideologies of Turkism and pan-Islamism prove as effective as he had hoped in rousing the people. Hard pressed by Bolshevik forces, brought in to deal with the uprising, he was in August 1922 killed in a skirmish fought in the neighbourhood of Baljuwan, north of old Bukhara, some 50 km from the Afghan border.

Talaat

Following his flight to Berlin, Talaat Pasha, like Enver, expected initially at least that he might yet be enabled to play a significant part in Ottoman politics. But unlike Enver he quickly concluded that his days of leadership were over; though he might yet remain influential. Like Enver, on first arriving in Berlin he visited Karl Radek, who he had met at the Brest-Litovsk peace conference, in Moabit prison; but he refused Radek's invitation to visit Moscow. Rather, he decided to assist Enver in his efforts to unite Muslim groups opposed to the imperial powers, publishing periodicals in Turkish, Persian and Arabic, supporting the dispatch of *Teşkilati Mahsusa* agents to Iran, Turkestan, India, Afghanistan and the Caucasus, and assisting in the organisation of the Union of Islamic Revolutionary Societies, which he helped set up. In July 1920 he

5. Yamauchi, *Green Crescent under the Red Star*, p. 68.

made contact with members of the Egyptian national movement in Constance; and in August he met Muhammad Ali, the leader of the caliphate movement, in Rome. Following the rise of the national movement in Anatolia he offered Mustafa Kemal his full support; and he rejected a proposal, put forward by Enver in January 1921, that they cooperate in an attempt to secure their political rehabilitation in Turkey.[6] In an elaborate scheme, allocating responsibility in the Union of Islamic Revolutionary Societies, drawn up by Enver, Talaat was allocated the task of representing the organisation in Berlin. His assassination, in March 1921, by the Armenian Soghomon Tehlirian, effectively marked, as one observer, no doubt with a degree of exaggeration, put it at the time, the end of an era: 'The existence of a society depends on the individual. If an individual passes away, the society is destined to die out. The Committee of Union and Progress has collapsed with the deceased's (Talaat Pasha's) immortal light. His companions in activity have dispersed.'[7]

Djemal

Following his flight from the Ottoman Empire in November 1918 Djemal Pasha, like Talaat, made initially for Berlin. He remained in Berlin for some months, but in July 1919 he moved to Klosters Platz in Switzerland. For a time he considered joining Enver in Moscow, but in the end he decided to make for Afghanistan where, hoping to promote resistance to British rule in India, he was to spend the rest of his life, attempting to organise an Afghan army. Throughout his travels he remained in close touch with Mustafa Kemal and the other CUP leaders. In June 1920 he asked Mustafa Kemal to dispatch competent officers to Kabul; and in November, acting on the instructions of King Amanullah, he contacted General Kress von Kressenstein, asking him to dispatch arms and ammunition for the use of the Afghan army. In the grandiose plan drawn up by Enver for the organisation of resistance to the imperial powers in Asia, Djemal was allocated responsibility for Afghanistan. Shortly before his assassination by Armenians in Tiflis in July 1922, it is said that he was contemplating a return to Anatolia.[8]

6. Ibid., pp. 9–53.
7. Ibid., p. 53.
8. *Encyclopaedia of Islam,* new edn, Djemal Pasha London: Luzac & Co, 1965.

A possible accommodation with the British

Throughout these years opposition to British imperial power in Asia remained a principal objective of the expatriate CUP leaders. Yet paradoxically both Enver and Talaat sought on several occasions to secure an accommodation with the British, which if realised might have radically altered the course of events. In February 1920, shortly before his departure for Moscow, Enver in an interview with Major Ivor Hedley, a member of the British military mission in Berlin, made it clear that, in return for certain concessions, he would be willing to abandon his plan of going to Moscow and organising a Bolshevik–Islamic alliance aimed at the British Empire in Asia. The concessions demanded would include independence for Egypt and the Sudan, self-determination for the Arab provinces, and the return of Izmir and Thrace to the Turks. Were Britain to come to terms with him, then he would remain in Berlin until everything was settled and then travel to the east, where he would seek to secure an improvement in Britain's relations with the Islamic world. The British response to Enver's approach was not encouraging. As W.S. Edmonds, a British foreign office official, noted, Enver's ambitions were clearly incompatible with British rule in Egypt and India. In any case, even if they were to stoop to treating with a man whom they regarded as a criminal, it would do no good, for the CUP and the Bolsheviks would continue to seek the destruction of British imperial power in Asia.[9]

Talaat's attempt to secure an accommodation with the British took place in February 1921. At the instigation of Sir Basil Thomson, a member of British intelligence, Talaat then met Aubrey Herbert, an old acquaintance, in Hamm, a small town near Düsseldorf, and in Düsseldorf itself. In the course of their discussions, he suggested that Britain and Turkey might form an alliance. In return for British assistance the Turks would give up their alliance with the Bolsheviks, cease to support pan-Islamism and pan-Turanism in Asia, and use their influence to calm the caliphate agitation in India; while the British would be expected to reconsider their position in Egypt and Mesopotamia, withdraw their support for the Greeks and return Izmir, eastern Thrace and the Aegean islands to Turkey. In the Armenian provinces, following a settlement, Britain might do as she liked, but it was to be doubted if she would succeed in

9. Sonyel, 'Mustafa Kemal and Enver in Conflict'.

creating an Armenian state there. As for the Straits, they might, as the British desired, be both neutralised and internationalised.

That Talaat's proposals were worth considering is not in doubt, for they were essentially the same as those put forward by Bekir Sami Bey, the nationalist foreign minister, at the London peace conference convened about that time. But there was in fact no chance that they would be accepted as the basis of a settlement, for at that time the Greeks, and to a lesser extent the Allied powers, remained convinced that they might yet secure their objectives by other means.[10]

10. A. Herbert, *Ben Kendim* London: Hutchinson, 1924, Pt. 6.

Conclusion

The destruction of the Ottoman Empire, brought about in the period 1908–23, marked a major turning point in the history of the Near and Middle East, a tectonic shift in the political and social structure of the area, comparable in the range and depth of its consequences with the break-up of the Habsburg, Tsarist and German empires that occurred in the same period. Out of the ruins of the empire emerged, by accident or design, in addition to the countries created in the nineteenth century (Serbia, Montenegro, Romania, Greece and Bulgaria) a series of states and mandated territories including Turkey, Albania, Syria, the Lebanon, Palestine (Israel), Transjordan (Jordan), Iraq and Saudi Arabia. Each of these countries was, in the following years, obliged, sometimes with the help of a mandatory appointed by the League of Nations, to establish a new government and administration, fortify and defend frontiers, few of which had been delineated in accordance with ethnic, strategic and geographical reality, and create from the crude rhetoric of race, nationality and culture, an ideology appropriate to its needs. These tasks were to preoccupy the rulers of the new states for many years to come.

The consequences of the end of the Ottoman Empire were by no means confined to the Near and Middle East. For the Great Powers the end of the empire marked the end of the Eastern Question, the great diplomatic, religious, economic and strategic question that had dominated European politics and diplomacy for a century and more. No longer would it be necessary for the rulers of Russia to approach their colleagues in Europe with elaborate schemes of partition, designed to forestall the worst consequences of an Ottoman collapse. No longer would it be necessary for the British and the French (themselves by no means immune to the temptations created by Ottoman decline) to prop up the ailing empire, whilst at the same time seeking to prevent a Russian and later a German take-over. Henceforth, the complex issues associated with the Eastern Question (the Bosnia-Herzegovina question, the Macedonian question, the Straits question, the Armenian question, the Kurdish question, the Suez Canal question, the Palestine question and a host of other associated questions) would have to be dealt with, not in the context of the Ottoman Empire, as heretofore, but in the context of the new state system. Not that the great strategic imperatives that had shaped the policies of the Great Powers in the period of the Eastern Question were radically affected by the change. On the contrary, magnified if anything by Great Power exploitation of the rich oil reserves of the area, they remained as significant as ever, as the events associated with the Suez Canal crisis of 1956 and the Kuwait War of 1993 prove.

That the end of the Ottoman Empire was an event of wide-ranging significance is not then in doubt. Yet many features of the Ottoman social and political order survived the collapse. These included the predominant part played by the military in the politics of the state, the significance of religion as a factor determining identity and the important part played by the notables in local politics. In Turkey, for instance, where nationalist rhetoric promoted an image of radical change in the state system, it has been estimated that as many as 85 per cent of Ottoman civil servants and 93 per cent of Ottoman staff officers remained in place following the creation of the republic; and to this day the Turkish army remains dominant. In Iraq, during the period of the British mandate, members of the Ottoman elite, many of whom had been trained in the Ottoman army and Ottoman bureaucracy, played a leading part in setting up the new state. In Syria, in the period of the French mandate, many of the great Sunni urban notable families, who had dominated the politics of the area in the Ottoman period, continued to function very much as before, maintaining their influence in the state system until the 1960s; while in Jebel Druze, the Druze, a fiercely tribal people never fully subjected to Ottoman rule, remained as independent as ever, launching a rebellion against the French in 1926–7. In the Lebanon, conflict between the Muslims (Sunni and Shiite), the Druzes and the Maronites remained endemic. In the Kurdish areas, divided between Turkey, Iraq and Persia, for long remote from any form of government control, inter-tribal conflict, sometimes accompanied by rebellion, flourished. Finally, in Arabia Ibn Saud and his successors continued to expand the frontiers of their Wahhabi state, much as they had done before under the Ottomans.

Controversy continues regarding the causes of Ottoman decline in the eighteenth and nineteenth centuries – as we have seen, Yapp even contends that in the nineteenth century the Ottoman Empire was not in decline at all – but with regard to the causes of the destruction of the Ottoman Empire in the last phase of its existence it is possible, with reasonable certainty, to identify four factors: economic failure brought about by the inability of the Ottoman Turks, as distinct from the Greeks and the Armenians, to adapt their culture to the requirements of capitalism and the market economy; the impact of nationalist ideologies, which helped undermine stability, not only in Macedonia, the Pontus region and the Armenian provinces, but also in Albania (though not as yet it would seem to any marked degree in the Kurdish and Arab provinces); Great Power intervention, certain to aggravate tension already present in the areas concerned; and finally, and most significantly, defeat in war. Of the four factors mentioned economic failure was, it may be supposed, the most important, for not only did it expose the Ottoman political and social system to the virus of nationalism, against which it might otherwise have remained, for some years at least, immune, it also created the conditions that led, first to Great Power intervention in the internal affairs of the empire, and then to defeat in war. Defeat in the Balkan Wars led to the loss of the Rumelian provinces, and defeat in the First World War led to the loss of the Arab provinces and eventually to partition. Not that the consequences of defeat in war were invariably adverse. As numerous commentators have remarked, defeat in the Balkan Wars may, paradoxically, have made the empire not weaker but stronger, for loss of the Rumelian provinces, mainly Christian, made the remaining parts of the empire more homogenous (Muslim). As a result, an Ottoman Empire, based on the ideology of Islam, might yet have survived, had the Ottoman government, led by Enver Pasha, not decided to enter the First World War on the side of the Central Powers.

Responsibility for the entry of the Ottoman Empire into the First World War on the side of the Central Powers had generally been laid at the door of the Germans, who are believed to have exercised a predominant influence in Istanbul, and on Enver and his faction, who from the beginning appear to have adopted a pro-German stance. Yet it may be doubted whether Enver and his colleagues would have prevailed in the argument regarding entry, had Ottoman opinion in general not been persuaded that the Entente Powers could no longer be relied on to secure the empire's survival. In 1878 Britain had occupied Cyprus; and in 1882 Egypt. In 1881 France had occupied Tunisia; and in 1911 Britain, France and Russia had permitted, if not actually encouraged, Italy's seizure of Tripolitania. Moreover in the Bosnia-Herzegovina crisis of 1908 the Entente Powers had failed to take effective steps to preserve Ottoman rights; and in the Balkan Wars they had failed to protect the empire from the assault launched by the Balkan states. Indeed, it was commonly believed at the time, possibly wrongly, that Russia had actually encouraged the assault. Meanwhile, in the Armenian provinces, the Russians were busy expanding their influence, as were the British in Iraq and the French in Syria. In these circumstances it is not surprising that the Ottomans should have decided to opt for an alliance, not with the Entente, but with the Central Powers.

Yet still, it may be presumed, the Ottomans might have been persuaded to opt for an alliance with the Entente Powers, or at least neutrality, had they not been made aware in the closing years of the nineteenth century and the opening years of the twentieth, of the radical change in the nature of Great Power relationships then taking place. For in that period the British, concerned regarding the future survival of their empire in Asia and the rise of German power in Europe, decided to abandon the policy of splendid isolation they had previously pursued and seek instead, first an entente with the French (1904), and then an entente with the Russians (1907), arrangements that led to the formation of the Triple Entente. Thereafter, British support for the preservation of the Ottoman Empire, sustained throughout the greater part of the nineteenth century and never in principle abandoned, became from the Ottoman point of view increasingly suspect, as the British, fearful that the Russians might abandon the Entente in favour of an alliance with the Germans (the worst British nightmare), sought by every means at their disposal, including hints and promises regarding a possible change in the Straits regime in a sense favourable to Russia, to keep the Russians loyal to the Entente. Again in these circumstances it is scarcely surprising that the Ottomans, in particular Enver and his colleagues, who may well have feared, with some justification, that in a European war the British would offer Russia Constantinople in return for support in Europe, should have decided to opt for an alliance with the Central Powers, seen as the strongest, the most dependable and the least threatening of the rival blocs then dividing Europe.

Even had the Ottomans not entered the First World War on the side of the Central Powers, or had the Central Powers emerged from the war victorious, the outcome that Enver clearly expected, it may be doubted whether the CUP-directed governments of the period could have succeeded in solving the problems faced by the empire in a manner likely to secure its long-term survival. Reforms based on the ideology of Ottomanism, introduced by the CUP, as by the statesmen of the *Tanzimat,* served merely to alienate the Muslim majority, who remained loyal to the principle of Muslim supremacy enshrined in the *Sheriat.* Wholehearted support for pan-Islamism, in effect a restoration of Muslim supremacy, clearly incompatible with Ottomanism, would inevitably have alienated the Christian minorities, now growing in wealth and self-confidence, and damaged relations with the Entente Powers; while support for pan-Turkism or Turkish nationalism would have alienated the Arabs, a powerful constituency, certain to be infected by the virus of nationalism in the future. What the empire clearly needed in the decade or so preceding the First World War was a period of relative peace and stability accompanied by rapid economic expansion. Economic expansion might, at least for a time, have eased the strains on the body politic inflicted by ethnic, religious and political conflict (though some would argue that economic expansion would merely have encouraged the spread of nationalist ideology among the minorities); but it is evident that in the period of the Young Turk Revolution, the counter-revolution, the Albanian uprising, the Tripolitanian War and the Balkan Wars, no such outcome was possible. Not that the position was necessarily hopeless. What the minorities, as distinct from the politically active members of the nationalist organisations, wanted, it would seem, was better government, based perhaps on the federal principle, the introduction of a fair system of taxation, the posting of conscripts to their home provinces, free use of local languages and scripts and the appointment of officials speaking those languages. What they were, for the most part, offered by the CUP-directed government of the period was a series of ill thought-out reforms, based for the most part on the principles of centralisation and autocracy, certain to lead, paradoxically, not to the 'unity' and 'progress' the CUP supposedly desired, but to further disintegration and in some cases even outright revolt. Had the CUP had the time and opportunity further to refine its policies, it might yet have succeeded in making them acceptable; but time and opportunity were, in the conditions prevailing, simply not available. As a result, in the period of the Balkan and First World Wars, CUP policy, increasingly driven by what one historian has referred to as a 'siege mentality', came to resemble that later pursued by national socialist regimes in Europe in the period of the Second World War. The results were, inevitably perhaps, the same: civil conflict, war, 'ethnic cleansing', massacre, famine and disease.

In the context of Ottoman decline, the Young Turk Revolution of 1908, like the end of the empire itself, has generally been seen as a major turning point, heralding a period of radical change, associated with the destruction of established values, the brutalisation of the political process, already to some extent accomplished by the troubles in Macedonia and the Armenian provinces, and territorial loss. Yet the achievements of the CUP, frequently referred to by its members as the 'sacred society', were by no means entirely negative. Roderick Davison, the American historian, has remarked, in his *Essays on Ottoman and Turkish History* (1990), that the *Tanzimat* period, during which the concepts of fatherland, sovereignty, citizenship, equality before the law and representative government were absorbed into the Ottoman political vocabulary, constituted the 'seed time' of the Turkish republic established by Mustafa Kemal and his colleagues in the post-war period. It can equally well be argued that, had the officers and officials associated with the CUP not secured the restoration of the constitution in 1908, defeated the counter-revolution of 1909, fought, frequently heroically, in the Tripolitanian and Balkan Wars, engaged in a fundamental reevaluation of Ottoman ideology, and forced through the wide-ranging military reforms that enabled Ottoman armies to win a series of important victories in the First World War, the later achievements of the nationalists (themselves virtually all long-standing members of the CUP) in securing the survival of an independent Turkish state in Anatolia and eastern Thrace, would have proved impossible. What, it may be enquired, would have happened to the Ottoman Empire had the Allies succeeded in their attempt to force the Straits in 1915? What would have happened had the Entente Powers, possibly including a resurgent Russia, saved from collapse by the opening of the Straits, occupied Anatolia in 1918? Merely to ask these questions is to indicate the significant service rendered by the CUP to the future survival of an independent Turkish state.

Further Reading

Useful bibliographical guides to the history of the Ottoman Empire in its final phase can be found in M. Heper, *Historical Dictionary of Turkey* (London: Scarecrow Press, 1994); M.E. Yapp, *The Making of the Modern Near East* (Harlow: Longman, 1981); E.J. Zürcher, *The Unionist Factor* (Leiden: E.J. Brill, 1984); and A.L. Macfie, *Atatürk* (Harlow: Longman, 1994).

Collections of documents concerning the foreign policies of the Great Powers in the late nineteenth and early twentieth centuries abound. These include *British Documents on the Origins of the War, 1898–1914* London: HMSO, 1926–38, *Documents on British Foreign Policy, 1919–39* London: HMSO, 1947–55, *Documents Diplomatiques Français, 1871–1914* Paris: Imprimerie Nationale, 1929–59, and *Die Grosse Politik der Europäischen Kabinette, 1871–1914* Berlin: Deutsche Verlags gesellschaft für Politik und Geschichte m.b.H., 1922–1927. Much more manageable, from the student's point of view, are J.C. Hurewitz, *Diplomacy in the Near and Middle East* (Princeton, New Jersey: D. Van Nostrand, 1956, Vol. 2, and K. Bourne and D.C. Watt, *British Documents on Foreign Affairs* (University Publications of America, 1981), in particular, Vol. 14, Pt. 1, Series B, Vol. 20. For the period of national struggle that followed the First World War in Turkey see B.N. Şimşir, *British Documents on Atatürk* (Ankara: Türk Tarih Kurumu, 1973–84), Vols 1–4. Mustapha Kemal Atatürk's account of the national struggle can be found in Mustafa Kemal, *A Speech Delivered by Ghazi Mustafa Kemal* (Leipzig: Koehler, 1929).

Wide-ranging accounts of the end of the Ottoman Empire and the emergence of modern Turkey and the other successor states include B. Lewis, *The Emergence of Modern Turkey* (Oxford: Oxford University Press, 1961); S. Shaw and E.K. Shaw, *History of the Ottoman Empire and Modern Turkey* (Cambridge: Cambridge University Press, 1977), Vol. 2; M.E. Yapp, *The Making of the Modern Near East* (Harlow: Longman, 1981); D. Fromkin, *A Peace to End All Peace* (Harmondsworth: Penguin Books, 1989); and H.M. Sacher, *The Emergence of the Middle East* (New York: Knopf, 1969). More specialised accounts include N. Berkes, *The Development of Secularism in Turkey* (Montreal: McGill University Press, 1964); A.L. Macfie, *The Straits Question, 1908–36* (Salonica: Institute for Balkan Studies, 1993); M.S. Anderson, *The Eastern Question* (London: Macmillan, 1966); H.J. Psomiades, *The Eastern Question: The Last Phase* (Salonica: Institute for Balkan Studies, 1968); M.L. Smith, *Ionian Vision: Greece in Asia Minor* (New York: St. Martin's Press, 1973); L. Evans, *United States Policy and the Partition of Turkey* (Baltimore: Johns Hopkins University Press, 1965); U. Heyd, *The Foundation of Turkish Nationalism* (Westport, Connecticut: Hyperion Press, 1979); D. Kushner, *The Rise of Turkish Nationalism* (London: Frank Cass, 1977); E. Kedourie, *Arabic Political Memoirs and Other Studies* (London: Frank Cass, 1974); M. Arai, *Turkish Nationalism in the Young Turk Era* (Leiden: E.J. Brill, 1992); M. Yamauchi, *The Green Crescent Under the Red Star: Enver Pasha in Soviet Russia* (Tokyo: Institute for the Study of Languages and Cultures of Asia and Africa, 1991); K. Tunçay and E.J. Zürcher, *Socialism and Nationalism in the Ottoman Empire* (London: British Academic Press, 1994); H. Nicolson, *Curzon, the Last Phase* (London: Constable, 1937); E. Kedourie, *England and the Middle East* (London: Bowes and Bowes, 1956); and *In the Anglo-Arab Labyrinth* (Cambridge: Cambridge University Press, 1976); U. Trumpener, *Germany and the Ottoman Empire, 1914–1918* (Princeton: Princeton University Press, 1968); A. Emin, *Turkey in the World War* (New Haven, Connecticut: Yale University Press, 1930); P. Kinross, *Atatürk: The Rebirth of a Nation* (London: Weidenfeld and Nicolson, 1964); D. McDowall, *A Modern History of the Kurds* (New York: J.B. Tauris, 1996); A. Nassibian, *Britain and the Armenian Question* (London: Croom Helm, 1985); J. Goldberg, *The Foreign Policy of Saudi Arabia* (Cambridge, Massachusetts: Harvard University Press, 1986); F. Ahmad, *The Young Turks* (Oxford: Oxford University Press, 1969); A. Kansu, *The Revolution of 1908 in Turkey* (Leiden: E.J. Brill, 1997).

Useful studies of the period, at present available only in Turkish, include H. Bayur, *Türk İnkilâbı Tarihi* (Istanbul: Maarif Matbaası, 1940); S. Akşin, *Jön Türkler ve İttihat ve Terrakhı* (Istanbul: Gerçek Yayinevi, 1980), and *Istanbul Hükümetleri ve Milli Mücadele* (Istanbul: Cam Yayinevi, 1992).

Recent researches into the history of the Ottoman Empire in its final phase have resulted in the publication of a series of excellent articles which have transformed our understanding of the period. These include K. Karpat, 'The Memoirs of N. Batzaria: The Young Turks and Nationalism', *International Journal of Middle Eastern Studies*, Vol. 6 (1975); G. Gawrych, 'The Culture and Politics of Violence in

Turkish Society, 1903–14', *Middle Eastern Studies*, Vol. 22 (1986); H. Kayali, 'Elections and the Electoral Process in the Ottoman Empire, 1876–1919', *International Journal of Middle Eastern Studies*, Vol. 27 (1995); M. Hakan Yavuz, 'Nationalism and Islam: Yusuf Akçura and Üç Tarz-i Siyaset', *Journal of Islamic Studies*, Vol. 4 (1993); E. Kedourie, 'Young Turks, Freemasons and Jews', *Middle Eastern Studies*, Vol. 7 (1971); M. Şükrü Hanioğlu, 'Notes on the Young Turks and Freemasons, 1875–1908', *Middle Eastern Studies*, Vol. 25 (1989); and 'The Young Turks on the Verge of the 1908 Revolution', *Varia Turcica*, Vol. 13 (1991); S. Akşin, 'Notes on Kâzim Karabekir's Committee of Union and Progress, 1896–1909', *Varia Turcica*, Vol. 13 (1991); M.Ş. Güzel, 'Prélude à la Revolution', *Varia Turcica*, Vol. 13 (1991); V.R. Swanson, 'The Military Rising in Istanbul, 1909', *Journal of Contemporary History*, Vol. 5 (1970); F. Ahmad, 'Unionist Relations with the Greek, Armenian and Jewish Communities of the Ottoman Empire, 1908–14', in B. Braude and B. Lewis (eds), *Christians and Jews in the Ottoman Empire* (London: Holmes and Meier, 1982); G.W. Swanson, 'A Note on the Ottoman Socio-Economic Response to the Balkan War of 1912', *Middle Eastern Studies*, Vol. 14 (1978); G. Dyer, 'The Turkish Armistice of 1908', *Middle Eastern Studies*, Vol. 8 (1972); Y.T. Kurat, 'How Turkey Drifted into World War I', in K. Bourne and D.C. Watt (eds), *Studies in International History*, 1967; S. Tanvir Wasti, 'The Defence of Medina, 1916–19', *Middle Eastern Studies*, Vol. 27 (1991); E. Karsh and I. Karsh, 'Myth in the Desert, or Not the Great Arab Revolt', *Middle Eastern Studies*, Vol. 33 (1997); J. Heller, 'Britain and the Armenian Question, 1912–14', *Middle Eastern Studies*, Vol. 16 (1980); E. Tauber, 'Sayyid Talib and the Young Turks in Basra', *Middle Eastern Studies*, Vol. 25 (1989); S. Akgün, 'Turkish–Greek Population Exchange, with a Selection from American Documents', *Turkish Review of Balkan Studies*, Vol. 1 (1993); H. Ünal, 'Young Turk Assessments of International Politics', *Middle Eastern Studies*, Vol. 32 (1996); and B. Gökay, 'Turkish Settlement and the Caucasus', *Middle Eastern Studies*, Vol. 32 (1996).

Glossary

Action Army: the army despatched by the CUP and its supporters to suppress the counter-revolution in Istanbul in 1909

agha: rural lord or master, landowner, title of a respected person

Anatolianism: the idea propounded by the Turkish nationalists that the Ottomans should concentrate their efforts on developing Anatolia

Armistice of Mudros: the armistice that ended the participation of the Ottoman Empire in the First World War (1918)

Army of Islam: the name of an army organised by the Ottomans in Transcaucasia towards the end of the First World War

autocephalous church: an independent church, appointing its own head

Baksheesh: gratuity

Balfour Declaration: declaration made in 1917 by the British Foreign Secretary, James Arthur Balfour, and authorised by the British War Cabinet, expressing British support for the establishment in Palestine of a National Home for the Jewish people

Balkan League: alliance of the Balkan powers, Serbia, Bulgaria, Greece and Montenegro, formed in 1912. Aimed at the Ottoman Empire

bashi-bazouk: irregular soldier

Bosnia-Herzegovina question: the question of what should become of the Ottoman provinces, Bosnia and Herzegovina

caliphate: office of the Chief Muslim religious leader, regarded as a successor to Mohammed. Traditionally held by the Ottoman Sultan. Abolished by Atatürk in March 1924

camarilla: cabal or clique

capitulations: grants or treaties establishing a system of extra-territorial jurisdiction and a tariff limitation in the Ottoman Empire

Central Powers: germany and Austria-Hungary

CUP: the Committee of Union and Progress. The name of a secret society, later a political party, which dominated Ottoman politics from the period of the Young Turk Revolution of 1908 until the end of the First World War

dervish: a form of Muslim mystic, who attempts to approach God through renunciation of the world

dhimmis: christians and Jews living under the protection of a Muslim ruler

dönme: converts, members of a Judaeo-Islamic syncretist sect

Dreikaiserbund: an informal alliance formed by Germany, Russia and Austria in 1872 as a result of a meeting of their respective emperors

durbar: a public levée

emir: title of a Muslim ruler or tribal chief

emirate: territory ruled by an emir

entente cordiale: understanding arrived at in 1904 by Britain and France. Later joined by Russia

fedai: one ready to sacrifice his life for a cause

fellahin: egyptian peasant

ferik: divisional general or army division

fetwa: opinion on legal matters furnished by an official expounder of Muslim law

fief: land held in return for feudal service or on condition of military service

Fourteen Points: peace plan proposed by President Woodrow Wilson before the US Congress in January 1918

ghazi state: state formed by Muslim warriors, in the borderlands of Islam

Ghiaur: non-Muslim

grand vizier: first minister in the Ottoman state

Great Powers: collective term for the major European states; usually Great Britain, France, Russia, Italy, Germany and Austria–Hungary

Green Army: a left-wing organisation set up in Anatolia in the period of the War of Independence to spread socialist ideas and fight the forces of reaction

Hashemite: member of the Hashimid dynasty that had ruled in Mecca for almost a thousand years

Hellenisation: making Greek

hodja: muslim teacher

imam: head of mosque and prayer leader in Sunni Islam. Head of community and ruler, in theory, in Shiite Islam

irade: decree or command

kaimakam: head official of a district

Karakol: a secret organisation set up in the Ottoman Empire in the closing months of the First World War to organise opposition to the victorious Entente Powers in the post-war period

khan: a title given to rulers and officials in Central Asia

khedive: viceroy of Egypt

khutba: sermon given at the Friday congregational prayer in a mosque

Kibrisli: coming from Cyprus

komitadji: member of an irregular band of soldiers in the Balkans

Macedonian question: the question of what should become of the Macedonian provinces in the Ottoman Empire

mandate: a commission from the League of Nations to a member state to administer a territory. In 1920 Britain was awarded mandates for Iraq, Palestine and Transjordan, and France mandates for Syria and Lebanon

mandatary: person or state receiving a mandate

March Agreement: agreement regarding the future of Constantinople, concluded by Britain, France and Russia in March 1915. According to the terms of the agreement Russia was to acquire possession of Constantinople and the Straits

millet: religious community or nation

mizan: balance, measure, justice, equality

Molotov Pact: a non-aggression pact concluded by Russia and Germany in August 1939

mutasarrif: governor of a sandjak

National Pact: statement of minimum peace terms acceptable to the Turkish Nationalists, approved by the Ottoman parliament in January 1920

riverain: on or of a riverbank. For example, on a river running into the Black Sea

Osmanli: Ottoman

padishah: sultan

pan-Islamism: a policy designed to rally support for the Ottoman Empire in the Muslim world

pan-Turkism: a policy designed to encourage the unification of the Turkish peoples of the world

the Porte: central Office of the Ottoman government

sanjak: sub-division of a province

Salanikli: from Salonica (Thessaloniki)

serasker: Ottoman commander-in-chief and minister of war

Senussi: member of an Islamic brotherhood, mainly located in Libya

sheikh: chief or head of an Arab tribe or family

Sheriat: Islamic religious canonical law

Shiite: one belonging to the branch of Islam that recognises Ali ibn Abi Talib (Mohammed's cousin and son-in-law) and his successors as the true imam. Shiites are the majority in Iran, are the largest group in Lebanon, and make up a considerable proportion of the populations of Iraq and Pakistan

Sunni: a member of the majority group of Muslims, who accept the *Sunna* (traditional law based on Muhammed's words or acts) as equal in authority to the Koran

sultan: ruler, sovereign. The ruler of Turkey

sultanate: office of sultan

Syncretism: reconciliation of different systems of belief

Tanin: an Ottoman newspaper. The organ of the CUP

Tanizimat: reorganisation or reform

Teshkilati Mahsusa: special organisation set up by the Ottoman government in the period of the Balkan Wars to strengthen the authority of the CUP government and promote the cause of pan-Islamism and pan-Turkism in the east

theocracy: government by God or his agents

Triple Alliance: alliance formed by Germany, Austria and Italy in 1882

Triple Entente: agreement between Great Britain, France and Russia to resolve their outstanding colonial differences; it became a military alliance in 1914

Triplice: *see* Triple Alliance

Trucial states: a series of small states bordering the Persian Gulf persuaded by the government of India to suspend hostilities in the area

ulema: doctors of Muslim canon law, tradition and theology

vali: governor of a *vilayet*

vilayet: province

Wahhabi: member of a sect of Muslim puritans, inhabiting central Arabia

Yildirim: a special army group set up by the Ottomans in 1917 to liberate Baghdad

Zionism: a movement for the re-establishment of the Jewish people in Palestine

Maps

1   The Balkan Wars

Source: Reproduced from Justin McCarthy, *The Ottoman Turks;
An Introductory History to 1923*, London, 1997.

N

2   The Balkans on the eve of the First World War
Source: Reproduced from M.E. Yapp, *The Making of the Modern Near East 1792–1923*, London, 1987.

3 Syria and Iraq on the eve of the First World War
Source: Reproduced from M.E. Yapp, *The Making of the Modern Near East 1792–1923*, London, 1987.

Kurds

Amadiyya

IRAN

Greater R. Zab

Ruwandaz

Mosul

Lower R. Zab

Sulaimaniyya

Kirkuk

R. Tigris

• Kirmanshah

• Khanaqin

Qizil
Ribat

R.Euphrates

Baghdad

• Ctesiphon

Karbala • • Hindiyya

Kut al-Amara

A Q

Najaf •

Khazā'il

Amara

Qurna •

Mohammerah

Muntafiq

Basra •

Umm Qasr •

Fao

Shammar

Kuwayt

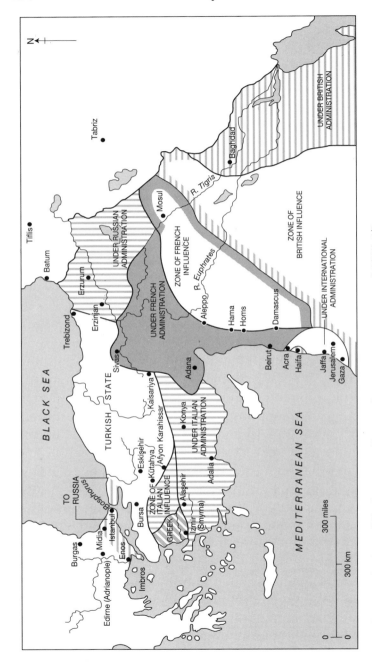

4 The partitioning of Turkey according to the secret agreements of 1915–17
Source: Reproduced from A.L. Macfie, *Atatürk*, London, 1994.

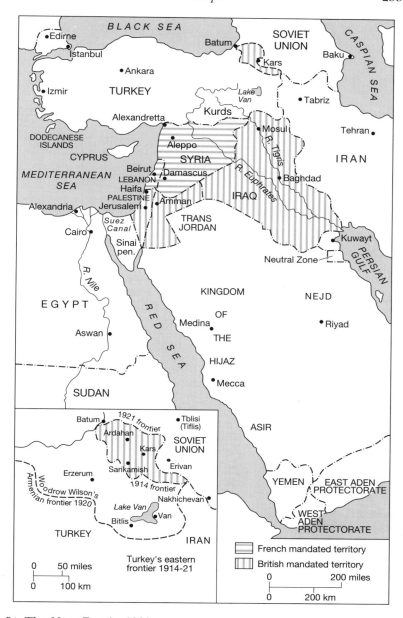

5 The Near East in 1923
Source: Reproduced from M.E. Yapp, *The Making of the Modern Near East 1792–1923*, London, 1987.

Index